The Earth and the Moon

THE SOLAR SYSTEM

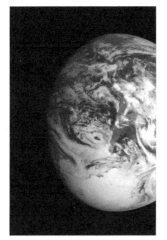

The Earth and the Moon

Linda T. Elkins-Tanton

CHELSEA HOUSE
PUBLISHERS

An imprint of Infobase Publishing

FoF   1/07   #32.00

The Earth and the Moon

Chelsea House
An imprint of Infobase Publishing
132 West 31st Street
New York NY 10001

Library of Congress Cataloging-in-Publication Data

Elkins-Tanton, Linda T.
The Earth and the moon / Linda T. Elkins-Tanton.
p. cm. — (Solar system)
Includes bibliographical references and index.
ISBN 0-8160-5194-1 (acid-free paper)
1. Earth—Popular works. 2. Moon—Popular works. I. Title.
QB631.2.E45 2006
525—dc22   2005014189

Chelsea House books are available at special discounts when purchased in bulk quantities for businesses, associations, institutions, or sales promotions. Please call our Special Sales Department in New York at (212) 967-8800 or (800) 322-8755.

You can find Chelsea House on the World Wide Web at http://www.chelseahouse.com

Text and cover design by Dorothy M. Preston
Illustrations by Richard Garratt

Printed in the United States of America
VB CH 10 9 8 7 6 5 4 3 2 1
This book is printed on acid-free paper.

To Tim Grove, Brad Hager,
Maria Zuber, Sam Bowring, and my
other friends at the Massachusetts
Institute of Technology who worked
at turning me into a scientist,
with special appreciation for the
research we did about the Moon.

Contents

Preface

The planets Mercury, Venus, Mars, Jupiter, and Saturn—all visible to the naked eye—were known to ancient peoples. In fact, the Romans gave these planets their names as they are known today. Mercury was named after their god Mercury, the fleet-footed messenger of the gods, because the planet seems especially fast moving when viewed from Earth. Venus was named for the beautiful goddess Venus, brighter than anything in the sky except the Sun and Moon. The planet Mars appears red even from Earth and so was named after Mars, the god of war. Jupiter was named for the king of the gods, the biggest and most powerful of all, and Saturn was named for Jupiter's father. The ancient Chinese and the ancient Jews recognized the planets as well, and the Maya (250–900 C.E., Mexico and environs) and Aztec (ca. 1100–1700 C.E., Mexico and environs) called the planet Venus "Quetzalcoatl," after their god of good and light.

These planets, small and sometimes faint in the night sky, commanded such importance that days were named after them. The seven-day week originated in Mesopotamia, which was perhaps the world's first organized civilization (beginning around 3500 B.C.E. in modern-day Iraq). The Romans adopted the seven-day week almost 4,000 years later, around 321 C.E., and the concept spread throughout western Europe. Though there are centuries of translations between their original names and current names, Sunday is still named for the Sun, Monday for the Moon, Tuesday for Mars, Wednesday for Mercury, Thursday for Jupiter, Friday for Venus, and Saturday for Saturn. The Germanic peoples substituted Germanic equivalents for the names of four of the Roman gods: For Tuesday, Tiw, the god of war, replaced Mars; for Wednesday, Woden, the god of wisdom, replaced Mercury; for Thursday, Thor, the god of thunder, replaced Jupiter; and for Friday, Frigg, the goddess of love, replaced Venus.

More planets, of course, have been discovered by modern man, thanks to advances in technology. Science is often driven forward by the development of new technology, allowing researchers to make measurements that were previously impossible. The dawn of the new age in astronomy, the study of the solar system, occurred in 1608, when Hans Lippershey, a Dutch eyeglass-maker, attached a lens to each end of a hollow tube, creating the first telescope. Galileo Galilei, born in Pisa, Italy, in 1564, made his first telescope in 1609 from Lippershey's model. Galileo soon had noticed that Venus has phases like the Moon and that Saturn appeared to have "handles." These of course were the edges of Saturn's rings, though the telescope was not strong enough to resolve the rings correctly. In 1610, Galileo discovered four of Jupiter's moons, which are still called the Galilean satellites. These four moons were proof that not every heavenly body orbited the Earth, as Ptolemy, a Greek philosopher, had asserted around 140 C.E. Galileo's discovery was the beginning of the end of the strongly held belief that the Earth is the center of the solar system, as well as a beautiful example of a case where improved technology drove science forward.

Most of the science presented in this set comes from the startlingly rapid developments of the last hundred years, brought about by technological development. The concept of the Earth-centered solar system is long gone, as is the notion that the "heavenly spheres" are unchanging and perfect. Looking down on the solar system from above the Sun's North Pole, the planets orbiting the Sun can be seen to be orbiting counterclockwise, in the manner of the original *protoplanetary disk* of material from which they formed. (This is called *prograde* rotation.) This simple statement, though, is almost the end of generalities about the solar system. The notion of planets spinning on their axes and orbiting around the Sun in an orderly way is incorrect: Some planets spin backward compared to the Earth, others planets are tipped over, and others orbit outside the *ecliptic* plane (the imaginary plane that contains the Earth's orbit) by substantial angles, Pluto in particular (see the accompanying figure on obliquity and orbital *inclination*). Some planets and moons are hot enough to be volcanic, and some produce *silicate* lava (for example, the Earth and Jupiter's moon Io), while others have exotic lavas made of molten ices (for example, Neptune's moon Triton). Some planets and even moons have atmospheres, with magnetic fields to protect them from the solar wind (for example, Venus, Earth, Mars, Io, Triton, and Saturn's moon Titan), while other planets have lost both their magnetic fields and their atmospheres and orbit the Sun fully exposed to its radiation and supersonic particles (for example, Mercury).

Size can be unexpected in the solar system: Saturn's moon Titan is larger than the planet Mercury, and Charon, Pluto's moon, is almost as big as Pluto itself. The figure on page xii shows the number of moons each planet has; large planets have far more than small planets, and every year scientists discover new celestial bodies orbiting the gas giant planets. Many large bodies orbit in the asteroid belt, or the Kuiper belt, and many sizable asteroids cross the orbits of planets as they make their way around the Sun. Some planets' moons are unstable and will make new ring systems as they crash into their hosts. Many moons, like Neptune's giant Triton, orbit their planets backward (clockwise when viewed from the North Pole, the opposite way that the planets orbit the Sun). Triton also has the coldest surface temperature of any moon or planet, including Pluto, which is much farther from the Sun. The solar system is made of bodies in a continuum of sizes and ages, and every rule has an exception.

Obliquity, orbital inclination, and rotation direction are three physical measurements used to describe a rotating, orbiting body.

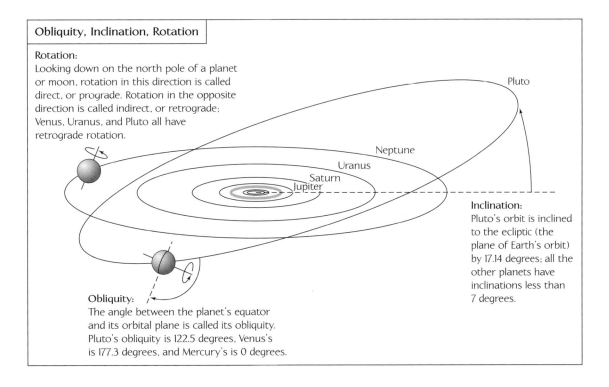

Obliquity, Inclination, Rotation

Rotation:
Looking down on the north pole of a planet or moon, rotation in this direction is called direct, or prograde. Rotation in the opposite direction is called indirect, or retrograde; Venus, Uranus, and Pluto all have retrograde rotation.

Pluto

Neptune

Uranus

Saturn

Jupiter

Inclination:
Pluto's orbit is inclined to the ecliptic (the plane of Earth's orbit) by 17.14 degrees; all the other planets have inclinations less than 7 degrees.

Obliquity:
The angle between the planet's equator and its orbital plane is called its obliquity. Pluto's obliquity is 122.5 degrees, Venus's is 177.3 degrees, and Mercury's is 0 degrees.

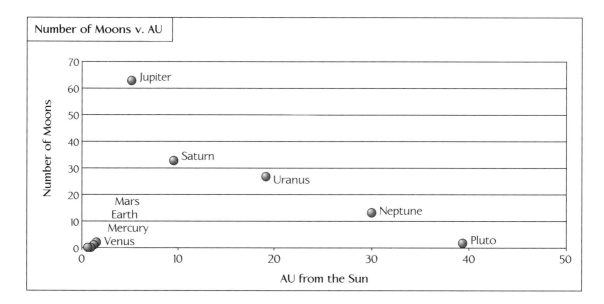

Number of Moons v. AU

As shown in this graph of number of moons versus planets, the large outer planets have far more moons than the smaller, inner planets.

Every day new data are streaming back to Earth from space missions to Mars. Early in 2004, scientists proved that there was once standing liquid water on Mars. Another unmanned mission, this time to a comet, determined that the material in a comet's nucleus is as strong as some *rocks* and not the loose pile of ice and dust expected. Information streams in from space observations and Earth-based experiments, and scientists attempt to explain what they see, producing an equivalent stream of hypotheses about the formation and evolution of the solar system and all its parts.

In this age of constant space missions and discoveries, how can a printed book on the solar system be produced that is not instantly outdated? New hypotheses are typically not accepted immediately by the scientific community. The choice of a leading hypothesis among competing ideas is really a matter of opinion, and arguments can go on for decades. Even when one idea has reached prominence in the scientific community, there will be researchers who disagree with it. At every point along the way, though, there are people writing books about science. Once an explanation reaches the popular press, it is often frozen as perpetual truth and persists for decades, even if the scientific community has long since abandoned that theory.

In this set, some statements will be given as facts: the gravitational acceleration of the Earth, the radius of Mars, the height of prominences from the Sun, for instance. Almost everything else is open to argumentation and change. The numbers of moons known to be orbiting Jupiter and Saturn, for example, are increasing every year as observers are able to detect smaller and dimmer objects. These volumes will present some of the thought processes that have brought people to their conclusions (for example, why scientists state that the Sun is fueled by nuclear reactions), as well as observations of the solar system for which no one has a satisfactory explanation (such as why there is no detectable heat flow out of the gas giant planet Uranus). Science is often taught as a series of facts for memorization—in fact, not until the second half of a doctoral degree do many scientists learn to question all aspects of science, from the accepted theory to the data itself. Readers should feel empowered to question every statement.

The Solar System set explores the vast and enigmatic Sun at the center of the solar system and also covers the planets, examining each and comparing them from the point of view of a planetary scientist. Space missions that produced critical data for the understanding of solar system bodies are introduced in each volume, and their data and images shown and discussed. The volumes *The Sun, Mercury, and Venus; The Earth and the Moon;* and *Mars* place emphasis on the areas of unknowns and the results of new space missions. The important fact that the solar system consists of a continuum of sizes and types of bodies is stressed in *Asteroids, Meteorites, and Comets.* This book discusses the roles of these small bodies as recorders of the formation of the solar system, as well as their threat as *impactors* of planets. In *Jupiter and Saturn,* the two largest planets are described and compared. In the final volume, *Uranus, Neptune, Pluto, and the Outer Solar System,* Pluto is presented not as the final lonely planet in the list but as the largest known of a extensive population of icy bodies that reach far out toward the closest stars, in effect linking the solar system to the galaxy itself.

In this set we hope to change the familiar litany Mercury, Venus, Earth, Mars, Jupiter, Saturn, Uranus, Neptune, and Pluto into a more complex understanding of the many sizes and types of bodies that orbit the Sun. Even a cursory study of each planet shows its uniqueness along with the great areas of knowledge that are unknown. These titles seek to make the familiar strange again.

Acknowledgments

Foremost, profound thanks to the following organizations for the great science and adventure they provide for humankind and, on a more prosaic note, for allowing the use of their images for these books: the National Aeronautics and Space Administration (NASA) and the National Oceanic and Atmospheric Administration (NOAA), in conjunction with the Jet Propulsion Laboratory (JPL) and Malin Space Science Systems (MSSS). A large number of missions and their teams have provided invaluable data and images, including the *Solar and Heliospheric Observer (SOHO), Mars Global Surveyor (MGS), Mars Odyssey,* the *Mars Exploration Rovers (MERs), Galileo, Stardust, Near-Earth Asteroid Rendezvous (NEAR),* and *Cassini.* Special thanks to Steele Hill, SOHO Media Specialist at NASA, who prepared a number of images from the SOHO mission, to the astronauts who took the photos found at Astronaut Photography of the Earth, and to the providers of the National Space Science Data Center, Great Images in NASA, and the NASA/JPL Planetary Photojournal, all available on the Web (addresses given in the reference section).

Many thanks also to Frank K. Darmstadt, executive editor at Chelsea House; to Jodie Rhodes, literary agent; and to E. Marc Parmentier at Brown University for his generous support.

Introduction

In geoscience texts the Earth is often treated as the beginning and almost the end of what is known about planets and geology; the other planets in the solar system are treated as brief addenda to the Earth itself. The study of geology started with the Earth and therefore Earth is the standard against which other planets are compared. As tempting as it is to discuss the Earth from the point of view of an Earth-bound geologist, in *The Earth and the Moon* the Earth will be compared equally with the other planets, and the Earth will be described from the point of view of a planetary scientist.

Earth belongs to the group of small, inner solar-system planets that also includes Mercury, Venus, and Mars, as shown in the following figure of the solar system. These planets, called the *terrestrial planets,* all consist of a *mantle* made of silica-based *minerals* above an iron-rich *core.* Their *crusts* all show evidence for meteorite bombardment and volcanic lava flows. Beyond these basic similarities, and despite their similar formation processes in the inner solar system, these four planets are strangely different from each other. While the Earth's surface temperatures are relatively constant, Mercury goes through daily cycles of heat high enough to melt lead and cold deep enough to freeze carbon dioxide gas, and its thoroughly cratered surface shows that it has not been volcanically active for about the last half of its existence.

Though the Earth is the only known planet in the universe to house life, Mars is a good candidate to have developed life at some point in its history. Mars once had liquid surface water, and it may still be volcanically active, providing surface warmth from geothermal systems in the crust. The red planet was gradually transformed through the loss of its magnetic field and the changing luminosity of the Sun from a wet planet with a significant atmosphere into a dry, cold desert. Though it began more like the Earth, Mars evolved away from that state.

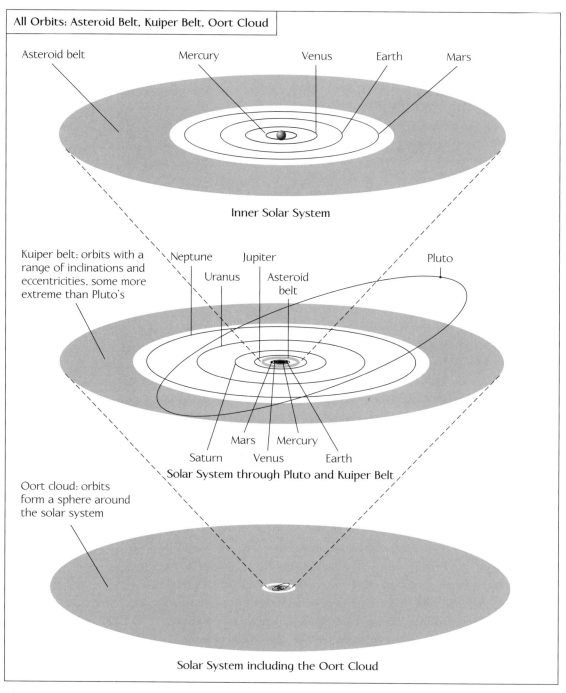

All Orbits: Asteroid Belt, Kuiper Belt, Oort Cloud

Asteroid belt

Mercury

Venus

Earth

Mars

Inner Solar System

Kuiper belt: orbits with a range of inclinations and eccentricities, some more extreme than Pluto's

Neptune

Jupiter

Pluto

Uranus

Asteroid belt

Mars

Mercury

Saturn

Venus

Earth

Solar System through Pluto and Kuiper Belt

Oort cloud: orbits form a sphere around the solar system

Solar System including the Oort Cloud

This book covers the Earth and the Moon. All the orbits are far closer to circular than shown in this oblique view, which was chosen to show the inclination of Pluto's orbit to the ecliptic.

Venus, however, should be the most similar of the four planets to Earth. The two planets are very close in size, density, composition, and distance from the Sun, but they have evolved in entirely different directions. Venus has a suffocatingly dense atmosphere consisting of carbon dioxide with clouds of sulfuric acid; its surface experiences such high atmospheric pressure, intense, unremitting heat, and toxic gases that no life similar to that on Earth could survive there. *The Earth and the Moon* will address the Earth in part 1. Unlike the other planets (with a slight exception for the Moon), there is some direct evidence about the Earth's interior, along with a great deal of indirect evidence from earthquake waves, heat flow measurements, and other physical observations. Chapter 1 covers fundamental aspects of the Earth as a planet: its size and mass, its orbit, and the causes of its seasons. Chapter 2 contains what is thought about the Earth's solid interior, including its probable composition and temperature, as well as its ability to flow like a liquid over very long periods of time. This ability to flow along with the action of liquid water on the surface and near-surface of the planet allows the process of *plate tectonics* to occur, with its attendant volcanoes, collisional mountain chains, earthquakes, and ocean basins.

A series of related hypotheses for the formation of the Earth and the other terrestrial planets has sprung from information on the composition and age of the Earth, as well as from studies of meteorites and the Moon. This fascinating subject, so remote in time as to be almost a branch of philosophy, is discussed in chapter 3. Finally, the most familiar aspects of the Earth, its surface appearance and atmosphere, are presented in chapter 4, followed in chapter 5 by a discussion of life, the most unique and important aspect of Earth. The Earth has several critical characteristics thought to have helped it stay hospitable to life. Earth is now the only terrestrial planet with

- Abundant liquid surface water, a requisite for life;
- An atmosphere rich in oxygen;
- Bimodal topography (low ocean basins and high continents);
- A strong magnetic field, which protects from solar radiation and preserves the atmosphere; and
- A large moon, keeping the Earth's orbit and therefore its climate stable.

Some of these attributes have helped Earth stay hospitable to life, but their efficacy may be limited in time. The Earth can sustain life now but its protective elements may not last forever, either because of natural physical or chemical processes, or because of the influence of humankind.

Biologists have trouble imagining a kind of life that does not depend on water; living creatures on Earth depend on water in many complex ways, and cannot have formed or survived without it. Water creates the unusual silica-rich rocks such as *granites* that appear to exist only on Earth, and water helps produce Earth's bimodal topography (on Mars, low and high topography may also be linked to water, but through different processes than occur on Earth). Earth's atmosphere is uniquely rich in oxygen, with just under 21 percent. Mars's atmosphere, by comparison, contains less than a half percent of oxygen, and Venus's atmosphere has none. Animals breathe oxygen, but the balance of oxygen and carbon dioxide in the atmosphere was created and is maintained by plants. Even the magnetic field is necessary for life: Without the magnetic field, the Sun's intense radiation would reach the surface with enough intensity to cause genetic mutations, cancers, and, eventually, extinctions. Without its magnetic field, the Earth's atmosphere would be blown away by the solar wind, and Earth would evolve toward the conditions of Mars.

The Moon, by contrast, is almost perfectly dry, has no currently active volcanism, no atmosphere, and no life. Its ancient surface is formed by impacts and by the constant flux of the solar wind, since it is unprotected by any significant magnetic field; it now stands virtually changeless on human timescales. Part 2 of *The Earth and the Moon* discusses the formation and evolution of the Moon, the body in the solar system about which the most is known outside the Earth. Chapter 6 describes the processes that link the Moon and Earth: tides, *synchronous rotation,* and eclipses. These physical links have been compelling to mankind for millennia, but the most exciting parts of the story of the Moon came about through space travel.

The Moon is the only body in the solar system outside Earth that a human has visited. There is over 840 pounds (382 kg) of lunar material brought by NASA and Soviet space missions to Earth for study. The information gleaned about the Moon from this relatively small pile of rocks is mind-boggling, and stands as the greatest proof that Martian planetary science would be greatly enhanced by returning samples to

The Lunar Orbiter 4 took this striking image of the lunar Orientale Basin, with portions of the mare basalt—filled Oceanus Procellarum visible on the upper right limb. (NASA/*Lunar Orbiter 4*)

Earth. Compositional studies of lunar rocks show that the Moon and Earth are made of similar material, and because lunar material has not been reworked through erosion and plate tectonics it also sheds light on the early formation of the Moon and its internal evolution. The Moon's light-colored highlands and dark mare basalts are shown in this image; the giant complex crater Orientale Basin is in the center.

Some moons in the solar system accreted from extra material orbiting around the main planet during planetary formation, and others are captured bodies that were orbiting past the main planet and were caught in its gravitational field. The Earth's Moon may have a unique provenance in all the solar system, intimately tied to the formation of the Earth: It is thought that during *accretion* of the Earth, a body the size of Mars collided with the proto-Earth, smashing most of it into a swirl of particles that re-formed into the Earth and the Moon. Thus, these two bodies are thought to share the material that makes them. The reasoning for this theory of lunar formation, presented in chapter 7, is followed by discussions of the Moon's interior and surface in chapter 8.

The Earth and Moon are the closest planet and moon in size except for Pluto and Charon. Unlike Pluto and Charon, the Earth and Moon are startlingly different. Their differences form a natural laboratory for understanding the importance of size in retaining atmosphere, trapping solar energy for warmth, allowing the growth of liquid oceans—and thus, in allowing life. In this book the Earth and Moon take their rightful places among the rest of the bodies in the solar system, as a small planetary system with what appears to be a highly unusual set of fortuitous circumstances that allowed for the development of life.

Part One: The Earth

The Earth: Fast Facts about a Planet in Orbit

Humankind has struggled throughout time to understand the shape of the Earth and its movements in the solar system. Understanding that the Earth is a sphere and that it orbits the Sun in a path shaped like an ellipse, governed by the forces of gravity, has been a journey consisting of long periods in which one model of the Earth was widely accepted, interrupted by periods of turmoil when a new idea was tested, argued against, and finally accepted. Space missions have produced some of the most recent confirming information: Few can contest that the Earth is a sphere once they have seen an image of it taken from space.

To a very close approximation, the Earth is a sphere. The sphericity of the Earth has been known and accepted by most peoples and civilizations since at least the second century B.C.E. This is a surprise to many students schooled in the United States, since the curriculum commonly states that Christopher Columbus discovered that the world is round in 1492. Jeffrey Burton Russell and other historians point to the American writer Washington Irving, among others, as the source of the flat-Earth story: Irving made the Columbus story into a tale of Columbus sailing against all advice that his ships would eventually fall off the edge of the Earth, and subsequently finding new continents and demonstrating there was no edge from which to fall. Irving may have had as his source Antoine-Jean Letronne, a French academician, who wrote that medieval Europeans widely believed in a flat Earth, and Irving's reputation was such that his statement was apparently never checked. In fact there have been only a few scholars in each age who believed in a flat Earth, and

Fundamental Information about the Earth

The Moon, Mars, and the Earth fall into a regular size order: Mars's radius is almost exactly twice that of the Moon, and Earth's is almost exactly twice that of Mars. Since the volume of a sphere is related to the cube of its radius ($V = 4/3 \pi r^3$), the bodies are far more different in terms of volume: Mars has 0.13 times the Earth's volume, and the Moon again 0.13 times Mars's volume. Earth and Mars are shown together in the upper color insert on page C-1 for a size comparison.

Though in many ways Mars resembles the Earth on its surface (deserts, volcanic flows, dry river valleys, ice caps), the small volume and resulting small internal pressures of Mars make its internal processes considerably different from the Earth's. The Earth's density and gravity are larger than Mars's, and Earth has its single large Moon while Mars has two very small moons. These and other physical parameters for the Earth are listed in the table below.

FUNDAMENTAL FACTS ABOUT THE EARTH

equatorial radius	3,963.19 miles (6,378.14 km)
polar radius	3,950.01 miles (6,356.75 km)
ellipticity	0.0034, meaning the planet's equator is about one-third of a percent longer than its polar radius
volume	2.59×10^{11} cubic miles (1.08×10^{12} km³)
mass	1.32×10^{25} pounds (5.9742×10^{24} kg)
average density	344 pounds per cubic foot (5,515 kg/m³)
acceleration of gravity on the surface at the equator	32 feet per square seconds (9.78 m/sec²)
magnetic field strength at the surface	varies from 2.2×10^{-5} to 6.6×10^{-5} T
rings	0
moons	1

their views have not been the most widely held at any time since the Greeks (though there have been a few scholars who believed in a square Earth). The Columbus myth is an example of how easily errors can be repeated and driven into the canon of fact without being checked; no one's word is above verification.

Sailors over two millennia ago noticed that a mountain or another ship seems to rise from the sea as it is approached, and this effect is most easily achieved by sailing on a sphere, and having the other object come above the horizon as it nears. The movement and shapes of shadows as the Sun passes from east to west is another obvious clue. Though the Earth was generally accepted to be spherical, a greater problem was measuring the size of the sphere. One of the earliest known experiments to measure the radius of the Earth was made by Eratosthenes, a Greek mathematician who lived from 276 to 194 B.C.E. in Cyrene, now a part of Libya, and Alexandria, Egypt. Eratosthenes noticed that on the longest day of the year, the summer solstice, a perfectly upright pole casts no shadow. He also noticed that on the same day the bottom of a well is perfectly lit by sunlight: Both these observations mean that the Sun is directly overhead. He realized that if the Earth were round, a pole placed elsewhere would cast a shadow when his pole did not. Eratosthenes placed a pole at Syene, modern-day Aswān, and another about 500 miles (800 km) away, at Alexandria. The lengths of the shadows were measured, and using relatively simple geometry, Eratosthenes was able to measure the circumference of the Earth. His calculation yielded 250,000 stadia, a measure of length used at that time. The length of the Greek stadium is debated and may have been anywhere from 515 to 548 feet (157 to 167 m). Given that unknown, it can still be said that Eratosthenes'

Symbol for Earth

Many solar system objects have simple symbols: this is the symbol for the Earth.

measurement was something between a few and less than a half percent in error from the currently accepted value of 24,901 miles (40,075 km) at the equator (see the sidebar "Fundamental Information about the Earth" on page 4).

Each planet and some other bodies in the solar system (the Sun and certain asteroids) have been given its own symbol as a shorthand in scientific writing. The symbol for the Earth is shown on page 5.

A planet's rotation prevents it from being a perfect sphere. Spinning around an axis creates forces that cause the planet to swell at the equator and flatten slightly at the poles. Planets are thus shapes called oblate spheroids, meaning that they have different equatorial radii and polar radii, as shown in the image here. If the planet's equatorial radius is called r_e, and its polar radius is called r_p, then its flattening (more commonly called ellipticity, e) is defined as

$$e = \frac{r_e - r_p}{r_e}.$$

Ellipticity is the measure of by how much a planet's shape deviates from a sphere.

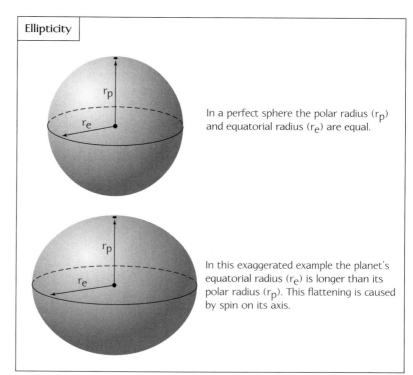

Ellipticity

In a perfect sphere the polar radius (r_p) and equatorial radius (r_e) are equal.

In this exaggerated example the planet's equatorial radius (r_e) is longer than its polar radius (r_p). This flattening is caused by spin on its axis.

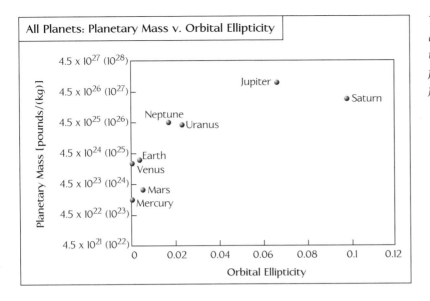

All Planets: Planetary Mass v. Orbital Ellipticity

The ellipticities of the planets differ largely as a function of their composition's ability to flow in response to rotational forces.

The larger radius, the equatorial, is also called the *semimajor axis,* and the polar radius is called the *semiminor axis.* The Earth's semimajor axis is 3,963.19 miles (6,378.14 km), and its semiminor axis is 3,950.01 miles (6,356.75 km), so its ellipticity (see the figure on page 6) is

$$e = \frac{3963.19 - 3950.01}{3963.19} = 0.00333.$$

Because every planet's equatorial radius is longer than its polar radius, the surface of the planet at its equator is farther from the planet's center than the surface of the planet at its poles.

To a lesser extent, the distance from the surface to the center of the Earth changes according to topography such as mountains or in valleys. Being at a different distance from the center of the planet means there is a different amount of mass between the surface and the center of the Earth. What effect does mass have? Mass pulls with its gravity. At the equator, where the radius of the Earth is larger and the amount of mass beneath them is relatively larger, the pull of gravity is actually stronger than it is at the poles. Gravity therefore, is not a perfect constant on any planet: Variations in radius, topography, as well as the density of the material beneath the surface make gravity vary slightly over the surface. This is why planetary gravitational accelerations are generally given as an average value on the planet's equator.

Gravity is among the least understood forces in nature. It is a fundamental attraction between all matter but it is also a very weak force: The gravitational attraction of objects smaller than planets and moons is so weak that electrical or magnetic forces can easily oppose it. At the moment, about the best that can be done with gravity is to describe its action: How much mass creates how much gravity? The question of what makes gravity itself is unanswered. This is part of the aim of a branch of mathematics and physics called string theory: to explain the relationships among the natural forces, and to explain what they are in a fundamental way. Sir Isaac Newton, the English physicist and mathematician who founded many of today's theories back in the mid-17th century, was the first to develop and record universal rules of gravitation. There is a legend that he was hit on the head by a falling apple while sitting under a tree thinking, and the fall of the apple under the force of Earth's gravity inspired him to think of matter attracting matter.

The most fundamental description of gravity is written in this way:

$$F = \frac{Gm_1 m_2}{r^2} \, ,$$

where F is the force of gravity, G is the universal gravitational constant (equal to 6.67×10^{-11} Nm^2/kg^2), m_1 and m_2 are the masses of the two objects that are attracting each other with gravity, and r is the distance between the two objects.

Immediately it is apparent that the larger the masses are, the larger the force of gravity. In addition, the closer together they are (r), the stronger the force of gravity, and because r is squared in the denominator, gravity diminishes very quickly as the distance between the objects increases. By substituting numbers for the mass of the Earth (5.9742×10^{24} kg), the mass of the Sun (1.989×10^{30} kg), and the distance between them, the force of gravity between the Earth and Sun is shown to be 8×10^{21} pounds per feet (3.56×10^{22} N). This is the force that keeps the Earth in orbit around the Sun. By comparison, the force of gravity between a piano player and her piano when she sits playing is about 6×10^{-7} pounds per feet (2.67×10^{-6} N). The force a pencil pressing down in the palm of a hand under the influence of

Earth's gravity is about 20,000 times stronger than the gravitational attraction between the player and the piano! So, although the player and the piano are attracted to each other by gravity, their masses are so small that the force is completely unimportant.

Gravity on Earth also affects the shape of the top of the ocean. If there is a large mountain at the bottom of the ocean, for example, the surface of the sea is actually depressed by the gravitational attraction of the mountain. Trenches in the ocean floor allow the surface of the ocean to rise up, because there is less mass pulling it down with gravity. The surface of the ocean deviates from horizontal for many reasons. The largest deviations are caused by tides, washing water from one side of the ocean basin to the other. Tides are a long wavelength phenomenon: Their wavelength is approximately the size of the ocean basin. Waves caused by wind have short wavelengths by comparison, and they are highly regular. By examining the average sea level only at small wavelengths while subtracting the effects of wind-driven waves, a picture of the topography of the ocean floor can be made.

Though trenches, mountains, and dense areas in the Earth's crust alter the gravity field on a small scale, the Earth's gravity field also changes on a large scale. The average value of gravity at the surface of the Earth is 32 feet per square seconds (9.8 m/sec^2), and variations in its strength are measured in units called galileos (Gal), or in this case, milliGals (0.001 of a galileo). One galileo is about 0.03 feet per square seconds (0.01 m/sec^2). Gravity is high over the Philippines, the Andes, and the North Atlantic, and low over Hudson Bay, the Indian Ocean, and the South Atlantic.

Conditions on the surface of the Earth, such as gravity, are controlled in part by the composition and size of the planet, but they are more significantly influenced by how the planet orbits the Sun. Day length, average, high, and low temperatures, the length of the seasons, and the length of the planet's year are all controlled in large part by the rotation of the planet, the tilt of its orbital axis, and the size and shape of its orbit around the Sun.

The length of a day on Earth varies constantly in response to changing interior and atmospheric motion, distance from the Sun, and through gravitational interactions with the Moon and other planets. A commission called the International Earth Rotation and Reference Systems Service was founded in 1987 by the International

Astronomical Union and the International Union of Geodesy and Geophysics to measure and record the rate of Earth's rotation, its celestial orientation, and changes in the Earth's mantle, core, and tides that affect its rotation. The value for day length given in this table, approximately equivalent to 23 hours, 56 minutes, and 4.09 seconds, is an average time for rotation. The time the Earth takes to rotate once on its axis is longest in the winter and shortest in the summer, varying around the average by about a millisecond.

Why, then, is the Earth's sidereal period ("year") listed as 1.0000174 Earth years? Each calendar year measured on Earth is a little bit shorter than the time it takes the Earth to actually orbit the Sun one time. Over four years this extra time adds up to one additional day, and that is the day that makes a leap year.

All orbits are ellipses, not circles. An ellipse can be thought of simply as a squashed circle, resembling an oval. Neptune's orbit is very close to circular, but it is still an ellipse. The proper definition of an ellipse is the set of all points that have the same sum of distances from two given fixed points, called foci. This definition is demonstrated by taking two pins and pushing them into a piece of stiff cardboard, and looping a string around the pins, as shown in the figure below. The two pins are the foci of the ellipse. Pull the string away from the pins with a pencil and draw the ellipse, keeping the string taut around the pins and the pencil all the way around. Adding the distance along the two string segments from the pencil to each of the pins will give the same answer each time: The ellipse is the set of all points that have the same sum of distances from the two foci.

Making an ellipse with string and two pins: Adding the distance along the two string segments from the pencil to each of the pins will give the same sum at every point around the ellipse. This method creates an ellipse with the pins at its foci.

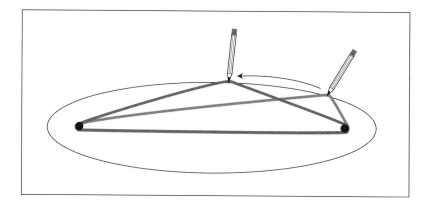

The mathematical equation for an ellipse is

$$\frac{x^2}{a^2} + \frac{y^2}{b^2} = 1,$$

where x and y are the coordinates of all the points on the ellipse, and a and b are the semimajor and semiminor axes, respectively. The semimajor axis and semiminor axis would both be the radius if the shape were a circle, but two are needed for an ellipse. If a and b are equal, then the equation for the ellipse becomes the equation for a circle:

$$x^2 + y^2 = n,$$

where n is any constant.

When drawing an ellipse with string and pins, it is obvious where the foci are (they are the pins). In the abstract, the foci can be calculated according to the following equations:

Coordinates of the first focus

$$= (+\sqrt{a^2 - b^2}, 0)$$

Coordinates of the second focus

$$= (-\sqrt{a^2 - b^2}, 0)$$

In the case of an orbit, the object being orbited (for example, the Sun) is located at one of the foci (see upper figure on page 12).

An important characteristic of an ellipse, perhaps the most important for orbital physics, is its eccentricity: the measure of how different the semimajor and semiminor axes are. Eccentricity is dimensionless and ranges from 0 to 1, where an eccentricity of zero means that the figure is a circle, and an eccentricity of 1 means that the ellipse has gone to its other extreme, a parabola (the reason an extreme ellipse becomes a parabola results from its definition as a conic section). One equation for eccentricity is

$$e = \sqrt{1 - \frac{b^2}{a^2}},$$

The semimajor and semiminor axes of an ellipse (or an orbit) are the elements used to calculate its eccentricity, and the body being orbited always lies at one of the foci.

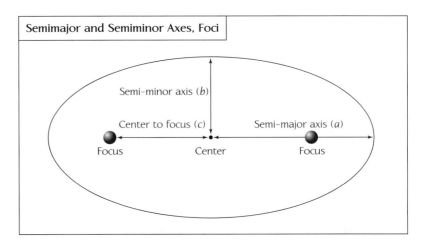

where *a* and *b* are the semimajor and semiminor axes, respectively. Another equation for eccentricity is

$$e = \frac{c}{a},$$

where *c* is the distance between the center of the ellipse and one focus. The eccentricities of the orbits of the planets vary widely, though most are very close to circles, as shown in the figure below. Pluto has the most eccentric orbit at 0.244, and Mercury's orbit is also very eccentric, but the rest have eccentricities below 0.09.

Though the orbits of planets are measurably eccentric, they deviate from circularity by very little. This figure shows the eccentricity of Pluto's orbit in comparison with a circle.

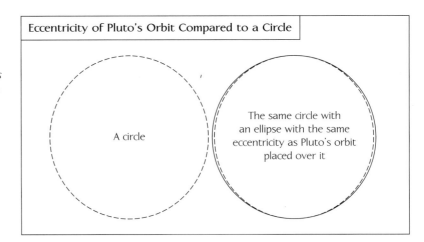

While the characteristics of an ellipse drawn on a sheet of paper can be measured, orbits in space are more difficult to characterize. The ellipse itself has to be described, and then the ellipse's position in space, and then the motion of the body as it travels around the ellipse. The shape of the ellipse and its relation to the Sun help determine the seasons, though the tilt of the planet on its axis is the most important determinant of seasons.

Seasons are created almost exclusively by the tilt of the planet's rotational axis, called its *obliquity*. While a planet rotates around the Sun, its axis always points in the same direction (the axis does wobble slightly, a movement called *precession*). The more extreme the obliquity, the more extreme the planet's seasons. The Earth's obliquity is not the most extreme in the solar system, as shown in the table below.

OBLIQUITY, ORBITAL INCLINATION, AND ROTATIONAL DIRECTION FOR ALL THE PLANETS

Planet	Obliquity (inclination of the planet's equator to its orbit; tilt); remarkable values are in italic	Orbital inclination to the ecliptic (angle between the planet's orbital plane and the Earth's orbital plane); remarkable values are in italic	Rotational direction
Mercury	0° (though some scientists believe the planet is flipped over, so this value may be 180°)	7.01°	prograde
Venus	*177.3°*	3.39°	retrograde
Earth	23.45°	0° (by definition)	prograde
Mars	25.2°	1.85°	prograde
Jupiter	3.12°	1.30°	prograde
Saturn	26.73°	2.48°	prograde
Uranus	*97.6°*	0.77°	retrograde
Neptune	29.56°	1.77°	prograde
Pluto	*122.5°*	*17.16°*	retrograde

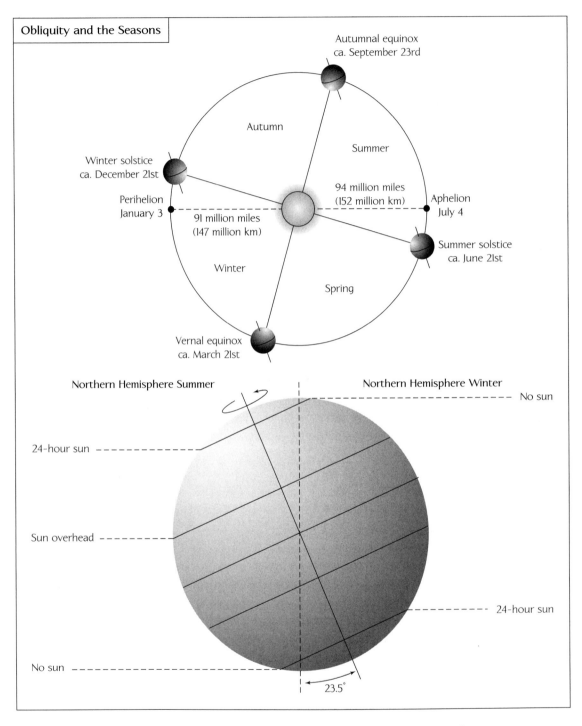

Obliquity and the Seasons

Autumnal equinox
ca. September 23rd

Autumn

Summer

Winter solstice
ca. December 21st

94 million miles
(152 million km)

Aphelion
July 4

Perihelion
January 3

91 million miles
(147 million km)

Summer solstice
ca. June 21st

Winter

Spring

Vernal equinox
ca. March 21st

Northern Hemisphere Summer

Northern Hemisphere Winter

No sun

24-hour sun

Sun overhead

24-hour sun

No sun

23.5°

A planet's obliquity (the inclination of its equator to its orbital plane) is the primary cause of seasons.

The Earth's obliquity, 23.45 degrees, is intermediate in the range of solar system values. The planet with the most extreme obliquity is Venus, with an obliquity of 177.3 degrees, followed by Pluto, with an obliquity of 122.5 degrees. An obliquity above 90 degrees means that the planet's North Pole has passed through its orbital plane and now points south. This is similar to Uranus's state, with a rotational axis tipped until it almost lies flat in its orbital plane. With the exceptions of Mercury and Jupiter, therefore, all the planets have significant seasons caused by obliquity.

Like its roundness, the Earth's obliquity has been recognized for millennia. In addition to his estimate of the circumference of the Earth, Eratosthenes calculated that the Moon is 780,000 stadia (124,800 km) from the Earth (the currently accepted value is 384,401 km, so in this case his calculation was not very accurate at all). However, Ptolemy records that Eratosthenes also measured the Earth's obliquity as 23.85 degrees, very close to the currently accepted 23.45 degrees.

Obliquity creates seasons by changing the amount of sunlight each hemisphere of the planet experiences from maximum to minimum during each orbit around the Sun (see figure on page 14). When a planet with obliquity has its North Pole tipped toward the Sun, the Northern Hemisphere receives more direct sunlight than does the Southern Hemisphere. The Northern Hemisphere then experiences summer, and the Southern Hemisphere is in winter. The planet progresses in its orbit, revolving around the Sun until it has moved 180 degrees, at which point the Southern Hemisphere gets more direct sunlight, and the Northern Hemisphere is in winter. The more oblique the rotation axis, the more severe the seasons—in summer one hemisphere receives even more sunlight and the other hemisphere even less, and vice versa in winter; summers are hotter and winters are colder. Basic statistics about Earth's orbit are given in the table on page 16.

The obliquity of a planet may change over time as well. Mars's obliquity may oscillate by as much as 20 degrees over time, creating seasons that are much more extreme. The Moon's stabilizing influence on the Earth has prevented large changes in obliquity and helped maintain a more constant climate, allowing life to continue and flourish.

At present the midpoint of summer on Earth for the Northern Hemisphere, when the North Pole points most toward the Sun, is

EARTH'S ORBIT

rotation on its axis ("day")	0.99726968 Earth days
rotation speed at equator	0.29 miles per second (0.47 km/sec)
rotation direction	prograde (counterclockwise when viewed from above the North Pole)
sidereal period ("year")	1.0000174 Earth years
orbital velocity (average)	18.5 miles per second (29.786 km/sec)
sunlight travel time (average)	8 minutes and 19 seconds to reach Earth
average distance from the Sun	92,958,361 miles (149,597,890 km), or 1 AU
perihelion	91,405,436 miles (147,098,768 km), or 0.9833 AU from the Sun
aphelion	94,511,989 miles (152,098,144 km) or 1.0167 AU from the Sun
orbital eccentricity	0.01671022
orbital inclination to the ecliptic	0.0 degrees (by definition of the ecliptic)
obliquity (inclination of equator to orbit)	23.45 degrees

June 21 plus or minus one day, depending on leap years. This is called the summer solstice, the longest day of the year, after which the days gradually become shorter. The Northern Hemisphere's winter solstice, the shortest day of the year, is around December 21. The reverse is true in the Southern Hemisphere: The summer solstice is in December and marks the longest day of the year, and the winter solstice is in June and marks the shortest day of the year.

Along with the summer and winter solstices, there are two other important days, and between these four days, the year is divided into quarters. The *vernal equinox* is the day in spring on which day and night are the same length (the word *equinox* means equal night). The autumnal equinox is the day in fall when day and night are the same length.

There are four movements in the Earth's orbit that change the severity of seasons over time. First, the Earth's rotation axis wobbles back and forth along a line of longitude on the Earth, slowly causing a slight change in obliquity. This is called *nutation*. The Earth's obliquity changes between approximately 22 and 25 degrees on a cycle of about 41,000 years. Nutation is thought to be caused by the Sun and Moon pulling on the Earth's tidal bulge. The Sun's torque on the Earth is at a maximum twice a year, at the solstices, when the Sun is 23.5 degrees above or below the Earth's equatorial plane. Solar torque is at a minimum at the equinoxes, when the Sun is directly above the Earth's equator. Lunar torque, on the other hand, reaches a maximum twice a month. The interaction of these torques causes the Earth's axis to bob in the motion of nutation.

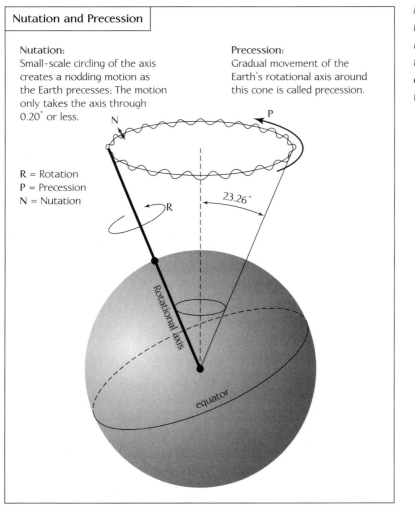

Nutation and Precession

Nutation:
Small-scale circling of the axis creates a nodding motion as the Earth precesses. The motion only takes the axis through 0.20˚ or less.

Precession:
Gradual movement of the Earth's rotational axis around this cone is called precession.

R = Rotation
P = Precession
N = Nutation

23.26˚

Rotational axis

equator

Nutation and precession are two movements of the Earth's rotational axis that change the severity of the seasons over time periods of thousands of years.

The direction of tilt of the Earth's axis also changes, much as a toy top does as it is slowing down. This circling of the axis, the second type of movement, is called *Chandler wobble* after its discoverer, or *axial precession.* Nutation and precession are shown in the figure on page 17. The cause of precession is not agreed upon, though both the Earth's ellipticity and the sloshing of the oceans due to tides may influence it. A complete circuit of the Earth's axis through precession takes about 25,000 years.

A third effect is called the *precession of the equinoxes.* Since in summer the Sun shines directly on the hemisphere in question, then the intensity of summer must depend in part on when summer occurs in the planet's orbit. If the planet's axis tilts such that the hemisphere has summer at *perihelion,* when the planet is closest to the Sun, then it will be a much hotter summer than if that hemisphere had summer at *aphelion,* when the planet is farthest from the Sun (also, a summer occurring at aphelion will be shorter, since the planet is moving faster). For the Earth, perihelion now occurs in January, making Northern Hemisphere winters slightly milder, and Southern Hemisphere summers slightly hotter. This change in timing of perihelion is known as the precession of the equinoxes, and occurs on a period of 22,000 years (the date of perihelion shifts by about one day in 58 years). Eleven thousand years ago, perihelion occurred in July, making the Northern Hemisphere's winter more severe than it is today.

The fourth effect on the severity of the seasons is a cyclical change in the eccentricity of Earth's orbit. Along with the precession of the equinoxes, the eccentricity of the earth's orbit varies on cycles of 100,000 and 400,000 years, affecting how important the timing of perihelion is to the strength of the seasons: A more eccentric orbit creates more extreme seasons.

The combination of the 41,000-year axial nutation cycle and the 25,000-year precession cycles affect the relative severity of summer and winter, and are thought to control the growth and retreat of ice sheets. The climate cycle caused by the combination of these effects is called the *Milankovitch cycle.* Cool summers in the Northern Hemisphere, where most of the Earth's landmass is located, appear to allow snow and ice to persist to the next winter, allowing the development of large ice sheets over hundreds to thousands of years. On the other hand, warmer summers shrink ice sheets by melting more ice than the amount accumulated during the winter.

An even more obscure change to the Earth's orbital and rotational cycles is caused by an interaction between the Earth's core and its atmosphere. In ways not entirely understood, the two flowing systems trade energy and can cause changes of day length on the order of two milliseconds per day. This corresponds to a 1 percent change in the average rate of Earth's rotation, and can cause a change in average global wind speed of about 11 miles per hour (18 km/hr). The fact that planetary orbits are ellipses, combined with the fact that the ellipses precess around the Sun slowly, allowed Mars and the Earth to come very close together on August 27, 2003. This close approach was at a distance of 34,776,000 miles (56 million km), not close

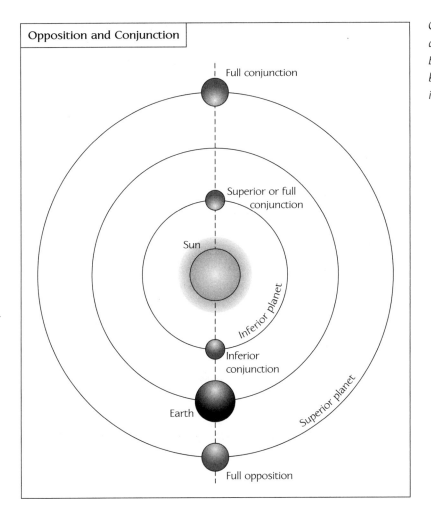

Opposition and conjunction are the two cases when the Earth, the Sun, and the body in question form a line in space.

enough to touch, but closer than the two planets have been in almost sixty thousand years. This kind of close approach is called a perihelic *opposition*. The orbits had precessed such that their long axes were almost perpendicular to each other. Mars was near perihelion, its closest approach to the Sun, while the Earth was very close to the autumnal equinox, on the side of its ellipse, directly between perihelion and aphelion. *Opposition* means that the Sun, Earth, and Mars were in a straight line, with Mars directly on the night side of the Earth (see the figure on page 19). The Earth orbits more quickly than Mars, lapping it around the Sun, and every two years the two planets are placed in their orbits in opposition. Normal oppositions occur every two years and bring the planets to within 0.4 to 0.68 AU of each other. Perihelic oppositions only occur about every 15 years, and bring the planets to within 0.37 to 0.4 AU of each other.

The closeness of the planets made Mars appear especially bright to viewers on Earth. The brightness of a celestial object when seen from a given distance is called its *apparent magnitude*. This scale has no dimensions but allows comparison between objects. The lower the magnitude number, the brighter the object. The brightest star is Sirius, with a magnitude of −1.4; the full Moon is −12.7; and the Sun is −26.7. The faintest stars visible under dark skies are around +6. During its close opposition, Mars rose to an apparent magnitude of −2.9, when normally it is as dim as +1.8.

Opposition is an optimal time to launch missions from the Earth to Mars. The spacecraft can be launched before opposition, make an arc between the two planets' orbits at an angle, and then land on Mars just after opposition. On particularly good oppositions the trip between the planets can be made in seven months. Because of the extreme closeness of this opposition, *Mars Express* and the two Mars Exploration Rover missions to Mars were launched at almost the same time, and all arrived at Mars in January 2004.

As knowledge increases and research continues, the questions scientists pose about the solar system become more complex and focused on more distant bodies. The physics of the sphericity of the Earth, its orbit around the Sun, and the force of gravity are all well understood; their fundamental functioning as described in this chapter are believed to have passed completely into the realm of what is known. Though scientists today might state that these facts and descriptions will stand for all time, perhaps scientists in the past thought the same thing about what they thought to be true. The Catholic Church up to the time of Galileo (the early 17th century) believed completely that the Sun orbited the Earth, and decades and in some cases centuries were required to convince people otherwise. Will modern science be similarly overturned?

With respect to the shape and orbit of the Earth, the answer is certainly no. So many measurements and observations have been taken that the shapes, sizes, and movements of the planets are completely known with such thoroughness that no doubt remains. Some details may still be modified, such as the effects that long-term changes in orbit and obliquity have on climate, but the fundamental physics is known.

The Interior of the Earth

Planetary geologists spend much of their time trying to understand how planets initially form and how their internal structures evolve. The temperatures and compositions of the interior of the Earth are well understood at shallow depths, and are less well understood as depth increases. The development of this knowledge has taken a lot of ingenuity and time because there are few ways to study the composition of the Earth directly.

The crust itself can be sampled at its surface, and volcanic eruptions sometimes bring up small pieces of the mantle. At certain places on the Earth's surface, rocks from the upper mantle have been pushed up onto the continents, either by collision or by deep volcanic explosions, and can be inspected directly. In these ways, there is direct evidence of only the very shallowest parts of the Earth, which may also be the parts of the Earth that have gone through the most alteration: repeated episodes of heating, melting, and mixing.

Other information on the Earth's composition comes from meteorite compositions, and from replicating deep-earth conditions in labs with high-pressure and high-temperature experimental equipment (see the sidebar "High-Pressure Experiments" on page 36). Scientists can begin to make estimates about what the mantle is made of based on the minerals that are stable in experiments at various pressures and temperatures. Experiments can give a large-scale idea of mineralogy, but the variation in compositions and therefore the variation in less common, or accessory, minerals in the Earth's mantle is not known. Gravity, magnetism, and seismic waves can be measured at the Earth's surface and allow scientists to learn more about the Earth's deep interior. Through the analysis of earthquake waves moving in the deep interior, scientists have been able to determine that the Earth's outer core is liquid, a crucial step in understanding the interior of the Earth.

Deep mines give us some information about composition and heat at depth, but even the deepest hole on Earth, the 7.5-mile- (12-km-) deep drill hole in Russia's Kola Peninsula, is still well within the crust and fails to approach even the upper mantle. As the writer Brad Lemley put it in *Discover* magazine, using the Kola drill hole to investigate the deep interior of the Earth is like learning about Alaska by driving from St. Petersburg, Florida, to nearby Tampa. Though 7.5 miles (12 km) is very deep by human standards, it does not reach through even the outermost, thinnest layer of the Earth.

Heat radiates away from the Earth into space, and the Earth is cooling through time. If the Earth had only the heat from its initial formation it could be calculated that the planet would have completely cooled by this time. *Radioactive* decay of *atoms* throughout the Earth produces heat, and the interior of the Earth is hotter than the surface. Heat flowing out of the Earth can be measured by placing thermal measuring devices in holes dug deeply into the soil, and heat flux (the amount of heat moving through a unit of surface area in a unit of time) has been found to be different in different parts of the world. Heat flux in areas of active volcanism, for example, is higher than heat flux in quiet areas. The likely internal temperatures of the Earth can be calculated based on heat flux at the surface. Such calculations lead to the conclusion that the Earth's shallow interior, not much deeper than the hard, cold crust, is 2,190 to 2,640°F (1,200 to 1,450°C).

Rocks at that temperature are able to flow over geologic time. Although they are not liquid, there is enough energy in the atoms that the crystals can deform and "creep" in response to pressure, over thousands or millions of years. The interior of the Earth is indeed creeping in this way, in giant circulation patterns driven by heat from the interior escaping toward the surface and radiating into space. This movement in response to heat is called *convection*. A small example of convection occurs in heating soup: In a glass pot, you can see upwelling plumes of hot soup, as well as soup that, having cooled at the surface, is now returning to the bottom of the pan.

Plate tectonics, the movement of the brittle outside of the Earth, is caused in part by these internal convective movements. At the surface this movement is only an inch or two (a few centimeters) a year, but over geologic time the movement is enough to give us the San

Andreas fault in California, where the edges of two plates are scraping past each other, along with the volcanoes around different parts of the Pacific Ocean's rim, where one plate is bending and being pushed beneath another.

Plate movement includes not only the crust at the surface, but also some portion of the Earth that lies beneath it. Below the crust, the planet's material is called the mantle. The uppermost mantle is too cool to be able to flow easily, even over millions of years, and so it moves as a unit with the crust. Together, these cool, connected layers are called the *lithosphere*. Beneath the lithosphere, the remaining mantle is hot enough to flow more quickly, perhaps at centimeters to tens of centimeters per year on average.

Seismologists studying the way earthquake waves move through the Earth have long known that the Earth has a core made of very different material than the mantle. Based on an analysis of the bulk silicate Earth (the mantle and crust, made mostly of minerals based on silicon atoms) compared to the composition of primitive meteorites that represent the material the inner planets were made of, we know that the silicate Earth is clearly missing a lot of iron and some nickel. Models of planetary formation also show that the heat of accretion (the original assembly of the planet) will cause iron to melt and sink into the deep interior of the Earth. Scientists are fairly certain, then, that the core of the Earth is made of iron with some nickel and a few percent of other elements. The density structure this implies also matches the planet's *moment of inertia,* which is a measure of the density structure inside a planet (for more, see the sidebar "Moment of Inertia" on page 26).

The structure of the Earth, used as the starting point in understanding the structures of other terrestrial planets, begins with the outermost cool, thin veneer of the Earth, the crust. The crust is coupled to the coolest, uppermost mantle, and together they are called the lithosphere. Under the lithosphere is the convecting mantle, and beneath that, the core. The outer core is liquid metal, and the inner core is solid metal. Though this structure is used as the starting point for understanding other terrestrial planets, it is different in one very important way: The Earth is the only known planet with plate tectonics (Mars may have had plate tectonics very early in its history). Mercury, Venus, and Mars are *one-plate planets:* Their crust and lithosphere form a single, solid spherical shell. Without

Moment of Inertia

The moment of inertia of a planet is a measure of how much force is required to increase the spin of the planet. (In more technical terms, the angular acceleration of an object is proportional to the torque acting on the object, and the proportional constant is called the moment of inertia of the object.)

The moment of inertia depends on the mass of the planet and on how this mass is distributed around the planet's center. The farther the bulk of the mass is from the center of the planet, the greater the moment of inertia. In other words, if all the mass is at the outside, it takes more force to spin the planet than if all the mass is at the center. This is similar to an example of two wheels with the same mass: one is a solid plate and the other is a bicycle wheel, with almost all the mass at the rim. The bicycle wheel has the greater moment of inertia and takes more force to create the same angular acceleration. The units of the moment of inertia are units of mass times distance squared; for example, lb $\times$ ft^2 or kg $\times$ m^2.

By definition, the moment of inertia I is defined as the sum of mr^2 for every piece of mass m of the object, where r is the radius for that mass m. In a planet, the density changes with radius, and so the moment of inertia needs to be calculated with an integral:

$$I = \int_0^{r_f} (\rho(r)) \, r^2 dr,$$

where r_o is the center of the planet and r_f is the total radius of the planet, $\rho(r)$ is the change of density with radius in the planet, and r is the radius of the planet and the variable of integration. To compare moments of inertia among planets, scientists calculate what is called the moment of inertia factor. By dividing the moment of inertia by the total mass of the planet M and the total radius squared R^2, the result is the part of the moment of inertia that is due entirely to radial changes in density in the planet.

plate tectonics, there are no volcanic arcs such as Japan or the Cascades, and there are no *mid-ocean ridges* from which oceanic crust is produced. Surface features on one-plate planets are therefore different from those on Earth.

What all the terrestrial planets seem to have in common are a cool outer crust and lithosphere, a silicate mantle, and an iron-rich core

This division also produces a non-dimensional number because all the units cancel. The equation for the moment of inertia factor, K, is as follows:

$$K = \frac{I}{MR^2}.$$

The issue with calculating the moment of inertia factor for a planet is that, aside from the Earth, there is no really specific information on the density gradients inside the planet. There is another equation, the rotation equation, that allows the calculation of moment of inertia factor by using parameters that can be measured. This equation gives a relationship between T, the rotation period of the planet; K, the moment of inertia factor of the planet; M, the mass of the planet; G, the gravitational constant; R, the planet's polar radius; D, the density for the large body; a, the planet's semimajor axis; i, the orbital inclination of the planet; m, the total mass of all satellites that orbit the large body; d, the mean density for the total satellites that orbit large body; and r, the mean polar radius of all satellites that orbit the large body:

$$T^2 = K\left(\frac{4\pi^2 D^3}{G(M+m)\cos^2 i}\right)\left(\left(\frac{m}{M}\right)\left(\frac{r}{R}\right) + \left(\frac{M}{m}\right)\left(\frac{D}{d}\right)\right)(4\pi a r K).$$

By getting more and more accurate measures of the moment of inertia factor of Mars, for example, from these external measurements, scientists can test their models for the interior of Mars. By integrating their modeled density structures, they can see whether the model creates a moment of inertia factor close to what is actually measured for Mars. On the Earth, the moment of inertia factor can be used to test for core densities, helping constrain the percentage of light elements that have to be mixed into the iron and nickel composition.

(see figure on page 28). How the crusts formed seems to differ among the planets, as does the composition of the mantle (though always silicate) and core (though always iron-dominated), and the heat and convective activity of the mantle. Theorizing about the degree of these differences and the reasons for their existence is a large part of planetary geology.

The Brittle Crust

The crust, the part of the Earth that humans tend to think of *as* the Earth, makes up only 0.5 percent of the Earth's total mass. The crust is made up of *igneous* rocks, *metamorphic* rocks, and *sedimentary* rocks. Sedimentary rocks, such as shale and limestone, can only be made at the surface of the planet, by surface processes such as rivers, glaciers, oceans, and wind. They make up the majority of rock outcrops at the surface but are not found at any depths in the planet. The crust of the Earth is significantly different from the crusts of other planets. On other terrestrial planets, the crust seems to made largely of igneous rocks low in silica and high in magnesium, like the dark lavas that erupt in Hawaii. There are exceptions: On the Moon, the white highlands seen so clearly from Earth seem to be made largely of the high-silica mineral plagioclase. In general, though, other planets are not covered with metamorphic rocks or high-silica igneous rocks, like

The fundamental layers of the Earth are the inner and outer core, the lower and upper mantle, and the lithosphere and crust. (Zaranek, modified after Beatty et al., 1999)

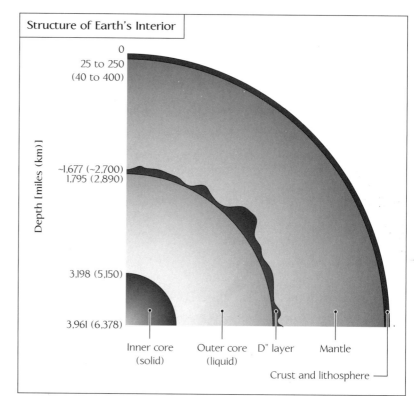

Structure of Earth's Interior

Depth [miles (km)]

0
25 to 250 (40 to 400)

~1,677 (~2,700)
1,795 (2,890)

3,198 (5,150)

3,961 (6,378)

Inner core (solid)   Outer core (liquid)   D" layer   Mantle

Crust and lithosphere

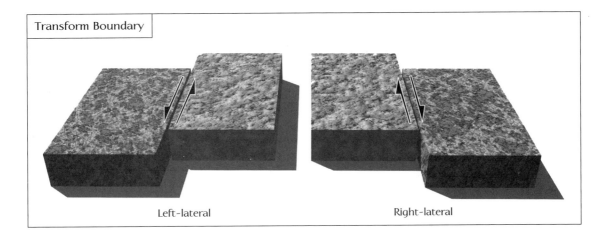

Transform Boundary

Left-lateral   Right-lateral

granites and andesites (these water-rich, high-silica magmas erupt at *subduction* zones). There are some sedimentary rocks on Mars, formed by ancient water movement and current wind storms.

On the Earth, oceanic crust consists of *basalt,* a dense, dark-colored igneous rock produced by melting the mantle, and of sediments deposited on the sea floor. The thickest oceanic lithosphere is about 40 miles (70 km) thick, and oceanic crust attains that thickness at an age of about 10 million years. Continental crust, on the other hand, is thicker and more buoyant, being made mainly of rocks that have a lower density than oceanic crust. Oceanic crust is eventually subducted back into the mantle, and so no oceanic crust is much older than 200 million years. Continental crust, on the other hand, has a wide range of ages. The oldest crustal rocks are almost 4 billion years old (discovered in the Canadian northwest by Sam Bowring, a professor at the Massachusetts Institute of Technology). There are no known crustal rocks older than 4 billion years, which raises the question: What was the Earth like in its first 560 million years? Was there little or no crust? Why was crust first formed? These questions remain unresolved. The lithosphere is divided into about 12 plates that move as individual units. There are a number of kinds of boundaries between plates. At one type of boundary, a transform boundary (see figure above), the plates move parallel to each other, creating long faults at the boundary (shown in the upper color insert on page C-2) where they meet. The San Andreas fault on the United States' west coast is one such place; movement at these boundaries create earthquakes.

At a transform boundary, plates slip horizontally past each other without significant convergence or divergence. The San Andreas fault between the North American and Pacific plates is an example of a right-lateral transform boundary.

At mid-ocean ridges, plates move away from each other (see figure below). These are called extensional boundaries. Mid-ocean ridges are marked by jagged lines of mountains down the center of the Atlantic, Pacific, and some other oceans, with a deep rift valley between the mountains. Beneath these rifts the mantle is flowing upward, and it melts as it depressurizes. This melt rises to the surface and cools as new oceanic crust. A total of about one cubic mile (~4 km³) of new oceanic crust is produced each year at mid-ocean ridges. As new melt rises, the crust moves away from the mid-ocean ridge, cooling, thickening, and settling more deeply into the mantle as it ages and moves away from the ridge. In this way, the deepest basins in the oceans are formed, by cooling, settling oceanic plates.

At compressional boundaries, the plates are moving toward each other. This kind of boundary creates a subduction zone, shown in the figure on page 31: Thinner, denser oceanic crust is pressed down underneath thicker, more buoyant continental crust, and the oceanic crust descends into the mantle (for more on subduction zones, see the mantle section below). Subduction zones create both earthquakes and volcanic eruptions, like those almost ringing the Pacific Ocean, including the Cascades, with many volcanoes, including Mount Saint Helens (shown in the lower color insert on page C-2); the Japanese islands, including Mount Fuji; and the Philippines, including Mount Pinatubo. When the oceanic plate subducts

At mid-ocean ridges, new crust is formed by upwelling and melting mantle, and the plates on each side of the ridge move away from each other.

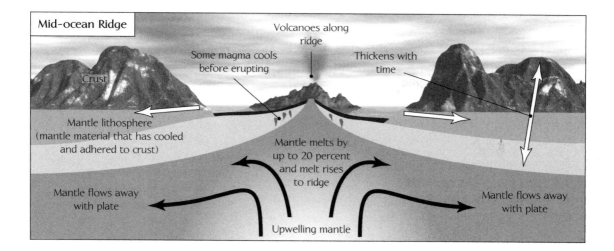

Mid-ocean Ridge

Volcanoes along ridge

Some magma cools before erupting

Thickens with time

Crust

Mantle lithosphere (mantle material that has cooled and adhered to crust)

Mantle melts by up to 20 percent and melt rises to ridge

Mantle flows away with plate

Mantle flows away with plate

Upwelling mantle

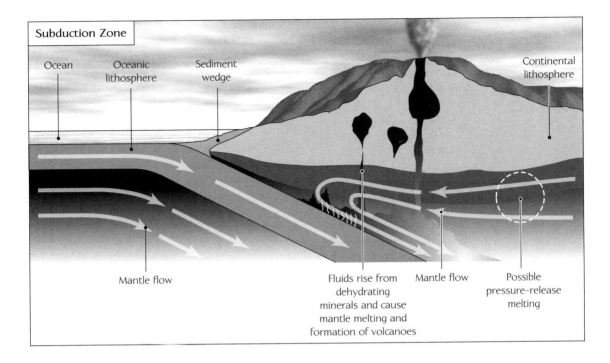

Subduction Zone

Ocean

Oceanic lithosphere

Sediment wedge

Continental lithosphere

Mantle flow

Fluids rise from dehydrating minerals and cause mantle melting and formation of volcanoes

Mantle flow

Possible pressure-release melting

beneath the continent, it sinks through its inherent density into the mantle and pulls the rest of the plate with it; this is thought to be the driving force for the formation of new crust at mid-ocean ridges, and is also thought to create the pattern of convection in the upper mantle. Clint Conrad, a researcher with Carolina Lithgow-Bertelloni at the University of Michigan, has created a model showing that some slabs remain attached as they sink into the mantle, pulling the plate behind them, and others detach but mantle flow continues to pull the plate down.

At some compressional boundaries the intervening ocean has been completely subducted and the two continents once separated by the ocean basin have collided. Neither can easily subduct beneath the other, and so large plateaus and mountain ranges are thrown up along complex systems of faults as the two continents are forced into each other. The collision of the Indian plate with the Asian plate is an example of this kind of compressional boundary, and has produced high mountains, including the Earth's highest, Mount Everest. Mount Everest is 5.5 miles (8.8 km) high. Astronaut Dan Bursch, a member of the Expedition 4 crew on the *International Space Station*, took this

At subduction zones, thinner, denser oceanic crust slides under more buoyant continental crust and sinks gradually into the mantle beneath.

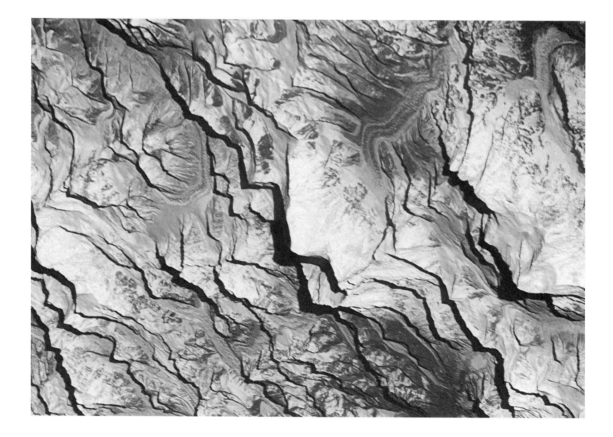

Astronaut Dan Bursch, a member of the Expedition 4 crew on the International Space Station, *took this photograph of Mount Everest from the space station in late March 2002.* (Earth Sciences and Image Analysis Laboratory, NASA Johnson Space Center, eol.jsc.nasa.gov, ISS04-E-8852)

photo of Mount Everest in late March 2002. In this image early morning light shines on the mountain's eastern Kangshung Face.

The Solid but Moving Mantle

It is necessary to stress here that the upper mantle of the Earth is not molten because this is a falsehood that has been propagated through textbooks for years. The uppermost mantle, in general, is solid, but because it is warm and at low pressure compared to the rest of the mantle, it is softer and flows more easily. Only small parts of the upper mantle melt as they rise and depressurize, or as they have water injected into them at subduction zones. The addition of water lowers the melting temperature of the mantle, and so melting and subsequent volcanism is triggered by the addition of water from sediments on the subducting slab. Only a small percent of the upper mantle is molten at any one time, and that melt rapidly moves upward through buoyant forces. Further, the areas of the mantle with melt in them are in specific geologic settings scattered around the Earth.

Based on what is suspected about the bulk composition of the Earth, what is known about the seismic properties of the mantle, and what is known from pieces of the mantle that are carried to the surface in volcanic eruptions (these are called xenoliths), the bulk composition of the mantle is approximately 46 percent silica (SiO_2), 38 percent magnesium oxide (MgO), 7 percent iron oxide (FeO), 4 percent alumina (Al_2O_3), 3 percent calcium oxide (CaO), 0.5 percent sodium oxide (Na_2O), and about 1 percent all other elements. Note that all these compounds are expressed as oxides: there is enough oxygen in the Earth to balance the charges of all the positively charged ions, such as silicon, magnesium, and so on. The oxides that make up the bulk composition are all organized into crystalline mineral grains in the mantle. Oxygen (O) and silicon (Si) form the framework of almost all the minerals that make up the mantle. Oxygen and silicon bonded together is called silica, and minerals with silica-based crystal structures are called silicates. These minerals determine the mantle's *viscosity,* density, seismic speed, and its melting behavior, which in turn determines the types and volumes of magma that erupt to the surface.

The mantle is divided into the upper mantle, including all material shallower than about 415 miles (670 km), and the lower mantle, reaching from 415 miles (670 km) to the core-mantle boundary at 1,800 miles (2,900 km) depth. The boundary between the upper and lower mantles, at 415 miles (670 km), is known throughout the geologic community as the 670 discontinuity. The upper mantle, which can be sampled through xenoliths, is made mainly of the minerals *olivine* (($Mg, Fe)_2SiO_4$), *clinopyroxene* (($Ca,Mg,Fe,Al)_2(Si,Al)_2O_6$), orthopyroxene (($Mg, Fe)SiO_3$), and one of several minerals that contains alumina, which cannot fit into the other three minerals in any great amount. The aluminous minerals change according to the pressure they are at. At the shallowest depths and lowest pressures, the aluminous mineral is plagioclase. At greater depths, the plagioclase ($NaAlSi_3O_8$ to $CaAl_2Si_2O_8$) transforms into spinel ($MgAl_2O_4$), and then at greater depths, into the beautiful mineral *garnet* ($[Ca,Mg,Fe Mn]_3[Al,Fe,Cr,Ti]_2[SiO_4]_3$). Because of this mineralogy, the mantle is an exceptionally beautiful material: The olivine is a bright olive green, usually making up over 50 percent of the rock, and the remainder of the mantle is made up of black orthopyroxenes, bottle-green clinopyroxenes, and brilliant ruby-colored garnets.

The boundary between the upper and lower mantle is clearly seen in seismic studies. Waves bounce off the boundary and change their qualities if they pass through the surface. This type of boundary is called a seismic discontinuity, and the 670 discontinuity is observed worldwide. To understand the nature of this boundary, how materials react to increasing pressure must be understood. The more pressure placed on a material, the closer the atoms are forced together. Some materials are compressible: With increasing pressure, their atoms move closer and the volume of the material decreases. Gases are compressible. They can be pushed into pressurized tanks, and balloons filled with gases expand as they go up in altitude, because the air pressure around them is lessening and allowing the interior gas to expand. Water is almost incompressible: Its molecules have slight charges, and the electrical charges repel each other, preventing water from being compressed too much. Crystalline substances, like the minerals that make up rocks, are generally close to incompressible. The crystal lattices are very stiff and are able to withstand large pressures without changing their shape or allowing their atoms to press more closely together (though pressure may cause defects, such as empty spaces or offsets in the crystal lattice, to migrate through the crystal, creating the creep phenomenon that leads to the mantle's ability to flow).

Raising temperature along with pressure enhances crystal's ability to change its properties. With increased temperature, the atoms in the crystal lattices vibrate faster and are more able to move out of position. As pressure and temperature are raised, the material eventually reaches a point where its current crystal structure is no longer stable, and it metamorphoses into a new, more compact crystal structure. The first such transformations in the mantle are in the aluminous phases, which transform from plagioclase to spinel to garnet with increasing pressure. These make up only a small percentage of the mantle, though, and their transformations do not change the way seismic waves travel through the Earth in any significant way. Olivine makes up the majority of the mantle, and when it transforms to a different crystal structure, the seismic properties of the mantle are significantly changed.

Within the upper mantle as pressure increases with depth olivine transforms to a higher-pressure phase called γ-olivine, and the pyroxene and garnet minerals transform into a garnet-like mineral with lower silica, called majorite. The pressures and temperatures for these transformations have been measured experimentally in high-pressure laboratory devices (see the sidebar "High-Pressure Experiments" on page 36), and they seem to correspond to a layer in the Earth weakly seen in seismic studies at 255 miles (410 km) and about 140,000 atmospheres pressure (14 GPa) (see the table "Derived Units" in appendix 1). The big transformation occurs at higher pressure when y-olivine transforms to perovskite. This transformation makes a great change in seismic qualities of the mantle, and it occurs at a pressure and temperature that corresponds to 415 miles (670 km) depth and about 220,000 atmospheres pressure (22 GPa) in the Earth. Seismologists have thus measured the internal properties of the Earth, and experimental scientists have recreated the changes in the laboratory, so scientists have a good idea of the cause of the seismic transformations in the mantle.

Perovskite, then, is probably the most common mineral in the Earth, since it is thought to make up the bulk of the mantle between 415 miles (670 km) and 1,800 miles (2,900 km) depth. The volume of mantle is more than half the volume of the Earth. Our knowledge of the deep mantle is sketchy, though. There is tremendous ongoing debate over how well mixed the mantle is, and though perovskite is thought to make up by far the bulk of the lower mantle, there may be many other high-pressure mineral phases that are not yet identified. High-pressure experimentalists regularly find new minerals, though they are hard to characterize in the tiny amounts that are made in experiments. They receive letters instead of names, such as phase L, phase M, and phase N, pending further information.

Other seismic boundaries can be seen in the deep mantle, including an especially interesting deep layer called D" (pronounced "D double prime"), found at about 1,700 miles (2,700 km) depth. There is significant topography on its surface, so its depth varies from place to place. The changes in seismic speed across this boundary cannot be explained entirely by a change in temperature, but require a change in composition as well. Is this a deep, sequestered layer that has not been mixed into the rest of the mantle? Louise Kellogg, Brad Hager, and Rob van der Hilst, three of the most noted geophysicists working today, believe that this layer may be the starting point of hot, buoyant

High-Pressure Experiments

Though it is possible to estimate the pressure, temperature, and even the bulk composition of materials in the Earth's deep interior, it is difficult to know the minerals that would exist deep inside the mantle. Even if the deep mantle moves upward through convection, and pieces are erupted onto the surface in volcanoes, the deep minerals would have reequilibrated into lower-pressure phases before they could be examined.

Scientists in a branch of geology called experimental petrology seek to answer questions about the Earth's unreachable interior. Over the course of the 20th century, scientists slowly developed sophisticated equipment to re-create conditions deep in the Earth. The apparatus that puts material under the greatest pressure is called a diamond anvil. Two small circular plates, each bearing a diamond with a flattened tip, are screwed together until the tips of the diamonds meet and press an experimental sample between them. The diamond anvil can create pressures up to about 100 GPa, close to the pressure at the core-mantle boundary in the Earth. The sample, however, can only be about 20 microns in diameter, so the means to inspect and analyze the experiment are largely limited to X-ray diffraction studies of crystal structure. In addition, diamond anvil cells cannot be heated significantly.

mantle plumes that rise through the entire mantle and create melt that erupts onto the surface (the Hawaii island chain is thought to be the product of such a plume).

The topic of plumes brings us to another subject: mantle convection. At the temperatures and pressures in the mantle, the rock can flow slowly over time. Heat escaping from the core heats the lower mantle, which makes it less dense. (In general, heating a substance increases its volume slightly, which makes it less dense.) The less dense parts of the mantle are then buoyant when compared to their cooler neighboring areas, and the hotter material rises, displacing cooler material downward. This is the process of convection. The mantle is thought to move at a few centimeters per year near the surface (this is estimated from plate motions and subduction zone speeds), and it may move faster at depth. The motions of

An apparatus called the multi-anvil is used to create high pressures and temperatures simultaneously. A huge press frame, weighing perhaps 10 tons, houses a hydraulic system. The hydraulic system pushes a set of carbide blocks together in such a way that they all press equally on a tiny octahedron in their center. This octahedron contains about a tenth of a gram of experimental sample inside a graphite tube that acts as a heater. Graphite has high resistance to electrical current, so when a current is passed through the graphite it heats up. This simple principle allows the sample to be heated to 3,200°F (1,800°C) or more, and to be controlled within about 10 degrees by placing thermocouple wires next to the experiment and running them out through the carbide blocks to an electrical controller. The experimental sample is large enough to be examined in an optical microscope or analyzed in an electron microprobe, but usually the apparatus can only reach about 30 GPa.

The multi-anvil, the diamond anvil, and a lower-pressure but more common apparatus called the piston-cylinder are the tools that allow experimental petrologists to approximate conditions inside the Earth and attempt to determine the mineral phases present and their behaviors. Using these techniques, scientists have discovered the mineral phase changes that create the 410 and 670 discontinuities in the Earth's mantle, the processes that may have formed the Earth's core, as well as the compositions and mineral assemblages that make up the interior of the Moon (much of the author's research has been in this area).

convection are controlled by viscosity, which is a measure of the ability of a material to flow (see the sidebar "Rheology, or How Solids Can Flow" on page 38).

The viscosity of the mantle cannot be measured directly, and could not be even if it could be reached with a drill. Viscosity of the mantle is strongly controlled by temperature. As soon as the mantle is cooled, it stops flowing, and in any case it only flows a few centimeters a year. However, scientists thought of a very clever method to help measure mantle viscosity. About 10,000 years ago, the Northern Hemisphere was covered by ice sheets as thick as two miles (3 km). The edge of one of the Earth's two current ice sheets, the Greenland ice sheet, is shown in this image from NASA's Terra satellite (the second ice sheet in existence today is the far larger Antarctic sheet). The Greenland ice sheet is two miles (3 km) thick at its greatest extent,

Rheology, or How Solids Can Flow

Rheology is the study of how materials deform, and the word is also used to describe the behavior of a specific material, as in "the rheology of ice on Ganymede." Both ice and rock, though they are solids, behave like liquids over long periods of time when they are warm or under pressure. They can both flow without melting, following the same laws of motion that govern fluid flow of liquids or gases, though the timescale is much longer. The key to solid flow is viscosity, the material's resistance to flowing.

Water has a very low viscosity: It takes no time at all to flow under the pull of gravity, as it does in sinks and streams and so on. Air has lower viscosity still. The viscosities of honey and molasses are higher. The higher the viscosity, the slower the flow. Obviously, the viscosities of ice and rock are much higher than those of water and molasses, and so it takes these materials far longer to flow. The viscosity of water at room temperature is about 0.001 Pas (pascal seconds), and the viscosity of honey is about 1,900 Pas. By comparison, the viscosity of window glass at room temperature is about 10^{27} Pas, the viscosity of warm rocks in the Earth's upper mantle is about 10^{19} Pas.

The viscosity of fluids can be measured easily in a laboratory. The liquid being measured is put in a container, and a plate is placed on its surface. The liquid sticks to the bottom of the plate, and when the plate is moved, the liquid is sheared (pulled to the side). Viscosity is literally the relationship between shear stress σ and the rate of deformation ϵ. Shear stress is pressure in the plane of a surface of the material, like pulling a spatula across the top brownie batter.

$$\eta = \frac{\sigma}{\epsilon}.$$

The higher the shear stress needed to cause the liquid to deform (flow), the higher the viscosity of the liquid.

The viscosity of different materials changes according to temperature, pressure, and sometimes shear stress. The viscosity of water is lowered by temperature and raised by pressure, but shear stress does not affect it. Honey has a similar viscosity relation with temperature: The hotter the honey, the lower its viscosity. Honey is 200 times less viscous at 160°F (70°C) than it is at 57°F (14°C). For glass, imagine its behavior at the glasshouse. Glass is technically a liquid even at room temperature, because its molecules are not organized into crystals. The flowing glass the glassblower works with is simply the result of high temperatures creating low viscosity. In rock-forming minerals, temperature drastically lowers viscosity, pressure raises it moderately, and shear stress lowers it, as shown in the accompanying figure.

Latex house paint is a good example of a material with shear-stress dependent viscosity. When painting it on with the brush, the brush applies shear stress to the paint, and its viscosity goes down. This allows the paint to be brushed on evenly. As soon as the shear stress is removed, the paint becomes more viscous and resists dripping. This is a material property that the paint companies purposefully give the paint to make it perform better. Materials that flow more easily when under shear stress but then return to a high viscosity when undisturbed are called thixotropic. Some strange materials, called dilatent materials, actually obtain higher viscosity when placed under shear stress. The most common example of a dilatent

(continues)

These graphs show the relationship of fluid flow to shear stress for different types of materials, showing how viscosity can change in the material with increased shear stress.

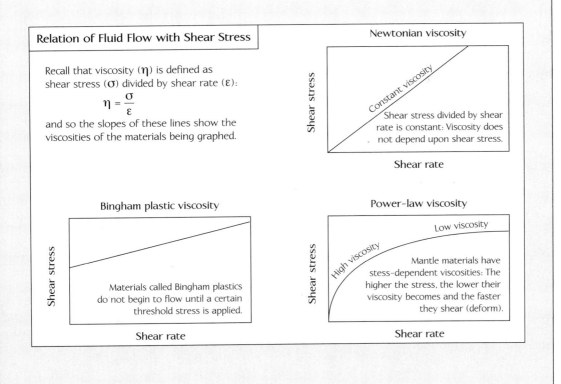

Relation of Fluid Flow with Shear Stress

Recall that viscosity (η) is defined as shear stress (σ) divided by shear rate (ε):

$$\eta = \frac{\sigma}{\varepsilon}$$

and so the slopes of these lines show the viscosities of the materials being graphed.

Newtonian viscosity

Constant viscosity

Shear stress divided by shear rate is constant: Viscosity does not depend upon shear stress.

Shear stress / Shear rate

Bingham plastic viscosity

Materials called Bingham plastics do not begin to flow until a certain threshold stress is applied.

Shear stress / Shear rate

Power-law viscosity

Low viscosity

High viscosity

Mantle materials have stess-dependent viscosities: The higher the stress, the lower their viscosity becomes and the faster they shear (deform).

Shear stress / Shear rate

Rheology, or How Solids Can Flow (continued)

material is a mixture of cornstarch and water. This mixture can be poured like a fluid and will flow slowly when left alone, but when pressed it immediately becomes hard, stops flowing, and cracks in a brittle manner. The viscosities of other materials do not change with stress: Their shear rate (flow rate) increases exactly with shear stress, maintaining a constant viscosity.

Temperature is by far the most important control on viscosity. Inside the Earth's upper mantle, where temperatures vary from about 2,000°F (1,100°C) to 2,500°F (1,400°C), the solid rocks are as much as 10 or 20 orders of magnitude less viscous than they are at room temperature. They are still solid, crystalline materials, but given enough time, they can flow like a thick liquid. The mantle flows for a number of reasons. Heating in the planet's interior makes warmer pieces of mantle move upward buoyantly, and parts that have cooled near the surface are denser and sink. The plates are also moving over the surface of the planet, dragging the upper mantle with them (this exerts shear stress on the upper mantle). The mantle flows in response to these and other forces at the rate of about one to four inches per year (2 to 10 cm per year).

Rocks on the planet's surface are much too cold to flow. If placed under pressure, cold, brittle surface rocks will fracture, not flow. Ice and hot rocks can flow because of their viscosities. Fluids flow by molecules sliding past each other, but the flow of solids is more complicated. The individual mineral grains in the mantle may flow by "dislocation creep," in which flaws in the crystals migrate across the crystals and effectively allow the crystal to deform or move slightly. This and other flow mechanisms for solids are called plastic deformations, since the crystals neither return to their original shape nor break.

and so is a modern analog to the last ice age, though at that time the ice sheets were far more extensive.

In Norway, Sweden, and Finland (together called Fennoscandia) in particular, because of the relatively small size and round shape of this land mass, the thick ice sheets pressed the continental crust down into the mantle just as one's hand can press a toy boat down into a bath of water. Now, with the ice sheets gone, Fennoscandia is rebounding, rising up again to its equilibrium height in the mantle. Since the mantle is highly viscous this rebound occurs slowly, unlike in the toy boat analogy. The viscosity of the mantle can be calculated by the speed of rebound of Fennoscandia. The area is rebounding about one-third of an inch (8 mm) per year at its center, and it is estimated that it has about 656 feet (200 m) of rebound to go. By using the following equation, the viscosity of the underlying mantle can be calculated:

$$\eta = 0.25\rho g R\tau,$$

The Greenland ice sheet is the smaller of the two ice sheets on the Earth today. (NASA's Earth Observatory)

where η is the viscosity of the mantle, ρ is the density of the mantle, g is the acceleration of gravity, R is the radius of the depressed area, and τ is the time required to approach equilibrium. In this way, it has been shown that the viscosity of the upper mantle is between 10^{19} and 10^{20} Pas (pascal-seconds). By comparison, the viscosity of water is about 10^{-3} Pas, and maple syrup is 2.5 Pas. Glass is also a liquid, no matter how hard and brittle it may seem on the short timescales of days, weeks, and years: The molecules that make up glass are not ordered, so the material is technically a liquid, and does in fact flow very slowly, over great amounts of time. Glass has a viscosity of about 10^{19} Pas. If the mantle were as cool as your window glass, it would be several orders of magnitude more viscous yet.

Much about convective motions in the Earth's mantle is unknown. The movement of the plates proves that the mantle in convecting at shallow depths, but the patterns of convection at depth are still a matter of debate. For years many scientists thought that the Earth had layered convection: The upper mantle convected in its own pattern, and beneath the 670 discontinuity, the lower mantle convected separately. This would make separate compositional reservoirs possible, since each convecting layer would eventually become well mixed, but the layers might remain separate.

In the last few years, a technique called *tomography* has been developed. Using seismic waves coming from earthquakes in several directions, material in the mantle that changes their speed can be pinpointed, and even outlined. Rob van der Hilst, a geophysicist at the Massachusetts Institute of Technology, and his colleagues have used tomographic techniques to locate and outline subducting slabs of oceanic crust as they sink in the mantle. The slabs remain cold for a long time as they sink, and their coldness slows down seismic waves that move through them, making it possible to create an image of the slab in the mantle. These researchers, and others, have found evidence that subducting slabs sometimes settle to rest on the 670 discontinuity, at least temporarily, but others plunge straight through that boundary and sink to the deepest mantle.

When these studies were published, they created shockwaves in the geologic community. Here was direct evidence for two things that geologists had speculated about for years: The first is whole-mantle convection, supported by the slabs' movement through the entire mantle, and the second is mantle heterogeneity. Using geochemical studies of volcanic rocks, it has been postulated for years that there are regions in the mantle that have distinct compositions. These distinct compositions are reflected in the compositions of the volcanic rocks that are produced from them. This was sometimes taken as evidence for layered mantle convection. Here, though, is a way to make the mantle compositionally heterogeneous on a small scale: The subducted plates have a very different composition than the mantle as a whole, and they could mix into the mantle over time, creating ribbons of varying composition in the mantle. Subducted slabs also carry sediment from the sea floor, and the uppermost slab and sediment are loaded with water. Subducting slabs are thus a way that water can be added to the mantle as well.

The Solid and Liquid Cores

The core of the Earth takes up about half the Earth's radius and 32.5 percent of its mass. Studies of the Earth's moment of inertia factor along with the movement of seismic waves through the Earth's interior show that the core is made of very dense material. The only real options, in terms of elements that are common enough in the inner solar system and also heavy enough to create the Earth's core, are iron (Fe) with the addition of a little nickel (Ni). These ideas are supported by finding iron meteorites made of mixtures of iron and nickel, thought to represent the broken-apart cores of *planetesimals* that did not survive the chaos of the early solar system.

To fit the constraints on the density of the core, knowing its radius, the core has to consist of 84.6 percent iron (about 27 percent of all the iron in the Earth), 7.7 percent nickel, and then an additional ~7.7 percent of some lighter element. Debate over what the lighter component might be is ongoing in the geological sciences. The best candidates are sulfur (S), potassium (K), oxygen (O), carbon (C), hydrogen (H), and silicon (Si). For each of these elements, there are reasons to support its existence in the core, and reasons to argue against it, and there are scientists who are protagonists for each and opponents of others. The light element in the core has to be soluble in the liquid iron in the outer core and abundant enough that some would be available to leave the mantle and enter the core during core formation. The fact that the outer core is liquid was first discovered by seismologists trying to understand the very complex waves caused by earthquakes. When two parts of the crust are being forced past each other, most often by plate tectonic forces, stress builds up in the rock to the point that the rock suddenly breaks and is able to slide past itself to relieve the pressure. This sudden breaking and slipping is the cause of the earthquake.

At the site of an earthquake, four kinds of waves are produced in the Earth as a result of the energy release and movement of the rocks. The first two are called body waves, because they move through the earth itself. The second two are called surface waves, because they propagate along the interface between the atmosphere and the earth. The two kinds of body waves are P-waves (P for primary, and also for pressure) and S-waves (S for secondary, and also for shear). P-waves move as fronts of compression and decompression, exactly like sound waves in the air. P-waves can move through liquids, gases, and solids (remember that you can hear while underwater, because this kind of wave can move through liquid). S-waves move as up-and-down shearing motions, like an oscillating string or a moving snake. The movement of this kind of wave requires that the material it is moving through holds together, having some strength. Shear waves cannot move through liquid. The two kinds of surface waves are called Love waves and Rayleigh waves, and they cause much of the earthquake damage experienced at the surface. Earthquakes also cause the whole Earth to oscillate, like a floating bubble after it has gently bumped into an object. These movements are called free oscillations and over

A major earthquake can cause the whole Earth to move according to patterns called free oscillations.

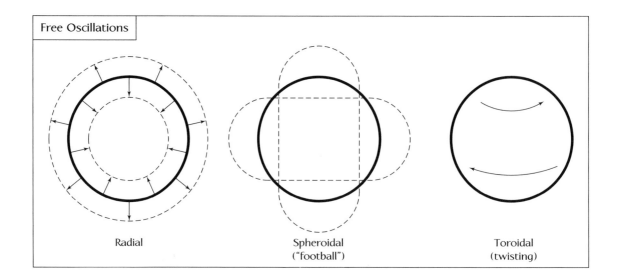

Free Oscillations

Radial

Spheroidal ("football")

Toroidal (twisting)

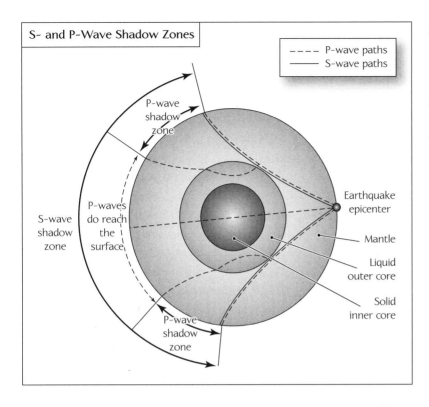

S- and P-Wave Shadow Zones

- - - - P-wave paths
——— S-wave paths

P-wave shadow zone

S-wave shadow zone

P-waves do reach the surface

Earthquake epicenter

Mantle

Liquid outer core

Solid inner core

P-wave shadow zone

S- and P-wave shadow zones are regions on the Earth's surface that cannot be reached by S- and P-waves from a given earthquake because of the inability of S-waves to move through the liquid outer core and by the refraction of P-waves through the same liquid.

1,000 modes have been found; a few of the simplest are shown in the figure on page 44. Sometimes the press announces that a huge earthquake has caused the Earth to "ring like a bell." This analogy refers to free oscillations, though they occur for all sizes of earthquakes, just less strongly for small earthquakes. (After major earthquakes the press has sometimes reported that the Earth moved out of its orbit, but it is physically impossible for earthquakes to cause that.)

So what do earthquake waves have to do with identifying the outer core? Since S-waves cannot pass through liquids, the S-waves from an earthquake are prevented from reaching the other side of the Earth if they have to pass through the outer core. There are zones on the surface of the Earth about 110 degrees from earthquakes where S-waves are not received at the surface. These are called shadow zones (see figure above). They were discovered in about 1910, and from them it was deduced that the outer core at least had to be liquid.

Inge Lehmann, a Danish geophysicist, subsequently discovered in 1936 that the Earth has a solid inner core. Her work is a great story of early success by a woman in a field traditionally populated only by men. By studying seismic waves she was able to discern the strange waves that had passed through the liquid outer core, through the solid inner core, and back out through the other side of the liquid core before traveling back up to the surface to be detected on seismometers. These waves had properties that could only be explained if they had passed through a solid inner core: The travel time of P-waves that go through the center of the core are appreciably faster then those that skirt the outside, indicating the center contains some dense, solid material through which waves travel faster. The discontinuity between the liquid outer core and the solid inner core, 3,200 miles (5,150 km) down, is named the Lehmann discontinuity. The name was given only recently, but Lehmann was still alive, in her nineties, and could enjoy the honor.

The liquid outer core convects much as the mantle convects, though 10^6 times faster and possibly more turbulently. Fluid motions in the outer core reach 10 to 100 kilometers per year, meaning that it is moving several meters per hour, movement fast enough to see if you were able to watch it.

Magnetic Field

The scientific community is fairly well united in the idea that the convective currents in the outer core combined with the planet's rotation cause the Earth's magnetic field. Sir Joseph Larmour, an Irish physicist and mathematician, first proposed the hypothesis that the Earth's active magnetic field might be explained by the way the moving fluid iron in Earth's outer core mimics electrical currents, and the fact that every electric current has an associated, enveloping magnetic field. The combination of convective currents and a spinning inner and outer core is called the dynamo effect. If the fluid motion is fast, large, and conductive enough, then a magnetic field can not only be created, but also carried and deformed by the moving fluid (this is also what happens in the Sun). The inner core rotates faster than the outer core, pulling field lines into itself and twisting them. Fluid upwelling from the boundary with the inner core is twisted by the Coriolis effect, and in turn twists the magnetic field. In these ways, it is thought that the field lines are made extremely complex. The exact patterns of the field at the core are not known. This theory works well for the Earth and for the Sun, and even for Jupiter and Saturn, though they are thought to have a dynamo made of metallic hydrogen, not iron.

The Earth's magnetic field is largely a bipolar field, meaning that it has a North and a South Pole with magnetic field lines that flow between them (see figure below). Magnetic fields are often thought of

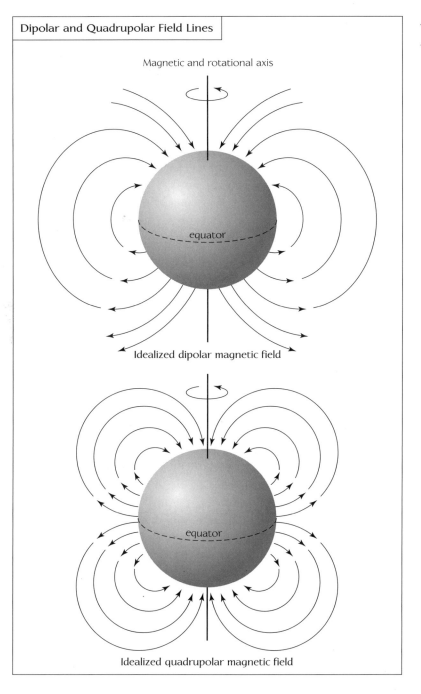

Dipolar and Quadrupolar Field Lines

Magnetic and rotational axis

equator

Idealized dipolar magnetic field

equator

Idealized quadrupolar magnetic field

A dipolar planetary magnetic field resembles the field of a bar magnet.

just in terms of *dipoles,* meaning a two-poled system like a bar magnet, with magnetic field lines flowing out of the south magnetic pole
and into the north magnetic pole, but there are other, more complex
configurations possible for magnetic fields. The next most complex
after the dipole is the quadrupole, in which the field has four poles
equally spaced around the sphere of the planet. After the quadrupole
comes the octupole, which has eight poles. Although the Earth's field
is largely a dipole field, it has fine, weak structure related to quadrupole, octupole, and higher order fields present as well. The dipole
field is the strongest, and the strength of the higher fields falls off by
nine orders of magnitude as the field complexity moves from quadrupole up through the next ten levels of field complexity.

The word *poles* was first used for the magnetic field in 1269 by a
man whose scholarly name was Petrius Peregrinus (actually Pierre de
Maricourt of France). Because the magnetic field points straight into
the North Pole of the Earth and straight out the South Pole, the magnetic field is also automatically aligned with the celestial poles, the
imaginary points in the sky directly above the north and South Poles
of the Earth. Peregrinus believed that the magnetic field was caused
by something extraterrestrial, and so named the high-flux points of
the magnetic field poles.

In 1600 William Gilbert of England was the first researcher who
wrote that the Earth itself was the giant magnet. Finally, in 1838, the
great mathematician C. F. Gauss developed the mathematics govern-
ing the magnetic field. Gauss also tried, without success, to understand the slow change in the magnetic field called secular variation
that had been known to navigators for over 200 years. The term
secular variation means change over time. The direction and intensity
of the Earth's magnetic field does change over many years (on the
Internet there are gorgeous animations of the field changing over
hundreds of years). At the moment, the north magnetic pole of the
Earth is changing location at about 25 miles per year (40 km/yr). The
secular variation of the field reveals complex magnetic configurations
underlying the basic dipole structure. The dominant dipole pattern is
especially apparent when magnetic field values are averaged over a
10,000-year period.

In general, the Earth's field is strongest near the poles and weakest
near the equator, though this generalization can be changed by secular
variations in the field. The average strength of the Earth's field at the

equator is about 30,300 nT (nanoteslas), stronger than the surface magnetic fields of any other planet except Jupiter, whose surface field is an immense 428,000 nT. Saturn, Uranus, and Neptune are close to the value of Earth, at 21,800, 22,800, and 13,300 nT, respectively. Mercury has a tiny field, at 300 nT, and Venus, the Moon, and Mars all have surface fields below 60 nT. The strength of the Earth's field sustains life on Earth by shielding us from radiation, but the strength of the field compared to those of Venus and Mars, is somewhat of a mystery. Why have those planets' internal dynamos ceased, while ours continues? The Earth's magnetic field actually completely reverses at intervals varying from about 10,000 to 100,000 years, putting magnetic north at the South Pole, and vice versa. By identifying which magnetic interval during which a rock was formed can even be used to date rocks in a relative sense. And the fact that the magnetic field reverses was first discovered by investigating patterns of remanent magnetism (magnetism frozen into the rock) in oceanic crust.

At mid-ocean rises, magma melts in the mantle and rises in sheets and tubes to form new oceanic crust as it cools. As the magma cools to form new oceanic crust, a few percent of the minerals that form are magnetites or other oxides that can hold a magnetic field. These tiny grains are aligned by the Earth's magnetic field as they cool, and when they have cooled past a certain temperature, the magnetic field that they were formed in is permanently locked into the rocks, and can be detected by instruments called magnetometers. Reversals of the magnetic field were first measured in patterns of magnetic rocks in the oceanic crust, and through this study, plate tectonics was first proven. The magnetic field recorded in oceanic crust produced at mid-ocean ridges has alternating bands in which the magnetic field is first in the same direction as it is today, and then in the opposite direction, back and forth in stripes of variable width across the entirety of all the oceanic basins.

The Earth's magnetic field can be measured with great precision, and currently the dipole field is weakening. It has been weakening for hundred of years, and it is weakening faster and faster. In the last 150 years the field has lost about 10 percent of its strength. This weakening shows, it is thought, that the field is preparing to reverse and may do so within about a thousand years. Complex computer models have been made to try to understand magnetic reversals, and it is thought that as a reversal approaches magnetic field strength dwindles by

The aurora australis is caused by charged particles from the solar wind spinning along the Earth's magnetic field and bombarding atmospheric particles. which then emit light. The aurora in the Northern Hemisphere is called the aurora borealis. (National Oceanic and Atmospheric Administration/ Department of Commerce)

orders of magnitude and also becomes much more complex. As the field weakens, it degenerates into quadrupole and octupole fields as it reverses, and then reforms into the reversed dipole field. A magnetic reversal will have an immense effect on life on Earth. The magnetic field protects us from the most dangerous kinds of solar and interstellar radiation. As the field weakens, more radiation will reach the Earth, cancer rates will soar, and some extinctions will probably occur. The aurora australis (seen in the Southern Hemisphere and shown above) and borealis (Northern Hemisphere) are bands and streaks of light caused by the high-energy particles of the solar wind striking the Earth's ionosphere. Energy from these charged particles is converted into light, usually greenish, but occasionally red or orange. Because the particles in the solar wind are charged, they are attracted by the magnetic field lines of the Earth. The Earth's magnetic field is strongest near the poles, and so the majority of charged particles are gathered there, and the strongest auroras are formed in circles around the north and south magnetic poles, following the magnetic field lines. The strength of the solar wind determines the brightness of the aurora, and since the solar wind is variable, the brightness of the auroras is also variable. The stronger the solar wind, the more likely the auroras are to be visible at lower latitudes.

The 11-year cycle in sunspot population creates an 11-year cycle in the strength of the solar wind, and therefore a similar cycle in the general strength of auroras on Earth (and on other planets with magnetic fields, which experience similar phenomena). Though this is an overarching cycle, there are local disturbances during unusual solar storms that temporarily strengthen the solar wind. During one recent strong solar storm the aurora was strikingly bright as far south in the United States as Massachusetts, while usually it is only visible much closer to the Arctic circle. As a strange and interesting sideline to the discussion of auroras, astronauts orbiting within the Earth's ionosphere can also view auroras, but in an unusual way: The tiny charged particles pass through their bodies, without creating any sensation, except that when the astronaut close their eyes they can see tiny, bright flashes of light from the solar wind striking their optic nerves.

Temperatures, Pressures, and Compositions

The temperature of the Earth rises from about 60°F (20°C) at the surface, to about 8,700°F (4,800°C) in the inner core. Pressure rises from one atmosphere pressure (10^{-4} GPa) at the surface to 4 million atmospheres (360 GPa) at center (see the sidebar "What Is Pressure?" on page 52). Diamonds, as an example, can be created at only 70,000 to 120 atmospheres (7 to 12 GPa). This corresponds to 125 to 250 miles (200 to 400 km) depth in the Earth. Though people think, from the Earth-surface perspective, that diamonds require impossibly high pressures for their formation, this is only scraping the surface when it comes to the pressures that exist inside the Earth.

The Earth is hotter inside, and heat is convected through the mantle and conducted through the lithosphere into the atmosphere and

What Is Pressure?

The simple definition of pressure (p) is that it is force (F) per area (a):

$$p = \frac{F}{a}.$$

Atmospheric pressure is the most familiar kind of pressure and will be discussed below. Pressure, though, is something felt and witnessed all the time, whenever there is a force being exerted on something. For example, the pressure that a woman's high heel exerts on the foot of a person she stands on is a force (her body being pulled down by Earth's gravity) over an area (the area of the bottom of her heel). The pressure exerted by her heel can be estimated by calculating the force she is exerting with her body in Earth's gravity (which is her weight, here guessed at 130 pounds, or 59 kg, times Earth's gravitational acceleration, 32 ft/sec², or 9.8 m/sec²) and dividing by the area of the bottom of the high heel (here estimated as one square centimeter):

$$p = \frac{(59 \ kg)\,(9.8 \ m/sec^2)}{(0.01^2 m^2)} = 5{,}782{,}000 \ kg/msec^2.$$

The resulting unit, kg/ms², is the same as N/m and is also known as the pascal (Pa), the standard unit of pressure (see appendix 1, "Units and Measurements," to understand more). Although here pressure is calculated in terms of pascals, many scientists refer to pressure in terms of a unit called the atmosphere. This is a sensible unit because one atmosphere is approximately the pressure felt from Earth's atmosphere at sea level, though of course weather patterns cause continuous fluctuation. (This fluctuation is why weather forecasters say "the barometer is falling" or "the barometer is rising": The measurement of air pressure in that particular place is changing in response to moving masses of air, and these changes help indicate the weather that is to come.) There are about 100,000 pascals in an atmosphere, so the pressure of the woman's high heel is about the same as 57.8 times atmospheric pressure.

What is atmospheric pressure, and what causes it? Atmospheric pressure is the force the atmosphere exerts by being pulled down toward the planet by the planet's gravity, per unit area. As creatures of the Earth's surface, human beings do not notice the pressure of the atmosphere until it changes; for example, when a person's ears pop during a plane ride because the atmospheric pressure lessens with altitude. The atmosphere is thickest (densest) at the planet's surface and gradually becomes thinner (less and less dense) with height above the planet's surface. There is no clear break between the atmosphere and space: the atmosphere just gets thinner and thinner and less and less detectable. Therefore, atmospheric pressure is greatest at the planet's surface and becomes less and less as the height above the planet increases. When the decreasing density of the atmosphere and gravity are taken into consideration, it turns out that atmospheric pressure decreases exponentially with altitude according to the following equation:

$$p(z) = p_o e^{-\alpha z},$$

where $p(z)$ is the atmospheric pressure at some height above the surface z, p_o is the pressure at the surface of the planet, and α is a number that is constant for each planet, and is calculated as follows:

$$\alpha = \frac{g\rho_0}{P_0},$$

where g is the gravitational acceleration of that planet, and ρ_o is the density of the atmosphere at the planet's surface.

Just as pressure diminishes in the atmosphere from the surface of a planet up into space, pressure inside the planet increases with depth. Pressure inside a planet can be approximated simply as the product of the weight of the column of solid material above the point in question and the gravitational acceleration of the planet. In other words, the pressure P an observer would feel if he or she were inside the planet is caused by the weight of the material over the observer's head (approximated as ρh, with h the depth you are beneath the surface and ρ the density of the material between the observer and the surface) being pulled toward the center of the planet by its gravity g:

$$P = \rho g h.$$

The deeper into the planet, the higher the pressure.

space. Heat flow through the crust can be measured, and it is higher where the lithosphere is thinnest and where there is volcanic activity. Fifty percent of heat flow through young continental crust is created by radioactive elements in the crust. Crustal materials are largely originally created from magmas, though they may have gone through enough further processing that they are now classified as metamorphic

Density, pressure, and temperature all rise with depth in the Earth.

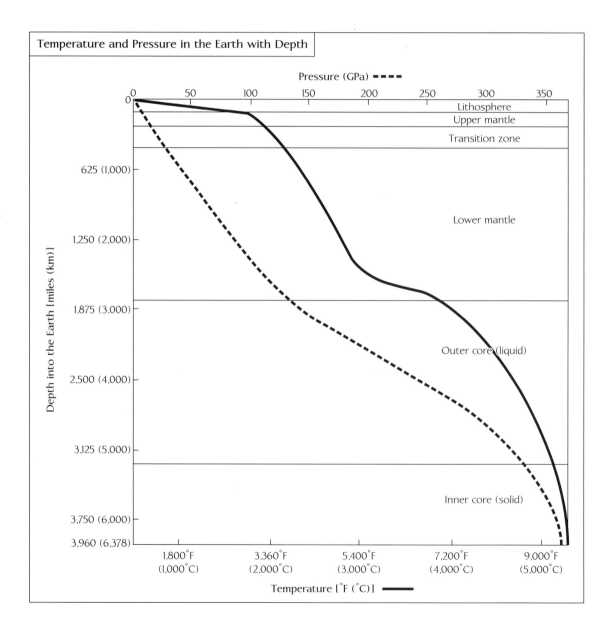

Temperature and Pressure in the Earth with Depth

or even sedimentary. When a rock is partially melted, all the elements that do not fit easily into the rock's crystal structure rush into the melt. These are called incompatible elements. The major heat-producing radioactive elements are ^{238}U, ^{235}U (*isotopes* of uranium), ^{232}Th (thorium), and ^{40}K (potassium), and all of these are incompatible. Granite is an igneous rock that is thought to be produced by two or more sequential melting events (though no one knows definitely how granite is made, which makes it a significant mystery since there is so much granite on Earth). Granite contains especially concentrated incompatible elements, and is thus by far the most radioactive common rock. If you ever have access to a Geiger counter, try measuring the radioactivity of a building built of granite.

Heat is also produced by the growth of the solid inner core. Cooler material sinking to the inner core releases gravitational potential energy, and the solidification of that material also releases energy. This heat is called the latent heat of solidification and results from the fact that a solid is more ordered than a liquid: Converting a disordered system to an ordered system releases heat. Conversely, to melt a solid, this same amount of heat must be added, and it all goes into the physics of melting and not into raising the temperature of the solid.

Two Earth scientists, Adam Dziewonski of Harvard University and Don Anderson of the California Institute of Technology, decided about 20 years ago that there was enough information about the Earth's interior to make a model of temperature, density, pressure, and a number of other parameters for the interior of the Earth, from the surface to the center (see figure on page 54). This model is called the Preliminary Reference Earth Model, or PREM. There is now a movement in the Earth sciences to update this model with a new model called the Reference Earth Model, or REM, but for the moment, the data from PREM is a fine place to start.

Though very little material from deep inside the Earth is directly accessible to scientists, a number of techniques are used to learn more about the Earth's interior. Seismic waves take the equivalent of an X-ray of the planetary interior, slowing when passing through hot or wet material, and speeding when passing through cold, stiff material. Shear waves (S-waves) cannot pass through liquid, and so revealed the presence of the liquid outer core of the Earth. This same liquid outer core forms the basis of theories for the formation of the magnetic field. While the crust of the Earth is accessible and provides samples of melts of the planet's interior, the bulk, unmelted composition of the mantle has to be inferred from a few samples, from information about meteorite bulk compositions that are thought to mirror the starting materials for forming the Earth, and from the results of laboratory experiments at high pressures. Even for this best-known of planets there are many outstanding questions about its interior, and new hypotheses are regularly presented for the structure and composition of the deep Earth.

The Early Evolution of the Planet Earth

T wo early thinkers about the formation of the solar system were Immanuel Kant, the German philosopher, and Pierre-Simon de Laplace, the French mathematician and astronomer. Though Kant was primarily a pure philosopher, he made forays into science, and among his most successful was his 1755 publication *Allgemeine Naturgeschichte und Theorie Des Himmels* (General natural history and theory of the heavens), in which he articulates the hypothesis of the formation of the universe from a spinning nebula. The nebula hypothesis was later developed independently by Laplace. Laplace presented his hypothesis in a 1796 publication titled *Exposition du systeme du monde* (Exposition of the system of the world), describing the origin of the solar system from a contracting, cooling, slowly rotating cloud of incandescent gas. These early formulations from a philosopher and a mathematician remain the fundamental understanding of the formation of the solar system. Laplace shows his clear understanding of the theoretical basis of these hypotheses, set so far back in time that few direct clues to their functioning remain:

> *If man were restricted to collecting facts the sciences were only a sterile nomenclature and he would never have known the great laws of nature. It is in comparing the phenomena with each other, in seeking to grasp their relationships, that he is led to discover these laws. . . .*

Though many calculations and correlations with planetary data have been made since the 18th century, the fundamental hypotheses of Kant and Laplace remain intact. The planets are thought to have grown from accumulations of matter in this early solar system nebula. Chunks of material collided and stayed together, eventually gathering enough mass to create significant gravity. Growing masses are often referred to as planetesimals, bodies that are too small and evolving too fast to be considered planets yet. These planetesimals continue to collide with each other and grow into a larger body, sweeping up the smaller matter available in the orbit of this growing planet. Some physicists believe that this process may have been completed within a few hundred thousand years.

The early planetesimals were probably irregular. The final planet Earth is round. When and how did that transformation occur? There are three main characteristics of a body that determine whether or not it will become round:

1. The first is its *viscosity*, that is, its ability to flow. Fluid bodies can be round because of surface tension, no matter their size; self-gravitation does not play a role. The force bonding together the molecules on the outside of a fluid drop pull the surface into the smallest possible area, which is a sphere. Solid material, like rock, can flow slowly if it is hot, so heat is an important aspect of viscosity. When planets are formed it is thought that they start as agglomerations of small bodies, and that more and more small bodies collide or are attracted gravitationally, making the main body larger and larger. The transformation of the original pile of rubble into a spherical planet is helped along significantly by the heat contributed by colliding planetesimals: The loss of their kinetic energy acts to heat up the main body. The hotter the main body, the easier it is for the material to flow into a sphere in response to its growing gravitational field.

2. The second main characteristic is *density*. Solid round bodies obtain their shape from gravity, which acts equally in all directions and therefore works to make a body a sphere. The same volume of a very dense material will create a stronger gravitational field than a less dense material, and the stronger the gravity of the object, the more likely it is to pull itself into a sphere.

3. The third characteristic is *mass*, which is really another aspect of density. If the object is made of low-density material, there just has to be a lot more of it to make the gravitational field required to make it round.

Bodies that are too small to heat up enough to allow any flow, or to have a large enough internal gravitational field, may retain irregular outlines. Their shapes are determined by mechanical strength, and response to outside forces such as meteorite impacts, rather than by their own self-gravity. In general, the largest asteroids, including all 100 or so that have diameters greater than 60 miles (100 km), and the larger moons are round from self-gravity. Most asteroids and moons with diameters larger than six miles (10 km) are round, but not all of them. Their ability to become round depends on their composition and the manner of their creation.

There is another stage of planetary evolution after attainment of a spherical shape: internal differentiation. All asteroids and the terrestrial planets probably started out made of primitive materials, such as the enstatite *chondrites,* which are an asteroidal composition that dates to the beginning of the solar system and seems to be among the least processed of solar system materials. The planets and some of the larger asteroids then became compositionally stratified in their interiors, a process called differentiation. In a differentiated terrestrial body, metals, mainly iron with some nickel and other minor impurities, have sunk to the middle of the body, forming a core. Lighter, silicate materials form a thick layer above the core, normally called the mantle. In some of these bodies, an even lighter crust covers the surface, such as the continents on Earth, and the white, anorthosite highlands on the Moon (anorthosite is a low-density mineral in a group of minerals called feldspars).

Terrestrial planets are therefore made up, in a rough sense, of concentric shells of materials with different compositions. The outermost shell is a crust, made mainly of material that has melted from the interior and risen buoyantly up to the surface. The mantle is made of silicate minerals, and the core is mainly of iron. The gas giant outer planets are similarly made of shells of material, though they are gaseous materials on the outside and rocky or icy in the interior. Planets with systematic shells like these are called differentiated planets. Their concentric spherical layers differ in terms of composition, heat, density, and even motion, and planets that are differentiated are more or less spherical. All the planets in the solar system seem to be thoroughly differentiated internally, with the possible exception of Pluto and Charon. What data there is for these two bodies indicates that they may not be fully differentiated. Some bodies in the solar system, though, are not differentiated; the material they are made of is still in a more primitive state, and the body may not be spherical. Undifferentiated bodies in the asteroid belt have their metal component still mixed through their silicate portions; it has not separated and flowed into the interior to form a core.

Among asteroids, the sizes of bodies that differentiated vary widely. Iron meteorites, thought to be the differentiated cores of rocky bodies that have since been shattered, consist of crystals that grow to different sizes directly depending upon their cooling rate, which in turn depends upon the size of the body that is cooling. Crystal sizes in iron meteorites indicate parent bodies from six to 30 miles (10 to 50 km) or more in diameter. Vesta, an asteroid with a basaltic crust and a diameter of 326 miles (525 km), seems to be the largest surviving *differentiated body* in the asteroid belt. Though the asteroid Ceres is much larger than Vesta, an unevenly shaped asteroid approximately 577 × 596 miles (930 × 960 km), seems from spectroscopic analyses to be largely undifferentiated. It is thought that the higher percentages of *volatiles* available at the distance of Ceres' orbit may have helped cool the asteroid faster, and prevent the buildup of heat required for differentiation. Ceres and Vesta are thought to be among the last surviving "protoplanets," and that almost all asteroids of smaller size are the shattered remains of larger bodies.

Where does the heat for differentiation come from? The larger asteroids generated enough internal heat from radioactive decay to melt (at least partially) and differentiate (for more on radioactive decay, see the sidebar "Elements and Isotopes" on page 64). Generally, bodies larger than about 300 miles (500 km) in diameter are needed, in order to be insulated enough to trap the heat from radioactive decay so that melting can occur. If the body is too small, it cools too fast and no differentiation can take place.

A source for heat to create differentiation, and perhaps the main source, is the heat of accretion. When smaller bodies, often called planetesimals, are colliding and sticking together, creating a single larger body (perhaps a planet), they are said to be accreting. Eventually the larger body may even have enough gravity itself to begin altering the paths of passing planetesimals and attracting them to it. In any case, the process of accretion adds tremendous heat to the body, by the transformation of the kinetic energy of the planetesimals into heat in the larger body. To understand kinetic energy, start with momentum, called *p,* and defined as the product of a body's mass *m* and its velocity *v:*

$$p = mv$$

Sir Isaac Newton called momentum "quality of movement." The greater the mass of the object, the greater its momentum is, and likewise, the greater its velocity, the greater its momentum is. A change in momentum creates a force, such as a person feels when something bumps into her. The object that bumps into her experiences a change in momentum because it has suddenly slowed down, and she experiences a force. The reason she feels more force when someone tosses a full soda to her than when they toss an empty soda can to her is that the full can has a greater mass, and therefore momentum, than the empty can, and when it hits her it loses all its momentum, transferring to her a greater force.

How does this relate to heating by accretion? Those incoming planetesimals have momentum due to their mass and velocity, and when they crash into the larger body, their momentum is converted into energy, in this case, heat. The energy of the body, created by its mass and velocity, is called its kinetic energy. Kinetic energy is the total effect of changing momentum of a body, in this case, as its velocity slows down to zero. Kinetic energy is expressed in terms of mass *m* and velocity *v:*

$$K = \frac{1}{2} mv^2$$

Students of calculus might note that kinetic energy is the integral of momentum with respect to velocity:

$$K = \int mv\, dv = \frac{1}{2} mv^2$$

The kinetic energy is converted from mass and velocity into heat energy when it strikes the growing body. This energy, and therefore heat, is considerable, and if accretion occurs fast enough, the larger body can be heated all the way to melting by accretional kinetic energy. If the larger body is melted even partially, it will differentiate.

How is energy transfigured into heat, and how is heat transformed into melting? To transfer energy into heat, the type of material has to be taken into consideration. Heat capacity describes how a material's temperature changes in response to added energy. Some materials go up in temperature easily in response to energy, while others take more energy to get hotter. Silicate minerals have a heat capacity of 245.2 cal/°lb (1,256.1 J/°kg). What this means is that 245.2 calories of energy are required to raise the temperature of one pound of silicate material one degree. Here is a sample calculation. A planetesimal is about to impact a larger body, and the planetesimal is a kilometer in radius. It would weigh roughly 3.7 × 10^{13} pounds (1.7 × 10^{13} kg), if its density were about 250 pounds per cubic foot (4,000 kg/m^3). If it were traveling at six miles per second (10 km/sec), then its kinetic energy would be

$$K = \frac{1}{2} mv^2 = (1.7 \times 10^{13} kg)(10,000 \text{ m/sec})^2$$
$$= 8.5 \times 10^{20} J = 2 \times 10^{20} cal.$$

Using the heat capacity, the temperature change created by an impact of a given mass can be calculated:

$$\frac{8.5 \times 10^{20} \text{ °kg}}{1,256.1 \text{ J/°kg}} = 6.8 \times 10^{17} \text{ °kg} = 8.3 \times 10^{17} \text{ °lb}.$$

How many kilograms of the larger body are going to be heated by the impact? Once this quantity is known, it can be divided by the number of kilograms being heated to determine how many degrees they will be heated. How widespread is the influence of this impact? How deeply does it heat, and how widely? Of course, the material closest to the impact will receive most of the energy, and the energy input will go down with distance from the impact, until finally the material is completely unheated. What is the pattern of energy dispersal? Energy dispersal is not well understood even by scientists who study impactors. Here is a simpler question: If all the energy were put into melting the impacted material, how much could it melt? To melt a silicate completely requires that its temperature be raised to about 2,700°F (1,500°C), as a rough estimate, so here is the mass of material that can be completely melted by this example impact:

$$\frac{6.8 \times 10^{17}\,{}^\circ kg}{1,500^\circ} = 4.5 \times 10^{14} kg = 9.9 \times 10^{14} lb$$

This means that the impactor can melt about 25 times its own mass ($4.5 \times 10^{14}/1.7 \times 10^{13} = 26$). Although this is a rough calculation, it shows how effective accretion can be in heating up a growing body, and how it can help the body to attain a spherical shape and to internally differentiate into different compositional shells.

Though they know that the Earth is differentiated, scientists continue to argue about when it happened. Was the heat of accretion enough to melt or partially melt the planet, such that differentiation happened immediately upon accretion? Did the planet differentiate during the giant impact that formed the Moon (more on this in the Moon section)? Was differentiation a more gradual process, moved along by the giant Late Heavy Bombardment, a period of heavy meteorite impact that lasted until about 3.8 billion years ago? On the Moon there is almost irrefutable geochemical evidence for early, complete differentiation, but no equivalently strong evidence exists on Earth. Various researchers are attempting to answer when the Earth differentiated by examining the isotopic systems that can be found in Earth and planetary materials.

Based on its size, it is likely that the Earth heated from accretion sufficiently to melt at least the outer 600 miles (1,000 km) of the planet. If the planet was hot enough in general to allow iron and nickel to flow downward and form a core, the loss of potential energy (energy stored by being away from the center of gravity, and therefore able to be released by falling into the center of gravity) might have been enough to raise the temperature of the planet by 2,700 to 3,600°F (1,500 to 2,000°C). Heat of this magnitude may have melted the entire silicate portion of the Earth, turning the mantle into a massive magma ocean. These are encouraging numbers for early differentiation, but many scientists argue that such heat was unlikely, as these processes occurred over a long enough time that heat was lost by radiation to space and so the early Earth never experienced the peak temperatures at one time.

Short-lived isotopes are radioactive isotopes of certain elements that have short half-lives, short enough to measure events that happen in tens of millions of years (as opposed to billions of years, which can be

Elements and Isotopes

All the materials in the solar system are made of *atoms* or of parts of atoms. A family of atoms that all have the same number of positively charged particles in their nuclei (the center of the atom) is called an *element*. Oxygen and iron are elements, as are aluminum, helium, carbon, silicon, platinum, gold, hydrogen, and well over 200 others. Every single atom of oxygen has eight positively charged particles, called protons, in its nucleus. The number of protons in an atom's nucleus is called its *atomic number*. All oxygen atoms have an atomic number of 8, and that is what makes them all oxygen atoms.

Naturally occurring nonradioactive oxygen, however, can have either eight, nine, or 10 uncharged particles, called neutrons, in its nucleus, as well. Different weights of the same element caused by addition of neutrons are called *isotopes*. The sum of the protons and neutrons in an atom's nucleus is called its *mass number*. Oxygen can have mass numbers of 16 (eight positively charged particles and eight uncharged particles), 17 (eight protons and nine neutrons), or 18 (eight protons and 10 neutrons). These isotopes are written as ^{16}O, ^{17}O, and ^{18}O. The first, ^{16}O, is by far the most common of the three isotopes of oxygen.

Atoms, regardless of their isotope, combine together to make molecules and compounds. For example, carbon (C) and hydrogen (H) molecules combine to make methane, a common gas constituent of the outer planets. Methane consists of one carbon atom and four hydrogen atoms and is shown symbolically as CH_4. Whenever a subscript is placed by the symbol of an element, it indicates how many of those atoms go into the makeup of that molecule or compound.

Quantities of elements in the various planets and moons, and ratios of isotopes, are important ways to determine whether the planets and moons formed from the same material or different materials. Oxygen again is a good example. If quantities of each of the oxygen isotopes are measured in every rock on Earth and a graph is made of the ratios of $^{17}O/^{16}O$ versus $^{18}O/^{16}O$, the points on the graph will form a line with a certain slope (the slope is 1/2, in fact). The fact that the data forms a line means that the material that formed the Earth was homogeneous; beyond rocks, the oxygen isotopes in every living thing and in the atmosphere also lie on this slope. The materials on the Moon also show this same slope. By measuring oxygen isotopes in many different kinds of solar system materials, it has now been shown that the slope of the plot $^{17}O/^{16}O$ versus $^{18}O/^{16}O$ is one-half for every object, but each object's line is offset from the others by some amount. Each solar system object lies along a different parallel line.

At first it was thought that the distribution of oxygen isotopes in the solar system was determined by their mass: The more massive isotopes stayed closer to the huge gravitational force of the Sun, and the lighter isotopes strayed farther out into the solar system. Studies of very primitive meteorites called chondrites, thought to be the most primitive, early material in the solar system, showed to the contrary that they have heterogeneous oxygen isotope ratios, and therefore oxygen isotopes were not evenly spread in the early solar system. Scientists then recognized that temperature also affects oxygen isotopic ratios: At different temperatures, different ratios of oxygen isotopes condense. As material in the early solar system cooled, it is thought that first aluminum oxide condensed, at a temperature of about 2,440°F (1,340°C), and then calcium-titanium oxide ($CaTiO_3$), at a temperature of about 2,300°F (1,260°C), and then a calcium–aluminum–silicon-oxide ($Ca_2Al_2SiO_7$), at a temperature of about 2,200°F (1,210°C), and so on through other compounds down to iron-nickel alloy at 1,800°F (990°C) and water, at –165°F (–110°C) (this low temperature for the condensation of water is caused by the very low pressure of space). Since oxygen isotopic ratios vary with temperature, each of these oxides would have a slightly different isotopic ratio, even if they came from the same place in the solar system.

The key process that determines the oxygen isotopes available at different points in the early solar system nebula seems to be that simple compounds created with ^{18}O are relatively stable at high temperatures, while those made with the other two isotopes break down more easily and at lower temperatures. Some scientists therefore think that ^{17}O and ^{18}O were concentrated in the middle of the nebular cloud, and ^{16}O was more common at the edge. Despite these details, though, the basic fact remains true: Each solar system body has its own slope on the graph of oxygen isotope ratios.

Most atoms are stable. A carbon-12 atom, for example, remains a carbon-12 atom forever, and an oxygen-16 atom remains an oxygen-16 atom forever, but certain atoms eventually disintegrate into a totally new atom. These atoms are said to be "unstable" or "radioactive." An unstable atom has excess internal energy, with the result that the nucleus can undergo a spontaneous change toward a more stable form. This is called "radioactive decay." Unstable isotopes (radioactive isotopes) are called "radioisotopes." Some elements, such as uranium, have no stable isotopes. The rate at which unstable elements decay is measured as a "half-life," the time it takes for half of the unstable

(continues)

Elements and Isotopes (continued)

atoms to have decayed. After one half-life, half the unstable atoms remain; after two half-lives, one-quarter remain, and so forth. Half-lives vary from parts of a second to millions of years, depending on the atom being considered. Whenever an isotope decays, it gives off energy, which can heat and also damage the material around it. Decay of radioisotopes is a major source of the internal heat of the Earth today: The heat generated by accreting the Earth out of smaller bodies and the heat generated by the giant impactor that formed the Moon have long since conducted away into space.

---

measured by the uranium-lead decay series). An example of a short-lived radioactive isotope is samarium with *mass number* 146, meaning samarium with a total of 146 protons plus neutrons in its *nucleus,* denoted ^{146}Sm. ^{146}Sm decays into ^{142}Nd (neodymium) with a *half-life* of 103 million years (for more on isotopes and half-lives, see the sidebar "Elements and Isotopes" on page 64). Half the ^{146}Sm decays to ^{142}Nd every 103 million years. If some differentiation event happened in the early solar system that could separate Sm from Nd before all the ^{146}Sm decayed, then the material with excess ^{146}Sm will end up with excess ^{142}Nd, and the material without the ^{146}Sm will end up with a deficit of ^{142}Nd, compared to undifferentiated material. Neodymium isotopes, therefore, can tell us something about early solar system processes.

Using the Sm-Nd system, scientists Charles Harper and Stein Jacobsen at Harvard University found an excess of ^{142}Nd in ancient crustal rocks that led them to conclude that there was a major terrestrial differentiation event, such as a magma ocean, 4.5 billion years ago, plus or minus 100 million years. This ^{142}Nd anomaly has been corroborated by Maud Boyet, a scientist at the Carnegie Institute of Washington, and a team of French and Danish scientists, but they argue that the differentiation event had to have happened within just a few tens of millions of years of planetary accretion. This is a blindingly short amount of time, and consistent with a magma ocean that crystallized without very much of an insulating atmosphere to slow its heat loss. Boyet also concludes that the samarium-neodymium data requires that the mantle be differentiated from the rest of the planet completely by 100 million years after planetary accretion.

A second isotopic system, ^{182}Hf-^{182}W (hafnium decaying to tungsten), is useful for studying the time interval between planetary accretion and core formation because tungsten is carried into the core by the iron and nickel, while hafnium tends to stay in the silicate mantle. If core formation occurred after all the hafnium had decayed, then almost all the tungsten would have been carried into the core and little left in the mantle. If core formation occurred before all the ^{182}Hf had decayed, then the mantle would contain more ^{182}W in the long run, after the hafnium has decayed. There are tungsten excesses in the silicate mantle that indicate that the core formed within about 15 million years after planetary accretion, lending support to the magma ocean hypothesis by showing that all the heat of core formation would be available in a short period of time to heat the planet.

Another much-debated issue is the composition of the planetesimals that accreted to make the Earth. As discussed in the previous chapter, scientists have some idea of what the composition of the bulk Earth is, though many aspects are still being argued over. Using what is known about the composition of the bulk Earth, and comparing the Earth's composition to the compositions of meteorites, which are thought to represent early solar system material from the asteroid belt, some guesses can be made about the most likely material to have collected together to form the Earth. The meteorite closest to the Earth's bulk composition is a type called an enstatite chondrite. (For more on ways to compare different solar system materials, see the sidebar "Elements and Isotopes" on page 64.)

There are two main categories of theories for the formation of the atmosphere and oceans on Earth: The accretion hypothesis (that the atmosphere came from gases trapped in the original accreting planetesimals that made up the Earth); and the capture hypothesis (that the atmosphere came from early solar nebula, or from solar wind, or from comets that impacted the Earth after its formation). There are now better and better computer models for the formation of the planets, and they do indicate that within a few tens of millions of years after core formation the terrestrial planets should have been completely solid and should have formed an early crust. These formation models do indicate that there was so much heat during accretion and solidification that there is a good chance that most of the volatiles (gases and liquids) were lost from the early Earth into space. This weakens the accretion hypotheses for atmospheric formation.

At about 1 million years after its formation, the Sun probably went through a special stage of its evolution called the T-Tauri stage. During its T-Tauri stage a star's early contraction slows or ends, and a very strong outflow of charged particles is released. This outflow was thought to have been strong enough to sweep away all the gaseous atmospheres of the inner solar-system planets. Some scientists think that this is compelling evidence that the inner planets had to obtain their gaseous atmospheres by later additions, such as from comets, or from later outgassing of their interiors. Recent models and work on extinct isotopic systems indicate that the cores of the Earth, Mars, and the Moon all formed within about 15 million years of the beginning of the solar system, but even this early formation may have been long after the Sun's T-Tauri stage. Now, therefore, there is disagreement over whether the evolution of the Sun could have had a significant controlling influence over the formation or retention of atmospheres in the terrestrial planets.

Some researchers, such as Kevin Zahnle at the NASA Ames Research Center, think that the early Earth was accreted from both rocky planetesimals and icy cometary matter. In this model, huge quantities of water were added to the early Earth, so much that the vast amounts lost to space during the heat and atmospheric disruption of giant impacts, and the evaporation into space due to the large quantities of accretional heat still present in the early Earth still left plenty of water to form oceans. Even if the Earth was accreted entirely from ordinary chondrite meteoritic material, it would have started with about one-tenth of a percent of water by weight (0.1 percent, the amount naturally existing in ordinary chondrites), and this is still two to four times as much water as the Earth is thought to have today (though the amount of water in oceans and in ice on the surface of the Earth is well known, the amount of water existing in trace amounts in deep minerals in the Earth's interior is not known).

There was a period of heavy bombardment of inner solar system bodies by large *bolides* that lasted until about 3.8 billion years ago. The giant basins on the Moon, filled with dark basalt and so visible to the eye from Earth, are left over from that period, called the Late Heavy Bombardment. Some scientists believe that the Late Heavy

Bombardment was a specific period of very heavy impact activity that lasted from about 4.2 to 3.8 billion years ago, while others believe that it was just the tail end of a continuously decreasing rate of bombardment that began at the beginning of the solar system. In this continual bombardment model, the last giant impacts from 4.2 to 3.8 billion years ago simply erased the evidence of all the earlier bombardment.

If, alternatively, the Late Heavy Bombardment was a discrete event, then some reason for the sudden invasion of the inner solar system by giant bolides must be discovered. Were they bodies perturbed from the outer solar system by the giant planets there? If they came from the outer solar system, then more of the material was likely to be water-rich cometary material. If as much as 25 percent of the Late Heavy Bombardment was cometary material, it would have contributed enough water to the Earth to create its oceans. There is some evidence that there was liquid water on the Earth's surface earlier than 4.2 billion years ago. In the section titled "How Old Is the Earth's Surface?" (see page 71) the compositions of some very ancient mineral grains of a type called zircon are discussed. These zircons are 4.4 billion years old, and their oxygen isotopic compositions appear to indicate that liquid water was present at that time.

The theory of cometary accretion for ocean formation has another problem. Recent observations of the comets Halley, Hyakutake, and Hale-Bopp have revealed that their water is twice as enriched in deuterium than water on Earth (deuterium is water made with hydrogen that contains a neutron as well as a proton in its nucleus; this is also called heavy water, because the neutron added to each hydrogen in the water molecule increases its mass by about 10 percent). There is no explanation of why, if the Earth's oceans came from heavy cometary water, they have since preferentially lost the heavy water and arrived at their current low-deuterium composition. This indicates that the water on Earth probably came from sources other than comets.

Venus and Mars probably received water in the same way Earth did, since they are near neighbors in the solar system. On Venus, the water was lost because of the high input of solar energy: The heat of the Sun evaporated the water high into the atmosphere, where the heavy bombardment of ultraviolet radiation broke the water molecules into their constituent water and hydrogen atoms, which were then light enough to escape into space. In this way Venus, closer to the Sun, lost its water. Being far from the Sun is equally bad for oceans: If the planet is colder, water will freeze. Frozen water reflects more energy away from the planet and back into space, making the planet colder still. This may be part of the reason that, though Mars may once have had oceans, its water is now frozen into the soil.

The optimal distance from the Sun for a planet to maintain a liquid ocean has also changed over time. When the Sun first burst into nuclear life, it is thought to have been about 30 percent dimmer than it is today. This means that the critical range of radii for planetary orbits that would allow the retention of liquid water was closer to the Sun, and that this zone habitable for water-based life is moving away from the Sun as it continues to heat up and give off more radiation. If there were oceans on Mars today, it is more likely that the planet could retain them and avoid freezing. Similarly, in about a billion years, the Sun will have heated up to the point that the Earth will be too close to it to retain its oceans, and the atmosphere here on Earth will convert to something more like Venus, and will be much less hospitable to life.

On the early Earth, the atmosphere is thought to have been much richer in carbon dioxide and methane, both chemicals that help retain heat in the atmosphere and keep the surface of the planet warm (they are so-called greenhouse gases). As life developed on Earth and more and more organisms used photosynthesis, the oxygen content of the atmosphere was built up. Because of the oceans of water on Earth, excess carbon dioxide can be converted into carbonate minerals, such as calcite ($CaCO_3$). Moderating the carbon dioxide content of the atmosphere helps keep the Earth's surface temperature within the range conducive to life.

The Visible Planet

The visible surface of the planet Earth has been studied the longest of any planetary subject and is the geologic field about which the most is known. The study of other planets begins with a comparison with the surface of the Earth. As long a time as humankind has been picking up rocks, looking at landforms, and attempting to predict the weather, infinitely more remains to be known about the surface of this planet. Looking back in time, geologists know how old the oldest rocks are on the planet's surface, but there is no consensus on what the surface of the Earth looked like before that earliest preserved record. Looking forward, climatologists clearly show that Earth conditions are variable and that humankind's contributions to the global environment are helping to push the Earth into an era of violent and extreme weather. In the present, volcanoes, earthquakes, and hurricanes are all the focus of research attempting to make people safer in the present day. Each of these phenomena can be found on other planets, as well, where their occurrence helps scientists understand their mechanisms here on Earth.

How Old Is the Earth's Surface?

The discovery of radioactivity and its application to determining the age of rocks all happened in the 20th century. Before then, geologists spent a couple of centuries working out the relative ages of rocks, that is, which ones were formed first, and in what order the others came. Between the years of 1785 and 1800, James Hutton, a Scottish geologist considered by many to be the founder of the modern field, and William Smith, a surveyor of limited education but great curiosity and intellect, introduced and labored over the idea of geologic time—that the rock record describes events that happened over a long time period.

Fossils were the best and easiest way to correlate between rocks that did not touch each other directly. Some species of fossil life can be found in many locations around the world, and so form important markers in the geologic record; when fossils of one species occur in rock layers all over the world, all those rock layers must have formed before that species went extinct. Relative time was broken into sections divided by changes in the rock record—for example, times when many species apparently went extinct, since their fossils were not found in younger rocks. This is why the extinction of the dinosaurs lies directly on the Cretaceous-Tertiary boundary; the boundary was set to mark their loss. The largest sections of geologic history were further divided into small sections, and so on, from epochs, to eras, to periods. For centuries a debate raged in the scientific community over how much time was represented by these geologic divisions.

With the development of radioactive dating methods, those relative time markers could be converted to absolute time. On Earth the age of a rock can often be exactly determined by measuring its radioactive isotopes and their daughter products, and thereby determining how long the radioactive elements have been in the rock, decaying to form their daughters (see the sidebar "Determining Age from Radioactive Isotopes" on page 76). Through radiodating it is now known that the Cretaceous-Tertiary boundary lies at about 66.5 million years ago, and that the greatest extinction in Earth history, at the Permian-Triassic boundary, occurred at 251 million years ago. The rocks that make up the Earth's surface are largely younger than 250 million years old. Oceanic crust is necessarily young, since it is made constantly and just as constantly lost into the mantle as it dives under continental crust at subduction zones. The oldest oceanic crust still in ocean basins (some slivers have been crushed into the continents during continental collisions) is about 200 million years old.

Because most of the rocks on the surface of the Earth were formed within the last 250 million years (only 5 percent of all of Earth's history!), scientists have difficulty in fully understanding and describing the state of the early Earth. How soon after its formation did the Earth form a crust, when did oceans form, and how long after that did plate tectonics begin? There is hardly a vestige of the early Earth's surface left for us to examine. Because of their importance to understanding the formation of the Earth and its early evolution, geologists are on a perpetual search to find the oldest remaining rocks on Earth. The obvious places to look are the ancient *cratons,* the stable interiors of the continents. Rocks older than 3 billion years have been found in Greenland; with each successive older find, the scientist responsible gained sudden fame, and the search went on. In the early 1990s, the geologist Sam Bowring from the Massachusetts Institute of Technology was working in the Slave craton in Canada's Northwest Territories. At the end of a stormy day of lake-hopping in a small plane across the tundra of northern Canada, Bowring used a sledge-hammer to break off some promising samples from a rock outcrop near a remote lake. These rocks lay awaiting analysis for some time in his lab back in Cambridge, Massachusetts, before they were found to be the oldest known rocks on Earth. Known as the Acasta gneiss, they date to 3.96 billion years, and contain a few stray mineral grains that are even older.

More recently, John Valley, a geologist from the University of Wisconsin at Madison, and his colleagues found a few tiny grains of a mineral called zircon in a sedimentary rock in the Jack Hills of Australia that date as far back as 4.4 billion years. These tiny, purple zircons were not formed in the sedimentary rock they were extracted from, which is much younger than 4.4 billion years old; they were weathered out of their original host rock and later laid down with the sediment that became the rocks found in central Australia today. By measuring the oxygen isotopic ratios in the zircons, some scientists have come to the conclusion that there had to be liquid water on the Earth when these zircons formed. If there was water on the Earth's surface 4.4 billion years ago, then the Earth must have cooled and solidified to the point that the crust was strong and cold enough to support oceans. Aside from the oxygen isotopes found in these zircons, the only evidence for early water are rocks made from sediments that were deposited in water between 3.8 and 3.6 billion years ago. There are only these tiny, tiny clues to what the surface of the Earth was like in the distant past.

The idea that the early Earth cooled fast and developed a crust and oceans much as there is today by as early as 100 million years after formation is a heretical idea to some geologists. In that early time radiogenic heat is estimated to have been five times higher than today's output, and some scientists think that much of the heat of early formation of the planet still existed. This early era in Earth

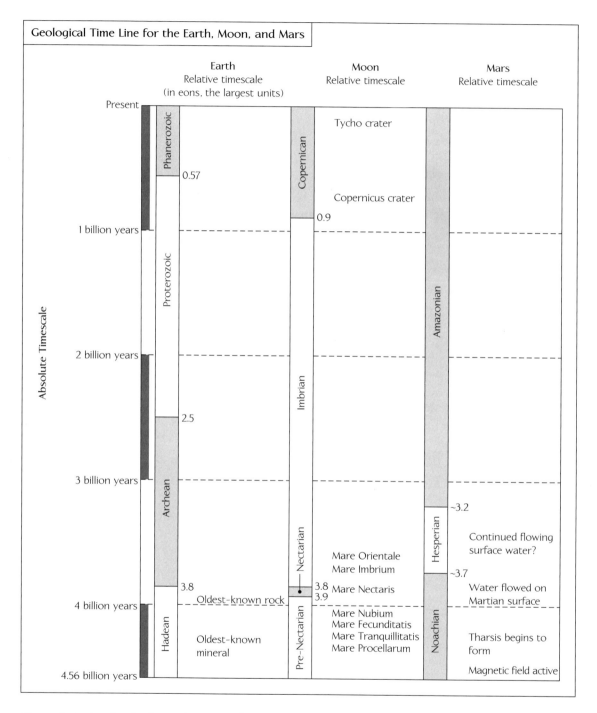

Geological Time Line for the Earth, Moon, and Mars

| Earth
Relative timescale
(in eons, the largest units) | Moon
Relative timescale | Mars
Relative timescale |

The geologic time line for the Earth compared with the Moon and Mars, as they are understood without further samples to date using radioisotopes history is actually named the Hadean, meaning "hell-like." The research of John Valley and his colleagues indicates that, far from being hell-like, the Earth cooled quickly and formed oceans. This theory is in agreement with the modeling efforts of the author and her colleagues at Brown University, which indicate that the Earth, the Moon, and Mars would all have formed a cool surface and a crust within about 60 million years of formation.

With the possible exception of the Moon, the Earth is the only body for which scientists can develop a detailed relative timescale because there has never been a field geologist on any other planet to do the necessary careful mapping of geologic units. A number of absolute radioisotope dates have been made for lunar rocks returned from the Apollo missions, forming the beginning of an absolute timescale for the Moon. Scientists cannot develop an absolute timescale for Mars because the only rocks available are the Martian meteorites, whose original locations on Mars are unknown. For other bodies there are no absolute dates. Using detailed images of other planets, though, it is possible to work out the relative ages of many of the crustal features. By carefully examining images researchers can determine "superposition," that is, which rock unit was formed first, and which later came to lie on top of it. Impact craters and canyons are very helpful in determining superposition. Through this sort of meticulous photogeology, scientists have developed relative timescales for other planets, as shown in the figure on page 74.

Surface Features

Earth's surface features are unique in the solar system because they are dominated by the movement and chemical action of water and the existence of life. Water and vegetation cover the majority of the planet, and even in deserts the landforms are shaped predominantly by the infrequent rainstorms and floods, and less by wind. Water and vegetation also act to erode rocks and change landforms: Sharp edges become dulled by weathering and wearing away the rock, soil slumps down steep slopes, and glaciers carve away the surface. The ability of ice to carve bedrock and carry sediment is shown in the image on page 79 of Viedma glacier in Argentina. This glacier flows into Lake Viedma, one of three major lakes on the Patagonian side of the southern Andean ice sheet, at 50 degrees south. The slender dark lines of rock material (moraine) are carried in the slowly flowing ice. Lighter

Determining Age from Radioactive Isotopes

Each element exists in the form of atoms with several different-sized nuclei, called isotopes. Consider the element carbon. All carbon atoms have six protons in their nuclei, but they can have different numbers of neutrons. Protons determine the kind of element the atom is because protons have a positive charge, and to balance their positive charge, the atom has negatively charged electrons orbiting around its nucleus. It is the structure and number of electrons and the size of the atom that determine how it interacts with other atoms, and thus makes all atoms with the same number of protons act alike. Neutrons, on the other hand, make an atom heavier, but do not change its chemical interactions very much. The atoms of an element that have different numbers of neutrons are called isotopes. Carbon has three isotopes, with atomic masses 12, 13, and 14. They are denoted ^{12}C, ^{13}C, and ^{14}C.

Most atoms are stable. A ^{12}C atom, for example, remains a ^{12}C atom forever, and an ^{16}O (oxygen) atom remains an ^{16}O atom forever, but certain atoms eventually disintegrate into a totally new atom. These atoms are said to be unstable or *radioactive*. An unstable atom has excess internal energy, with the result that the nucleus can undergo a spontaneous change toward a more stable form. This is called radioactive decay.

Unstable isotopes (which are thus radioactive) are called radioisotopes. Some elements, such as uranium, have no stable isotopes. Other elements have no radioactive isotopes. The rate at which unstable elements decay is measured as a *half-life*, the time it takes for half of the unstable atoms to have decayed. After one half-life, half the unstable atoms remain; after two half-lives, one-quarter remain, and so forth. Half-lives vary from parts of a second to billions of years, depending on the atom being considered. The radioactive element is called the parent, and the product of decay is called the daughter.

When rocks form, their crystals contain some amount of radioactive isotopes. Different crystals have differently sized spaces in their lattices, so some minerals are more likely to incorporate certain isotopes than others. The mineral zircon, for example, usually contains a measurable amount of radioactive lead (atomic abbreviation Pb). When the crystal forms, it contains some ratio of parent and daughter atoms. As time passes, the parent atoms continue to decay according to the rate given by their half-life, and the population of daughter atoms in the crystal increases. By measuring the concentrations of parent and daughter atoms, the age of the rock can be determined.

To learn the math to calculate the age of materials based on radioactive decay, read this section. Otherwise, skip to the end of the math section to learn about the ages of objects in the solar system.

Consider the case of the radioactive decay system ^{87}Rb (rubidium). It decays to ^{87}Sr (strontium) with a half-life of 49 billion years. In a given crystal, the amount of ^{87}Sr existing now is equal to the original ^{87}Sr that was incorporated in the crystal when it formed, plus the amount of ^{87}Rb that has decayed since the crystal formed. This can be written mathematically as:

$$^{87}Sr_{now} = {}^{87}Sr_{original} + ({}^{87}Rb_{original} - {}^{87}Rb_{now}).$$

The amount of rubidium now is related to the original amount by its rate of decay. This can be expressed in a simple relationship that shows that the change in the number of parent atoms n is equal to the original number n_o times one over the rate of decay, called λ (the equations will now be generalized for use with any isotope system):

$$\frac{-dn}{dt} = \lambda n_0,$$

where dn means the change in n, the original number of atoms, and dt means the change in time. To get the number of atoms present now, the expression needs to be rearranged so that the time terms are on one side, and the n terms on the other, and then integrated, and the final result is:

$$n_0 = ne^{\lambda t}.$$

The number of daughter atoms formed by decay, D, is equal to the number of parent atoms that decayed:

$$D = n_0 - n.$$

Also, from the previous equation, $n_o = ne^{\lambda t}$. That expression can be substituted into the equation for D in order to remove the term n_o:

$$D = n(e^{\lambda t} - 1).$$

(continues)

Determining Age from Radioactive Isotopes (continued)

Then, finally, if the number of daughter atoms when the system began was D_0, then the number of daughter atoms now is

$$D = D_0 + n(e^{\lambda t} - 1).$$

This is the equation that allows geologists to determine the age of materials based on radiogenic systems. The material in question is ground up, dissolved in acid, and vaporized in an instrument called a mass spectrometer. The mass spectrometer measures the relative abundances of the isotopes in question, and then the time over which they have been decaying can be calculated.

The values of D and n are measured for a number of minerals in the same rock, or a number of rocks from the same outcrop, and the data is plotted on a graph of D vs. n (often D and n are measured as ratios of some stable isotope, simply because it is easier for the mass spectrometer to measure ratios accurately than it is to measure absolute abundances). The slope of the line the data forms is $e^{\lambda t} - 1$. This relation can be solved for t, the time since the rocks formed. This technique also neatly gets around the problem of knowing D_0 the initial concentration of daughter isotopes: D_0 ends up being the y-intercept of the graph.

Radiodating, as the technique is sometimes called, is tremendously powerful in determining how fast and when processes happened on the Earth and in the early solar system. Samples of most geological material has been dated: the lunar crustal rocks and basalts returned by the Apollo and Luna missions, all the kinds of meteorites including those from Mars, and tens of thousands of samples from all over the Earth. While the surface of the Moon has been shown to be between 3.5 and 4.6 billion years old for the most part, the Earth's surface is largely younger than 250 Ma (million years old). The oldest rock found on Earth is the Acasta gneiss, from northwestern Canada, which is 3.96 billion years old.

If the oldest rock on Earth is 3.96 billion years old, does that mean that the Earth is 3.96 billion years old? No, because older rocks probably have simply been destroyed by the processes of erosion and plate tectonics, and there is reason to believe that the Earth and Moon formed at nearly the same time. Many meteorites, especially the primitive chondritic meteorites, have ages of 4.56 billion years. Scientists believe that this is the age of the solar system. How, a critical reader should ask, is it known that this is when the solar system formed, and not some later formation event?

The answer is found by using another set of radioactive elements. These have half-lives so short that virtually all the original parent atoms have decayed into daughters long since. They are called extinct nuclides (nuclide is a synonym for isotope). An important example is ^{129}I (an isotope of iodine), which decays into ^{129}Xe (xenon) with a half-life of only 16 million years. All the ^{129}I that the solar system would ever have was formed when the original solar nebula was formed, just before the planets began to form. If a rock found today contains excess ^{129}Xe, above the solar system average, then it formed very early in solar system time, when ^{129}I was still live. The meteorites that date to 4.56 Ga (billion years) have excess ^{129}Xe, so 4.56 Ga is the age of the beginning of the solar system.

lines at right angles are patterns of crevasses. The glacier diverges into two lakes where calved icebergs can be seen floating in the lakes. The glacier here is about 1.1 miles (1.8 km) wide.

Because of this continuous action and the destructive work of plate tectonics, very little of early Earth history is left on the surface. Though other planets and moons are covered with impact craters from meteorite bombardment, the Earth has relatively few recognizable

The Viedma glacier flows down the Andes in Argentina. (Earth Sciences and Image Analysis Laboratory, NASA Johnson Space Center, eol.jsc.nasa.gov, image number ISS008-E-12390)

craters. They have been eroded away over time. Because there are so few to be seen on the Earth, it took centuries for scientists to agree that giant meteorites have in fact struck the Earth. The reigning paradigm for the previous three centuries had been gradualism and uniformitarianism, the ideas that Earth processes happened gradually and incrementally over vast amounts of time, leading in the end to the dramatic formations seen today. Now scientists think there are several good examples of the converse, catastrophism. Shown in the lower color insert on page C-1, sudden catastrophic processes that alter landforms include meteorite impacts, volcanic explosions, giant landslides, earthquakes, and storms. On Earth erosion generally acts against the ability to recognize craters. There are about 170 terrestrial craters known, ranging in age from a few thousand years old to 2 billion years old, and in size up to several hundred kilometers in diameter. Newly verified impact sites are presented at scientific conferences every year. The largest known craters are in the accompanying table. Not all can be seen at the surface of the Earth; Chicxulub, for example, is best detected by anomalies in the gravity field.

One of the most famous and most studied craters on Earth is Meteor crater. Meteor crater, also called Barringer crater, after the man who bought the rights to the land around it, is a clean, round crater three-quarters of a mile (1.2 km) in diameter, 560 feet (170 m) deep, and has a rim of rock blocks 150 feet (45 m) high around its edge. Meteor crater lies in the middle of a great flat plain in Arizona. When first found by Europeans, the crater had about 30 tons of pieces of iron meteorite scattered it over a diameter of about six miles (10 km). The view on page 82 of Meteor crater was taken by an astronaut on the *International Space Station* on February 11, 2004. The crater looks much as a lunar crater might appear through a telescope. The prominent gully meandering across the scene is known as Canyon Diablo, which drains northward toward the Little Colorado River and eventually to the Grand Canyon. The Interstate 40 highway crosses and nearly parallels the northern edge of the scene.

A good example of how hard it can be to confirm a circular feature as an impact crater on Earth is the five-mile (8-km) feature known as the Iturralde Structure. It is possibly the Earth's most recent large impact event, recording an impact that might have occurred between 11,000 and 30,000 years ago. Iturralde is in an isolated part of the Bolivian Amazon. Although the structure was identified on satellite

SELECTED TERRESTRIAL IMPACT CRATERS

Crater name	State/Province	Country	Diameter (miles [km])	Approximate age (millions of years)
Vredefort		South Africa	190 (300)	2020
Sudbury	Ontario	Canada	150 (250)	1850
Chicxulub	Yucatán	Mexico	110 (180)	65
Manicouagan	Quebec	Canada	60 (100)	214
Popigai		Russia	60 (100)	35
Acraman	South Australia	Australia	55 (90)	450
Chesapeake Bay	Virginia	U.S.	53 (85)	35
Puchezh-Katunki		Russia	50 (80)	175
Morokweng		South Africa	44 (70)	145
Kara		Russia	40 (65)	73
Beaverhead	Montana	U.S.	38 (60)	625
Tookoonooka	Queensland	Australia	34 (55)	130
Charlevoix	Quebec	Canada	34 (54)	360
Kara-Kul		Tajikistan	33 (52)	within 5 Myr of present
Siljan		Sweden	33 (52)	368
Montagnais	Nova Scotia	Canada	28 (45)	50

photographs in the mid-1980s, its location is so remote that it has only been visited by scientific investigators twice, most recently by a team from NASA's Goddard Space Flight Center in September 2002. The feature is a closed depression only about 66 feet (20 m) in depth. Its rim cuts into the heavily vegetated soft sediments of this part of Bolivia. Thick vegetation makes its identification doubly difficult, since there are few hard rocks to preserve shock features.

Gosses Bluff, an impact crater sandwiched between the Macdonnell Range to the north and the James Range to the south in Australia's Northern Territory, is about 100 miles (160 km) west of Alice Springs. Australia makes a great natural laboratory for impact structure

Canyon Diablo and Meteor crater, one of the youngest and freshest craters on Earth, were photographed from the International Space Station. (Earth Sciences and Image Analysis Laboratory, NASA Johnson Space Center, eol.jsc.nasa.gov, image number ISS008-E-15268)

study, since it is so dry and old that many craters have been preserved on its surface. Gosses Bluff is one of the most studied (see image on page 83). The impactor, probably about 0.6 miles (1 km) in diameter, created the crater about 142 million years ago. The isolated circular feature within the crater consists of a central ring of hills about 2.8 miles (4.5 km) in diameter. The grayish feature surrounding the inner ring probably marks the original boundary of the outer rim.

Not all perfectly round features with concentric terraces are impact craters. This prominent circular feature, known as the Richat Structure, is in the Sahara of Mauritania. Richat has a diameter of 30 miles (50 km) and was, understandably, initially mistaken for a possible impact crater. It is now known to be an eroded circular dome of layered sedimentary rocks. Shown in the upper color insert on page C-4, this view, generated from a Landsat satellite image, exaggerates vertical expression by a factor of six to make the structure more apparent. The height of the mesa ridge in the center of the view is about 935 feet (285 m).

The runoff that erodes away the evidence of meteorite impacts on Earth eventually drains into the planet's oceans. Oceans cover nearly 70 percent of the planet, and the action of the water that flows down to them controls much of the shape of continents, the patterns of vegetation, and of human population. Seen in the upper color insert on page C-3, of the Earth's surface water, 97.2 percent is in the oceans, 2.15 percent in ice caps and glaciers, and only 0.65 percent in lakes, streams, ground water, and the atmosphere combined (this tiny percentage emphasizes the importance of preserving clean ground-water supplies for drinking).

Oceans are thought to have formed as early as 100 million years after the Earth formed, at 4.4 billion years before the present. They have not always existed in the places and shapes they do now, though; as shown in the upper color insert on page C-5, plate tectonics controls the shapes, ages, and positions of the ocean basins on Earth. At the moment on Earth, the Pacific Ocean is surrounded by subduction zones, while the Atlantic Ocean is surrounded for the most part by passive margins, where no relative movement is occurring between

The 142-million-year-old Gosses Bluff impact crater lies about 100 miles (160 km) west of Alice Springs in Australia. (Earth Sciences and Image Analysis Laboratory. NASA Johnson Space Center. eol.jsc.nasa.gov. image number ISS07-E-5697)

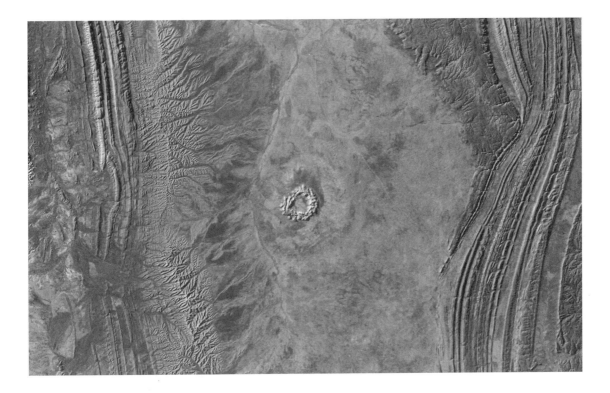

the oceanic plates and the continents. The Atlantic Ocean is growing in area at the rate at which new crust is produced at its mid-ocean ridges. The Pacific Ocean, on the other hand, is losing area all the time to the subduction zones around its perimeter. In this way the sizes of oceans wax and wane.

About 200 million years ago, the Atlantic Ocean was closed. The continents on each side had been driven toward each other because of tectonic forces on their opposite sides and because of mantle convention currents, and the ocean basin had gradually disappeared as the continents were driven to the point that they collided into one giant land mass. At 200 million years ago, for reasons that are not well understood, a great rift began to open more or less along the suture zone where the continents collided. Immense volumes of lava poured out, forming basaltic rocks that now line the shores of the continents along their lengths. A mid-ocean ridge began to form, creating new oceanic crust and pushing the continents apart again. The new ocean basin did not form exactly where the old one had been: Part of New England used to belong to Africa but remained on this side when the ocean basin opened.

The Nile River, Earth's longest river, meanders across its floodplain. Both Mars and Venus have longer channel systems, but those on Venus are thought to have been caused by flowing lava rather than by water. (Image courtesy of Earth Sciences and Image Analysis Laboratory, NASA Johnson Space Center, eol.jsc.nasa.gov. ISS009_E_8271)

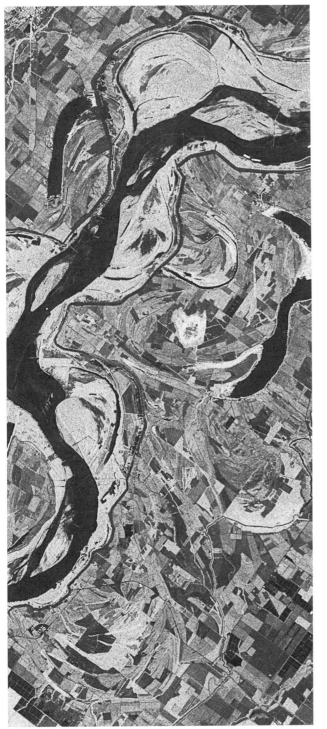

The Mississippi River displays meander bends and oxbow lakes, which are characteristic of water flow. (NASA)

By reconstructing the original types and ages of rocks found on North and South American, Europe, and Africa, it is now known that the Atlantic had gone through this cycle previously as well. The opening and closing of ocean basins was first developed in a paper by J. Tuzo Wilson, a professor of geophysics at the University of Toronto, published in 1963. In it he began to describe the cycle: A rift forms in a continent, developing into a mid-ocean ridge and the growth of oceanic crust. The two continents move farther apart. Eventually, tectonic forces from their other sides begin to push them together again, and subduction zones form on one side or both of the ocean. Finally, the two continents collide. When continents collide, neither one subducts; they are too rigid and too buoyant. Instead, as seen in the lower color insert on page C-4, mountains are thrust up where the continents meet, as the Himalayas are forming today in the continued collision of Asia and India. The idea of the Wilson cycle was critical in the development of plate tectonics.

Plate tectonics form and remove oceans and also take an important role in the water cycle of the planet. Sediments that sink to the bottom of the ocean carry water bound into their crystal structures. When oceanic plates subduct under continental plates at volcanic arcs, the plates carry some percentage of their

This large distributary fan on Mars is evidence for long-term water flow. (NASA/JPL/ Malin Space Science Systems)

wet sediments into the Earth. Some of this water is released from the sediments by pressure and heat and helps the overlying mantle melt, eventually being erupted onto the surface in volcanic flows. Some other percentage of the water is carried down into the mantle with the subducting plate and mantle. Some scientists estimate that there is the equivalent of 10 oceans' worth of water dissolved in minerals in the mantle.

Unique in all the solar system, oceans on Earth are fed by rivers carrying surface and ground water off the continents, by melting ice caps and glaciers, and by precipitation from clouds. Rivers erode and redistribute sediments, in addition to transporting water to oceans. Rivers are classified as meandering when they run mainly in a single channel which winds back and forth across the river's floodplain, and as a braided river when many channels combine and split across a floodplain. The image of the Nile River on page 84, taken from the

International Space Station, clearly shows its floodplain, as well as the pattern of meanders in the current river channel.

Rivers drop sediment along their beds where the water slows. When the beds build up to a certain level, the river flows out of its banks during a flood and forges a new channel. The patterns of channels and distribution of sediments make patterns unique to water transport, distinct from the other materials that can create channels (for example, lava on Venus).

The Mississippi River is the longest river in North America and one of the longest in the world, at 2,350 miles (3,750 km) (the Nile is the world's longest river). It begins at Lake Itaska in Minnesota and ends in the Gulf of Mexico. Along its length it displays all the characteristic forms of water transport, including the meander bends (curves in the river) and oxbow lakes (meander bends that have been abandoned when the river leaped its banks during a flood and assumed a new channel). Meander bends and oxbow lakes are shown in the image on page 85. Along the course of a river smaller rivers, called tributaries, empty into the main channel. When the river comes to its end, it slows as the slope it is flowing down becomes less steep and the river drops its sediment. As the sediment builds up in the river's bed the flow eventually splits and forms a new bed at a lower elevation. A river tends to split into many channels at its end, called distributaries, shown in the lower color insert on page C-3 for the Mississippi River.

Mars is the only other planet in the solar system now known to show evidence for having had flowing surface water at some point in its past. The image on page 86 shows meander loops and distributaries from an ancient water river on Mars, similar to those shown for the Mississippi River.

Volcanism

Volcanoes are mountains built up by the eruption of liquid rock, called magma, onto the Earth's surface. Magma is formed by a variety of processes deep in the Earth, and when it erupts onto the Earth's surface it is known as lava. Volcanoes and volcanism do not occur randomly over the Earth's surface but rather in striking patterns—along the edges of some continents and island chains, along mid-ocean ridges, and in lines along the ocean floors. These patterns reflect the mechanisms inside the Earth that are causing the mantle to melt.

The rock of the Earth's mantle is solid almost everywhere (only the outer core is always liquid, and it made mainly of iron and not silicates). Yet this is the rock that melts to make magmas that erupt through volcanoes, and scientists have spent centuries putting together evidence for how and why these melting events occur. The answers are not all known. First, mantle can melt if it is depressurized. As the mantle flows upward, it largely retains its temperature but progresses to lower and lower pressures. As pressure is released from the rock, eventually it can melt. Depressurization melting occurs at mid-ocean ridges. Second, mantle can melt if other materials are added to it which lower its melting temperature. Water and carbon dioxide are prime examples: Mantle material with a little of either of these volatiles added to it melts far more easily than the dry material alone. Melting by addition of water occurs at subduction zones. Third, mantle can melt if it is heated to higher temperatures. This seems to be the least common way of melting the mantle.

Mid-ocean ridges are the sources of the crust that lines ocean basins. The underlying mantle rises up beneath mid-ocean ridges and melts through decompression. The magma rises as sheets along vertical cracks near the line where the two oceanic plates are moving apart, creating new crust. Some of the magma bubbles to the surface and rolls out into the cold ocean water forming what are called pillow basalts. Pillow basalts form in humps as their surfaces freeze in the cold water and the hot rising magma pushes out of the bottom of the hump, forming a new hump, called a toe. These shapes are definitive of magma that erupted underwater. Magma is rising and forming new crust along the length of all the world's mid-ocean ridges all the time, and each year the new crust totals about one cubic mile ($\sim$4 km³).

The new oceanic crust moves away from the mid-ocean ridge. Because the area of the surface of the Earth is a fixed quantity new crust creates a space problem, so the other edges of each oceanic plate necessarily push against neighboring plates where oceanic crust pushes against continental crust, the oceanic crust is forced down into the mantle by the much thicker, more buoyant, and rigid continental crust. The process of a plate sinking down into the mantle when pressing against another plate is called subduction. When oceanic crust presses against another plate made of oceanic crust, one or the other plate will begin to subduct. The top of oceanic crust is filled with minerals holding water, from circulating ocean water heated in the new crust near mid-ocean ridges. The crust is also covered with water-holding sediments that settled onto it as it moved away from the ridge. When the oceanic crust subducts, the water-holding minerals give up their water at a variety of depths and temperatures. The sodium- and potassium-filled water released from these minerals rises buoyantly into the mantle above the subducting crust. Water reduces the melting temperature of mantle rocks, and so when the water percolates upward through the mantle, the mantle at some point begins to melt.

The resulting magma is also more buoyant than the mantle rock it melted from, and it, too, percolates upward. The magma eventually erupts, forming volcanoes that are explosive because they have water under pressure dissolved in the magma, bursting out as the pressure drops during eruption, and also because magmas formed in subduction zones tend to have more silica in them, making them highly viscous. The high viscosity also means that a large amount of pressure is required to force the eruption, also leading to explosive eruptions. These eruptions may also consist more of dry ash (flakes of silicate minerals that look like wood ash) or blocks of pumice (solidified magma laced with bubbles). Subduction zones form island arcs like Japan, the Philippines, and parts of the Caribbean. Subduction zones also form continental arcs like the Cascades on the west coast of North America, and the volcanoes that line the western edge of Central and South America.

Large-scale climate changes on Earth have occurred because of terrestrial effects. Volcanic eruptions inject ash and gas into the atmosphere, blocking the Sun's energy from reaching the Earth to the point that climate is changed. Two famous recent examples of catastrophic volcanic eruptions are Tambora, in Indonesia, which erupted in 1815, and Krakatau, also in Indonesia, which erupted in 1883. When Tambora erupted, the top of the volcano collapsed and the volcano ejected about 10 cubic miles (~40 km³) of ash and about double that amount in magma. Tambora's eruption produced pyroclastic flows, in which superheated clouds of ash and volcanic gas flow down the sides of the volcano like waterfalls, faster than a person can outrun. While about 10,000 people were killed by the eruption itself, the ash that blanketed plants or stayed in the atmosphere, blocking the Sun, killed another 80,000 people from crop loss and famine. The reduction of solar energy from ash in the atmosphere caused temperatures across the Northern Hemisphere to drop by three degrees, virtually eliminating summer. Krakatau killed the majority of its victims in another way: The extreme seismic shock of its immense explosion created tsunamis that killed 36,000 people. Mount Saint Helens, on the other hand, killed only 57 people when it erupted in 1980.

The many smaller volcanoes usually threaten fewer people, but the sizes and intensities of their eruptions are not always easily predictable. Shown here is an image of the 1994 eruption plume of the Rabaul volcano, in New Britain, Papua New Guinea. This eruption plume is estimated at 60,000 feet (18,300 m) tall. Many volcanoes are erupting on Earth on any given day, most of which are located in the Pacific ring, where multiple subduction zones create explosive volcanoes.

Italy has a long history of active volcanoes and danger to citizens. Mount Etna has been erupting for years, as shown in the lower color insert on page C-5. The view looks southeast over the island of Sicily.

The volcanic eruption cloud from Rabaul Caldera, Papua New Guinea, was estimated to be 60,000 feet (18,300 m) tall, but it was not the largest eruption plume of the decade when it erupted in 1994: Mount Pinatubo's 1991 eruption plume was larger. (Earth Sciences and Image Analysis Laboratory, NASA Johnson Space Center, eol.jsc.nasa.gov, STS064-116-64)

The high ash cloud curves south toward Africa, and ashfall was reported in Libya.

Volcanoes can be studied closely on Earth, and their effects can be seen on other planets. The large, dark portions of the Moon that are easily visible from Earth are giant pools of magma that erupted early in lunar history. Venus, Mercury, and Mars all have volcanoes and lava flows visible on their surfaces. These planets apparently all have internal processes that allow their silicate mantles to melt, as on Earth. Jupiter's moon Io is the most volcanically active body in the solar system, and erupts lavas consisting of both silicates and sulfur. While the gas and ice planets cannot have volcanism in the same way, some of their icy moons are volcanically active (volcanism consisting of ices is called cryovolcanism). Tiny moons cannot hold enough internal heat to create volcanism, but larger moons sometimes do. None of Jupiter's other moons show any signs of volcanism, even Ganymede, the largest moon in the solar system. Icy eruptions on Neptune's moon Triton were actually witnessed by spacecraft, and judging from their smooth, new surfaces, Jupiter's Europa, Uranus's Ariel, and Saturn's Titan and Enceladus probably experience cryovolcanism. While other moons may have been volcanically active in the past, the evidence for this has not yet been discovered.

Earthquakes

On Earth, earthquakes are concentrated on long narrow bands, often at the edges of continents. Until the theory of plate tectonics was developed in the 1960s, no one knew why this was, but now the movement of plates relative to each other is accepted as the cause of most earthquakes. Earthquakes are caused by a sudden release of stress from within a body of rock or between two bodies of rock moving relative to each other. The slow rate of movement at the Earth's surface generally allows the interface between the rocks to remain stationary for some time, while stress builds up, and then the rocks move suddenly to relieve the stress. This movement creates the earthquake.

Earthquakes can occur in the interior of plates due to plate flexure, for example, when a plate is rebounding from the weight of a recently removed ice cap. Intraplate earthquakes are relatively uncommon and not well understood. The great majority of earthquakes occur along the boundaries of tectonic plates. Plates moving parallel to each other form long faults that stick and rupture at intervals, creating seismic zones such as the San Andreas fault. Subduction zones, plate boundaries at which an oceanic plate moves under a continental plate, are another fertile ground for earthquakes. In subduction zones earthquakes can occur to depths of about 400 miles (700 km), below which the rock is too plastic from heat to allow stress to build up or to allow the rock to fail in a brittle manner. The deep earthquakes along linear trends were noticed in the early 20th century and named Wadati-Benioff zones, but it was not until the advent of plate tectonic theory that their cause was understood. Earthquakes occur at the interface between the subducting plate and the mantle it is moving through, as well as in the middle of the flexing, subducting plate. Mapping these earthquakes actually makes a picture of the location of the slab in the mantle.

About 3,000 seismic stations around the world are constantly monitoring for earthquakes. Seismic stations contain instruments that measure movement in the two horizontal directions and in the vertical direction. As waves of energy radiate from the site of the earthquake, the surface and subsurface of the Earth literally wave up and down or back and forth. The frequency of these waves varies from 0.001 to about 10 Hertz, depending on the size and distance of the earthquake and the material the energy is moving through. Though many scientists are working on earthquake prediction, it has proven impossible to date, even in the most reliable and well-studied simple fault zones.

Dr. Charles Richter, a professor at the California Institute of Technology, realized during the 1930s that the waves given off by an earthquake are proportional to the earthquake's energy, and thus can be used to compare the sizes of earthquakes around the world. By measuring the heights and frequencies of the waves as recorded by a seismic station, scientists can assign earthquakes a magnitude. The most commonly known scale for earthquakes is Dr. Richter's original work, the Richter scale, though there are a number of other earthquake magnitude scales. The formula for the Richter magnitude of an earthquake is to add the logarithm of the height of the earthquake's wave in millimeters to a factor taking into consideration the distance to the earthquake. Each increment on the Richter scale indicates a thirtyfold increase in earthquake energy. An earthquake designated 3 on the Richter scale is 900 times as strong as an earthquake designated 1. Comparisons of events with Richter scale magnitudes are given in the table below. Each year several hundred earthquakes with a magnitude of 3 occur, but only one or two with magnitude 7 or 8. A magnitude 9 event is thought to happen about every hundred years.

Earthquakes can cause immense damage simply by earth movement breaking roads, electrical, gas, and water lines, and knocking down buildings. Faults sometimes break all the way to the surface of the Earth and cause offsets in height or in lateral distance, leaving a scarp across the landscape or offsetting the line of a road, a fence, or even a river. Earthquakes near coasts can transfer their energy to the water, where waves form tsunamis that sometimes travel across entire ocean basins. Tsunamis can travel as fast as 650 feet per second (200 m/sec) across deep water. When they arrive at coastlines their energy is confined to shallower water and causes the wave to slow down but to increase in height. Tsunamis can be tens of feet tall as they hit a coast, and can run up over the land as far as a couple of miles (a few kilometers).

On Monday, December 27, 2004, the world's most powerful earthquake in 40 years (since the 1964 Good Friday earthquake in Alaska) occurred in the oceanic crust off the Indonesian island of Sumatra. The quake gave off waves that caused the Earth's surface to

THE RICHTER SCALE

Richter magnitude	Corresponding event
1	blast at a construction site
3	earthquakes of 3 and below are not generally felt by people
4	detonation of a small nuclear weapon
6	earthquakes in this range can cause significant damage within about 60 miles (100 km) of the event
8	1906 San Francisco earthquake
9.0	2004 Sumatran earthquake
9.2	1964 Good Friday earthquake in Alaska
9.7	the largest recorded earthquake, Chile, May 1960
12	thought to be the strongest earthquake sustainable by the Earth

move vertically by at least a half-inch (1 cm) as they passed by even at the greatest distances from the quake, and by at least four inches (10 cm) along the coastline of the Indian Ocean. The huge quake immediately triggered alarms in seismic monitoring stations around the world, notably in Hawaii, where a central monitoring station runs a warning system for countries around the Pacific Ocean. This monitoring station uses tide gauges set in deep water to confirm when an oceanic quake is creating a tidal wave. In the Indian Ocean, where the December 27 quake occurred, there is no such monitoring system, and there are no tide gauges. Immediately after the quake, its magnitude was estimated at less than the 9.0 magnitude that later, more careful analysis revealed it to be. This lower magnitude, combined with the lack of tide gauges, led scientists to consider the possibility of a tsunami but to have no certainty that one would result.

The size of an earthquake is not in itself a definitive indication of a tsunami. Water has to be significantly displaced to create a wave, so a landslide or large crustal movement is required. Deeper earthquakes, for example, do not usually cause significant crustal movement. Catastrophically for the residents of the Indian Ocean basin, the Sumatran earthquake occurred shallowly and created crustal movements at the site of up to 65 feet (20 m), initiating an immense tsunami (see the upper color insert on page C-6). The tsunami traveled as fast as 500 miles per hour (800 km/hr) in the open ocean, and then built to heights of 40 to 50 feet (~14 m) as they reached shallower water. Without a warning system or tide gauges, no advance word reached any waterfront. Over 250,000 people were killed by the tsunami throughout Southeast Asia, and a few were killed as far away as the coast of Somalia, 3,000 miles (4,800 km) from the quake.

As with any wave disruption in a water basin, the waves come in sets and not as a single event. Shown in the lower color insert on page C-7, residents who avoided the first wave were sometimes killed by the later sudden rises in sea level, which rose and fell at least four times with great enough magnitude to endanger people. The quake also disrupted the Earth into free oscillations, shown in the figure on page 44. The longest-period free oscillation distorts the Earth into a more football-shaped figure, and this quake created an oscillation in this mode with an average height of about 0.1 mm. A second free oscillation, in which the Earth moves radially in and out as if breathing, is slow to die away and was still detectable four months later.

In the immediate wake of this disaster, scientists and governments began working together to create warning systems for oceans other than the Pacific. Earthquakes of this magnitude occur on the order of several times per hundred years, so fast action to prevent another such disaster was necessary. Given just a half hour warning, almost every life could have been saved simply by moving to higher ground.

Atmosphere, Surface Conditions, and Weather

Earth's atmosphere is divided into five layers: the *troposphere,* from 0 to about six miles (0 to 10 km); the *stratosphere,* from six to 31 miles (10 to 50 km); the *mesosphere,* from 31 to 50 miles (50 to 80 km); the ionosphere, from 50 to 310 miles (80 to 500 km); and the *exosphere,* from 310 miles and up (500 km and up). Most of the atmosphere is close to the surface of the Earth, and there is no clear top to the atmosphere, as it simply becomes thinner and thinner with height as it merges into space. In the United States people who travel above an altitude of 50 miles (80 km) are designated as astronauts. The altitude of 62 miles (100 km) is often used as the boundary between atmosphere and space. For spacecraft traveling back to Earth, at 75 miles (120 km) atmospheric effects become noticeable during reentry.

The troposphere contains approximately 80 percent of the total mass of the atmosphere. Jet planes generally fly near the top of this layer. In the Earth's troposphere there is strong convection, that is, mixing due to temperature or density differences in a liquid or gas. One example of convection is boiling oatmeal in a pot: Heat put in at the bottom of the pot causes the water and oatmeal at the bottom to expand (some water is converted into gas, which rises as bubbles). Almost every material expands when it is heated, and since it retains its original mass, it becomes less dense. Lowing the density of the material at the bottom makes it buoyant, and it rises to the top. Cooler material from the top sinks to the bottom to take its place, and the cycle continues. Gentle convection can create "cells," regular patterns of circulation with one side moving up and the other down. More violent convection can become turbulent, with currents moving on many length scales. In general, though, convection is caused by a density difference between adjacent pieces of material; the light piece will rise, and the denser piece will sink, initiating a cycle. The differences in density can be caused by temperature, as in the boiling oatmeal case, or the differences in density can be caused by differing compositions. In the troposphere temperature falls with increasing altitude, from a global average of approximately 60°F (17°C) at sea level to approximately −61°F (−52°C). This means that colder, denser gases from the upper troposphere will be continuously sinking down to displace the more buoyant, warmer, lower atmosphere. The troposphere is thus always mixing, and its currents are wind, creating weather. In addition to the density differences in a given column of the troposphere, the differences in temperature between the polar regions and the equatorial regions also cause density differences that drive winds, and therefore weather. The top of the troposphere is known as the *tropopause,* marking the height at which the temperature in the atmosphere begins to rise again. The height of the tropopause varies with pressure and weather, from four to 10 miles (6 to 16 km). Temperature increases in and above the stratosphere because of solar heating, and since each higher layer is hotter than the one below it the layers are unlikely to mix: Higher temperatures create less dense material, so the higher material is buoyant with respect to all that lies beneath it. All planets with atmospheres have a troposphere in which temperature falls with height, and a stratosphere where the temperature rises with heat (see figure on page 98).

Above the stratosphere lies the mesosphere, which reaches from 31 to 50 miles (50 to 80 km) altitude. Temperatures in the upper mesosphere fall as low as −99°F (−73°C), though as do temperatures at other altitudes they vary with latitude, weather, and season. Many meteors burn up in the mesosphere; there are enough gas particles in the mesophere to create sufficient friction to burn the tiny grains of interplanetary dust that are seen from the surface as shooting stars.

The two highest layer of the atmosphere, the ionosphere and exosphere, together are called the *thermosphere.* In the ionosphere strong solar radiation energizes the atmospheric gases to the point that they ionize and become electrically charged and heated. Temperatures in the ionosphere are highly dependent on solar activity, and can rise to 3,600°F (2,000°C). The electrical charges in the ionosphere also bounce radio waves, allowing radio transmissions to travel above the Earth, bounce off the ionosphere, and travel back to a point beyond the horizon from their origination.

The exosphere extends to 6,250 miles (10,000 km) above the Earth's surface, where it merges into space. Atoms and molecules are constantly escaping to space from the exosphere if they have enough energy to overcome the pull of gravity. Hydrogen and helium are the major components of the sparse atmosphere at this great height. This is also the height at which many satellites orbit the Earth, and so the exosphere is often thought of as space.

The *POLAR* spacecraft is orbiting the Earth at a distance of 3,700 to 17,000 miles (6,000 to 28,000 km or 2 to 9 Earth radii), in the ionosphere, the exosphere, and slightly beyond. After averaging measurements over 93 orbits, the researchers found that there is an average electron density of one electron every 10 cubic centimeters near the poles, and about one electron every three cubic centimeters near the equator. These plasma densities in the remote atmosphere of

ATMOSPHERIC CONSTITUENTS OF THE EARTH

Constituent	Chemical symbol	Fraction	Fraction on Mars
nitrogen	N_2	0.7808	0.027
oxygen	O_2	0.2095	0.013
argon	Ar	0.0093	0.016
water	H_2O	0.3 to 0.04 ppm	300 ppm
carbon dioxide	CO_2	345 pm	0.95
neon	Ne	18 ppm	2.5 ppm
ozone	O_3	0 to 12 ppm	0.1 ppm
helium	He	5 ppm	
methane	CH_4	1.7 ppm	
krypton	Kr	1 ppm	0.3 ppm
hydrogen	H_2	500 ppb	
nitrous oxide	N_2O	300 ppb	
carbon monoxide	CO	100 ppb	700 ppm
chlorofluorocarbon	CFC–12	380 ppt	
chlorofluorocarbon	CFC–11	220 ppt	

(Note: ppm means parts per million; 1 ppm is equal to 0.000001 or 1×10^{-6}; ppb means parts per billion; 1 ppb is equal to 0.000000001 or 1×10^{-9}; ppt means parts per trillion; 1 ppt is equal to 0.000000000001 or 1×10^{-12}.)

the Earth are controlled by the interactions between the magnetic field and the solar wind, and these are the source regions of the plasma that creates the aurora borealis and aurora australis.

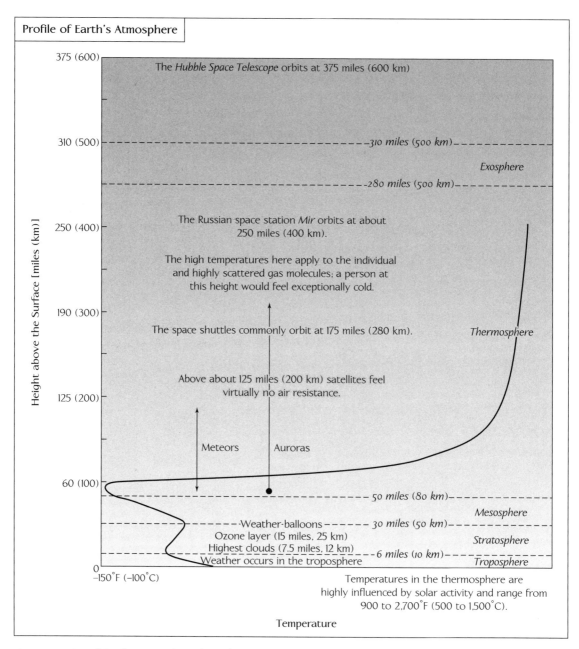

Profile of Earth's Atmosphere

The *Hubble Space Telescope* orbits at 375 miles (600 km)

310 miles (500 km)

Exosphere

280 miles (500 km)

The Russian space station *Mir* orbits at about 250 miles (400 km).

The high temperatures here apply to the individual and highly scattered gas molecules; a person at this height would feel exceptionally cold.

The space shuttles commonly orbit at 175 miles (280 km).

Thermosphere

Above about 125 miles (200 km) satellites feel virtually no air resistance.

Meteors   Auroras

50 miles (80 km)

Mesosphere

Weather balloons *30 miles (50 km)*

Ozone layer (15 miles, 25 km)

Stratosphere

Highest clouds (7.5 miles, 12 km)

6 miles (10 km)

Weather occurs in the troposphere

Troposphere

0
−150°F (−100°C)

Height above the Surface [miles (km)]

375 (600)
310 (500)
250 (400)
190 (300)
125 (200)
60 (100)

Temperatures in the thermosphere are highly influenced by solar activity and range from 900 to 2,700°F (500 to 1,500°C).

Temperature

A cross section of Earth's atmosphere shows how it merges into space.

The atmosphere on Earth is dominated by nitrogen, and Earth is one of the very few planetary bodies for which this is true (the others are Neptune's moon Triton, Saturn's moon Titan, and Pluto). While the atmosphere of Earth's neighbor Venus is rich in carbon dioxide, on Earth most of the carbon dioxide is tied up in carbonate rocks. The water content of Earth's atmosphere is highly variable; a given molecule of water has a residence time of about one week in the atmosphere before it is precipitated out. The main constituents of Earth's atmosphere are listed in the table on page 97, "Atmospheric Constituents of the Earth," where they are compared to the atmosphere of Mars. The life on Earth has made its atmosphere rich in nitrogen and oxygen, setting it apart from the atmospheres of its nearest neighbors.

The familiar forms of weather on Earth are, for the most part, duplicated on other planets. Hurricanes and typhoons are seen clearly on the gas giant planets, in particular Jupiter. Dust storms are common on Mars. Lightning is seen on Jupiter as well as other planets. Water rain appears to be unique in the solar system at the present time, though it probably occurred on Mars in the past. On Earth, water rain can freeze incrementally in the upper atmosphere into hailstones, like the huge example of a compound stone shown in the upper color insert on page C-7.

Storms and rain, along with snow and hail, create excitement and destruction on a daily basis somewhere in the world. Shown in the upper color insert on page C-8, some of the largest storms are tropical *cyclones,* low-pressure systems with circular (or "cyclonic") surface winds and rain and thunderstorms. If these storms have surface winds of less than 39 miles per hour (17 m/sec), they are known as tropical depressions. With higher sustained surface wind speeds, the storms are known as tropical storms, and if winds reach 74 miles per hour (33 m/sec), the storms are known by a bewildering number of terms. They are hurricanes if they are in the North Atlantic Ocean, the Northeast Pacific Ocean east of the dateline, or the South Pacific Ocean east of 160E, but they are known as typhoons in the Northwest Pacific Ocean west of the dateline, as severe tropical cyclones in the Southwest Pacific Ocean west of 160E or Southeast Indian Ocean east of 90E, as severe cyclonic storms in the North Indian Ocean, and as tropical cyclones in the Southwest Indian Ocean. The satellite image of the 1977 hurricane Heather shows the typical cyclonic pattern of

This satellite image of Hurricane Heather, taken in 1977, clearly shows the storm's typical spinning structure. (National Oceanic and Atmospheric Administration/Department of Commerce)

these storms, as does the above image of the 1979 typhoon Kerry, off the coast of Australia (also on page 101).

One of the most destructive hurricanes was Andrew, which hit the Bahamas, Florida, and Louisiana in 1992. Examples of damage by the hurricane are shown in two images. In the first image (on page 102), one of the cars belonged to a CNN reporter, and the other to a Hurricane Center employee, who learned of the damage to the car by watching CNN. The second image (shown in the lower color insert on page C-6) depicts a one-by-four-inch board that was driven through the trunk of a Royal Palm in the high winds of the hurricane.

The daily weather of the Earth is violent enough, but climate scientists have demonstrated that weather was more violent and extreme at times in the past, and is likely to become more violent and extreme in the future, as well.

For the last several hundred years people have known that the energetic output of the Sun is variable. This can be seen in sunspot and aurora variations, as well as in the amount of solar wind that makes it past the Earth's magnetic field and reach the Earth's surface. Over the

Typhoon Kerry was one of the Pacific's major storms in 1979. (National Oceanic and Atmospheric Administration/ Department of Commerce)

past 1,800 years, there have been nine cycles of solar energy output. Some of the periods of lowest solar output have names, such as the Oort, Wolf, Sporer, Maunder, and Dalton Minima. The Maunder Minimum is perhaps the most famous, because of its strong effects on civilization in Europe during recorded time. It occurred between 1645 and 1715, and even dedicated scientists with observatories were hard-pressed to see more than one or two sunspots per decade. At the same time, the Earth experienced what is called the Little Ice Age, from about 1600 to 1800 (scientists disagree about the proper beginning of the Little Ice Age; some put the start as early as 1400). Throughout the world glaciers in mountainous areas advanced. In many parts of the world average temperatures fell and harsh weather was more common. It was a time of repeated famine and cultural dislocation as many people fled regions that had become hostile even to subsistence agriculture.

In 1645 the glacier Mer de Glace on Mont Blanc in France was advancing on Chamonix due to the unusually cold temperatures. In warmer times there was less winter snow and more of it melted in the summer, leaving the glacier stationary. During the Little Ice Age, heavier winter snows and less summer melting weighed the glacier with additional layers of snow, pressing the deeper layers into ice, and the glacier moved more rapidly, deforming and flowing downhill under the force of its own weight like a spreading pile of bread dough. The advancing glacier had already engulfed and destroyed farms and even small villages. The Chamonix villagers wrote to the Catholic bishop of Geneva for help. The bishop actually came to Chamonix and performed a rite of exorcism, after which the glacier receded for some time, before once again inexorably advancing. Similar scenes of fear and destruction happened in other mountain areas. The North Atlantic was filled with icebergs both farther south and for more of the year than in current times, changing the cycles of fisheries and the availability of food. Eskimos came in kayaks as far south as Scotland. In China severe winters killed orange groves that had survived in Jiangxi province, around the lower Yangzi River, for centuries.

Temperatures during the Maunder Minimum period were only about one-half of a degree Celsius lower than the mean for the 1970s,

These cars were lifted and spun by the high winds of Hurricane Andrew in 1992. (National Oceanic and Atmospheric Administration/ Department of Commerce)

pointing out humankind's extreme sensitivity to small changes in average temperature, and the scientists Pang and Yau found that temperature decline consistent with the decrease in average solar radiance. Then, from 1795 to 1825, came the Dalton Minimum, along with another dip in Northern Hemispheric temperatures. Since that time, however, the Sun has gradually brightened to the current Modern Warm Period.

The small temperature variations in the Maunder Minimum caused violent changes in weather that strongly influenced human civilization. At the present time on Earth, average temperatures are rising. The overall average surface temperature on Earth is between 59 and 68°F (15 to 20°C), though at different places on the surface the average temperature varies between about −40 and 104°F (−40 to 40°C). About 31 degrees of the heat on Earth is due to the insulation of the atmosphere, called the greenhouse effect. Some amount of greenhouse effect is normal, caused primarily by the presence of carbon dioxide in the atmosphere. Venus's surface is hot enough to melt lead because of the greenhouse effects of carbon dioxide in its atmosphere. On Earth, the greenhouse effect is controlled by a cycle in which carbon dioxide is released continually from volcanoes, combines with calcium from weathered continental rocks, and is deposited as limestone (primarily as calcium carbonate, or $CaCO_3$) into the oceans. When oceanic plates subduct into the mantle, their carbon, in the form of calcium carbonate, is erupted back onto the surface through the volcanoes at subduction zones. Water is among the controlling factors of this cycle: Both Venus and Mars lost their water, and so their atmospheres are dominated by carbon dioxide.

Though carbon dioxide is the dominant natural greenhouse gas, there are other chemicals that control climate when they are in the atmosphere. Many of these, including chlorofluorocarbons, are produced by humans. Over the past 100 years the average temperature on Earth has risen by between one-half and one degree due to an increased greenhouse effect caused by chemical input from man. Though this addition may seem tiny, it already appears to be having an effect. Increased average temperature does not in the short run necessarily cause the weather to be hotter; instead it causes greater variations in temperature across the globe and therefore stronger driving forces for winds and weather. As the greenhouse effect increases weather is likely to get more violent and more erratic; some scientists believe these effects are already apparent in the increased numbers of hurricanes.

Human contributions to the environment are inexorably driving the climate on Earth to extremes. Though the rock record and chemical data from ice cores show that the Earth's climate has often been at extremes in the past, this is little consolation to the people who have to find a way to live through it. Adversaries of change in the habits of society correctly state that the Earth is well within the range of climates that have existed in the past, but these are not climates that humankind has shown any ability to cope with. Many times in Earth's past the climate has moved into periods of heat (with attendant violent storms) or complete freezing, and has recovered, but never has humankind had to live through these periods. The surface of the Earth is already a challenging place, full of volcanoes, mountains, hurricanes, and other marvels full of scientific interest; it is necessary for the future of our civilization that we do what is possible to prevent further climate change.

Life on Earth

5

A billion years after the formation of the Earth, simple blue-green algae (prokaryotic cells) developed and were the only life on the planet for another 2 billion years. Examples of these algae cells were discovered in northwestern Australia in a silica-rich sedimentary rock called chert dated at 3.77 billion years old. A billion and a half years ago, the cells then evolved nuclei, and became eukaryotic cells. Another billion years passed before multicellular living things evolved, and all the rest of the profusion of life has developed in the last 500,000 years, just one-ninth of the age of the Earth.

Once life developed the ability to photosynthesize, cells began to give off oxygen as they created energy. During the Proterozoic Eon, from 2.5 billion to 542 million years ago, the oxygen content of the atmosphere rose from about 1 to 10 percent because of this input. Not until the Devonian Period, about 400 million years ago, did the oxygen content of the atmosphere reach its current 21 percent. As oxygen increased in the atmosphere thanks to early life, fish developed in the Cambrian Period, about 500 million years ago. Land plants developed in the mid-Silurian Period, about 420 million years ago. Reptiles developed in the early Pennsylvanian Epoch, about 360 million years ago, and amphibians developed in the Devonian Period, about 340 million years ago. The earliest primates did not appear until about 57 million years ago.

Though there has been an overall increase of the numbers and diversity of species over the age of the Earth, life on Earth has gone through violent cycles, involving periods of development and diversity punctuated by extinctions. The greatest of the extinctions occurred 250 million years ago, at the boundary between the Permian and Triassic periods. At that moment in time, 95 percent of marine species and 70 percent of land-based species

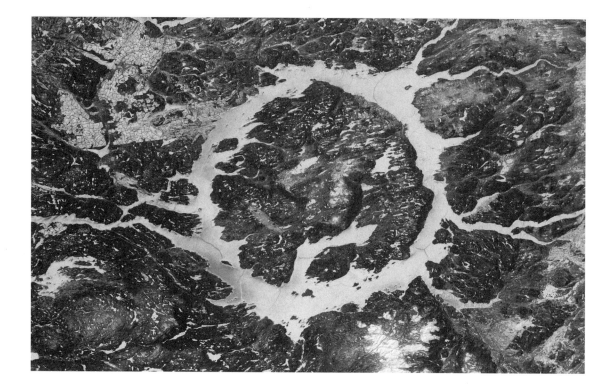

The Manicouagan impact crater in eastern Canada has been so eroded over time that only a circular depression, filled here with frozen water, remains. (Earth Sciences and Image Analysis Laboratory, NASA Johnson Space Center, eol.jsc.nasa.gov, image number ISS06-E-47702)

existing on Earth were wiped out. At the same time, the geologic rock record shows us, there was both a huge volcanic eruption in Siberia, a great fall in sea level, and changes in oceanic chemistry.

The interactions and causes of these simultaneous events are hotly debated in the scientific community. Some think a plume of hot material from the lowest mantle rose, melted, and erupted, changing climate violently enough to cause the extinctions, while others suggest that a huge meteorite impact both changed the climate and caused the volcanic eruptions. Giant impacts are the only known natural disaster that can wipe out all life on Earth. The image here shows the Manicouagan impact crater in eastern Canada, an impact large enough to have caused significant climatic disruption, but not enough to cause a global extinction. This photo of Manicouagan was taken from the *International Space Station* and shows the water filling the outer rim of the original crater has frozen in winter. The Manicouagan crater is an excellent example of an ancient crater partly erased by erosion until it consists of nothing but a circular lake. This image shows the reservoir now filling the crater frozen in winter.

▲ In this composite image the Earth and Mars can be compared directly: the size and water content of the Earth are apparent. (NASA/JPL)

▲ About 20 million years ago a large bolide impact struck near this site in Canada's arctic Devon Islands, ejecting material that fell to create these hills. Few hills on Earth are caused by impacts, though almost all hills on the Moon are created in this way. (NASA/JPL/ASU)

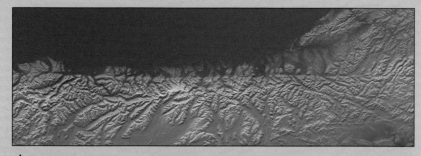

▲ *The Alpine fault, a major plate boundary, runs parallel to and just inland of a large section of the west coast of New Zealand's South Island. The false color in this image (just over 300 miles [500 km] wide) indicates elevation: green is the lowest, grading through tan to white at the highest.* (NASA/JPL/NGA)

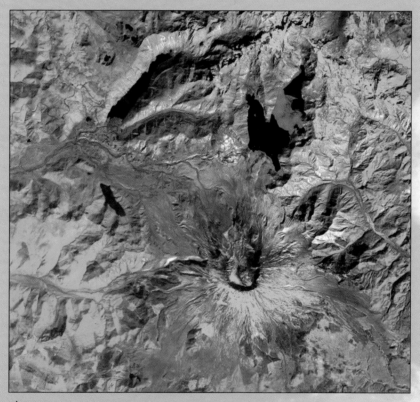

▲ *Red hotspots from lava show clearly in this thermal emission image of Mount Saint Helens, captured one week after the March 8, 2005, ash and steam eruption.* (NASA/GSFC/METI/ERSDAC/JAROS, and U.S./Japan ASTER Science Team)

◀ *The full Earth showing Africa and Antarctica, taken from the Apollo 17 spacecraft using a handheld Hasselblad camera.* (NASA/Apollo 17, NSSDC a17_h_148_22727)

▼ *The Mississippi Delta showing its distributary fan formed by sediment dropped from the river water as the flow slows.* (NASA)

▲ The round Richat Structure in Mauritania is formed by a pattern of eroded sedimentary rocks, not by an impact crater. (NASA/JPL/NIMA)

◄ Two major faults in western Tibet stand out in the topography and satellite imagery. The Karakoram fault runs from top left to lower right across this image, through the Karakoram mountain range and southern Tibet. The Altyn Tagh fault is the slightly curved line running along the northern edge of the plateau from top left to top right. (NASA/JPL)

◀ *The Sinai Peninsula is a result of those two continents moving apart to create new oceanic crust. Thinner crust forms the two northern branches of the Red Sea (the Gulf of Suez, west, and the Gulf of Aqaba, east). The Mediterranean Sea forms the northern side of the triangle. The false color indicates elevation: green is the lowest, grading through tan to white at the highest.* (NASA/JPL/NIMA)

▼ *This 2002 volcanic plume from Mount Etna, Italy, reached Africa.* (Earth Sciences and Image Analysis Laboratory, NASA Johnson Space Center, eol.jsc.nasa.gov, ISS005-E-19016)

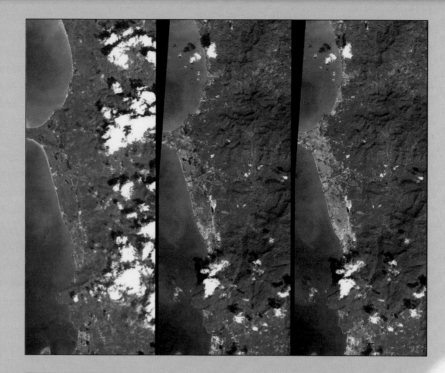

▲ *These simulated color images show a 17-mile (27-km) stretch of coast about 50 miles (80 km) north of the Phuket airport in Thailand on December 31, 2004 (middle), and also two years earlier (left). The changes to gray along the coast are caused by vegetation stripped away by the giant tsunami. The image on the right is a copy of the middle scene but shows as red areas with elevations below 33 feet (10 m).* (NASA/GSFC/ METI/ERSDAC/JAROS, and U.S./Japan ASTER Science Team/JPL/NGA)

◄ *High winds from Hurricane Andrew speared this palm tree with a piece of lumber.* (National Oceanic and Atmospheric Administration/ Department of Commerce)

▲ *This large compound hailstone formed high in the atmosphere.* (National Oceanic and Atmospheric Administration/Department of Commerce)

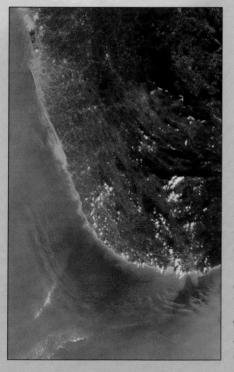

◀ *The initial tsunami waves from the earthquake that occurred on December 26, 2004, off the island of Sumatra, Indonesia, took just over two hours to reach Sri Lanka. Waves continued to arrive for hours afterward, during which NASA's Terra satellite captured this image of tsunami waves about 20 to 25 miles (30 to 40 km) from Sri Lanka.* (NASA/GSFC/LaRC/JPL, MISR Team)

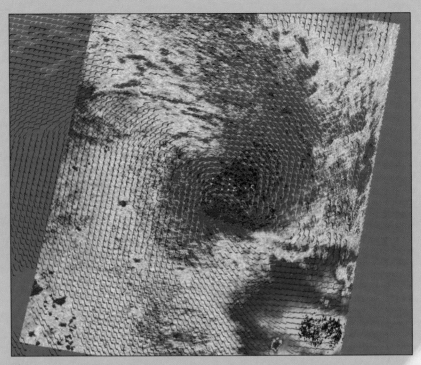

▲ Data from NASA's QuikSCAT satellite was used to create this image of Cyclone Olaf in the South Pacific on February 16, 2005. The colored background shows the near-surface wind speeds. The strongest winds (purple) are at the center of the storm. The black barbs indicate wind speed and direction, and white barbs indicate areas of heavy rain. (NASA/JPL)

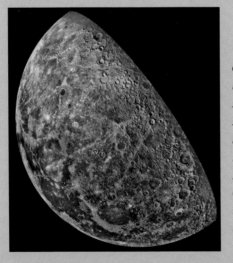

◄ This false-color mosaic was constructed from a series of 53 images taken by Galileo's imaging system on December 7, 1992. Colors show compositional variations. Bright pinkish areas are highlands materials, such as those surrounding the oval lava-filled Crisium impact basin toward the bottom of the picture. Blue to orange shades indicate volcanic lava flows. (NASA/JPL/Galileo)

Though the causes and interactions remain incompletely understood, study of extinctions does show that life on Earth is fragile. Extinctions have occurred regularly throughout Earth history and all of life is vulnerable to the violent actions of this mobile planet and to the effects of giant meteorite impacts. A list of the five largest extinctions in Earth history is given in the table on page 108. Many more of smaller magnitudes have occurred. In relatively small ways, earthquakes form hazards: The most deadly earthquake in recorded history took place in China's Shaanxi province in 1556, killing 800,000 people. Volcanoes, on the other hand, can change the entire planet's climate: 73,500 years ago a volcanic supereruption occurred in Sumatra, filling the atmosphere with sulfur, ash, and carbon dioxide, blocking the Sun's energy to such an extent that plants couldn't sufficiently photosynthesize, and the global ecosystem almost collapsed. Studies of human DNA suggest that there were only a few thousand early human survivors of that catastrophe. Much more recently, in 1815, Mount Tambora, on the Indonesian island of Sumbawa, erupted with an explosion that was heard 875 miles (1,400 km) away. Twelve thousand Indonesians died immediately from the eruption, and another 80,000 died later as a result of famine, as crops were wiped out. Another volcanic winter was caused by the ash cloud that enveloped the Earth, and in England and the United States, frosts occurred all summer.

The perennial question of why life developed on Earth has no clear answer. Key factors were present, including a moderate temperature and the presence of water, but perhaps mankind thinks of these as necessities for life simply because they are necessities for the life that has developed on Earth. Though many scientists hope and think that primitive life may have developed on Mars at some point in the past, no evidence for such life has been found. The only place in the universe that life is known to exist is here on Earth.

Reseachers have developed a number of interwoven and complex theories for how the solar system formed. The cloud of material orbiting the young Sun is supposed to have been composed of different materials depending on the distance from the Sun. The closest materials were rocky and metallic, able to withstand the intense heat near the new star. At a distance between where Mars and Jupiter now orbit, temperatures fell sufficiently to allow more volatile compounds to condense into ices. The point where ices could condense is often referred to as the snow line. As the planets accreted out of smaller

THE MOST EXTREME EXTINCTIONS IN EARTH HISTORY

Name	Time	Effect
Cretaceous–Tertiary	65 million years before present	possibly caused by a meteorite impact; 16 percent of marine families, 47 percent of marine genera, and 18 percent of land vertebrate families, including the dinosaurs, went extinct
End–Triassic	199 to 214 million years before present	possibly caused by volcanism at the opening of the Atlantic ocean; 22 percent of marine families, 52 percent of marine genera went extinct
Permian–Triassic	251 million years before present	possibly caused by the Siberian flood basalts or by a giant impact; 95 percent of marine species, including the trilobites, and 70 percent of land species went extinct
Late Devonian	364 million years before present	22 percent of marine families and 57 percent of marine genera went extinct
Ordovician–Silurian	439 million years before present	25 percent of marine families and 60 percent of marine genera went extinct

pieces of material and increasingly attracted new material to themselves by their increasing gravitational fields, they came to be made of averages of the compositions available to them at their distance from the Sun. The inner, terrestrial planets are therefore made of rocky and metallic material, and the planets outside the snow line contain a large fraction of ices. In this way scientists made a theory for the formation of planetary systems that depended exclusively on one example only: This solar system. There was no other example for comparison.

When *extrasolar* planets began to be discovered, the overarching theories for the formation of planetary systems were exploded. The largest of planets are the easiest to discover, since they influence their stars the most, by pulling the star with their gravity as they orbit so that the star wobbles, or by blocking a portion of the star's light if they pass between the star and Earth. Scientists began to discover a large number of giant planets orbiting distant stars. More than 100 extrasolar planets have been discovered; their masses range from one-tenth to 13 Jupiter masses (at about 15 Jupiter masses, the object will have the gravity necessary to become a star). All of the extrasolar planets now known orbit their stars more closely than 5 AU. In this solar system, 5 AU reaches just to Jupiter. The largest number of extrasolar planets orbit much closer to their stars, and the number of planets drops off steeply toward orbits of 5 AU. Out there was a large population of planetary systems that looked and behaved nothing like this solar system. This solar system is the only known example with giant planets orbiting far away, and now there are more than 100 that are completely different. What are the general laws for forming planetary systems? Scientists obviously need to think again! These giant extrasolar planets are thought to have formed further away from their stars; up close to the star, there is not enough material to make a giant planet. Did they form a core first, and then attract other materials gravitationally, as the Earth probably did, or did they collapse out of the early nebula like a new star does? If they formed farther away from the star, where there was more material to make a giant planet, why did they migrate inward to a tiny, close orbit? Why have the giant planets Jupiter and Saturn not done the same?

By studying extrasolar planets scientists hope to discover more about the Earth and how this solar system formed, and also to search for likely places to find life elsewhere in the universe. They hope to get a sense for the inventory of solar systems in the universe. Are there a continuum of planet sizes between small terrestrial planets like Earth and the giant planets that can now be detected orbiting distant stars, or are there really two populations of planet sizes? Where do ocean planets fit in this inventory? What is the inventory of solar systems? This is the big, central question: Since life requires water (if there are kinds of life that do not, they have not been discovered or imagined), scientists want to find planets with oceans. If there are other planets with oceans, can humans find life elsewhere in the universe?

Extrasolar planets can be detected by looking for stars that wobble from the gravitational pull of large planets that are circling them. More rarely, the planets pass between the star and Earth in their orbit, called a transit. Transiting takes a particular range of orientations and orbits. Observers could be looking down on the planetary system, for example, and the planet would appear to orbit around its

Dr. Sara Seager and the Search for Extrasolar Planets

For scientists studying the formation of planetary systems and the presence of life, there is one big problem: Humankind has only a single example, this solar system and life on Earth. To learn the most about a subject, it is best to study a number of cases. Where can other examples to compare to Earth be found? Other planets must be found orbiting other stars. Finding these extrasolar planets, and trying to understand what their surface environment is like and what they are made of, is the challenge and pursuit taken on by Dr. Sara Seager.

Extrasolar planets are necessarily far away and thus difficult to detect: The planets do not produce light, like stars do, and must be detected by their influences on the star they orbit. Before recent advances in telescopes, digital photography, and computer analysis, these planets could not be detected from Earth. In 1991 Alexander Wolszczan and Dale Frail at the National Radio Astronomy Observatory discovered the first real extrasolar planet. This planet is closely orbiting a pulsar star 978 light-years from Earth. A pulsar star constantly emits high levels of energetic radiation, so this new planet, which orbits at only 0.19 AU (closer to its star than Mercury is to ours), is extremely inhospitable to life. This planet is not an analog of Earth or of any of the other planets in this solar system.

In the mid-1990s Seager was a graduate student at Harvard University, ready to choose her thesis topic, when the first several extrasolar planets orbit Sun-like stars were discovered and confirmed. These planets are all far larger than the Earth and orbit much closer to their stars. Seager was fascinated by the discovery and made a risky choice, deciding to carry out her doctoral thesis research in the area of extrasolar planets. The content of a scientist's doctoral thesis is a dominant influence on their career; they become experts in the field of their original doctoral research, and will be hired for their first jobs on the basis of this work. In the case of extrasolar planets, the question remained whether the field would develop and become a legitimate area of study at all. Very few planets had been found, none Earth-like or even resembling the giant planets in this solar system. The four planets orbiting Sun-like stars are all of the type referred to as "hot Jupiters": giant planets close to their stars, and not in the least resembling the Earth. If the field did not prove to be a topic large and tractable enough for many scientists to pursue, with interesting and relevant results, Seager risked largely wasting her years of work toward a doctoral thesis. She completed her thesis in 1999, and her gamble paid off. The field is fascinating, fruitful, and relevant, and she is one of its first and most prominent researchers.

Dr. Seager is now a research scientist at the Carnegie Institute of Washington. To search for extrasolar planets Dr. Seager and her research team collect digital photos of a wide field of stars, taking snapshots every few minutes through a telescope. The digital photos are downloaded into computer clusters, where programs compare the amount of light emitted over time (the flux) by each star in each snapshot. The programs are written to look for stars that show short-term decreases in the flux of a star. A planet moving in front of the star (known as transiting) and blocking some of its light from coming to Earth may create decreases in flux. Once the computer programs locate stars with short-term decreases in flux, the scientists study the candidates in much more detail to make sure the cause of the dip is a transiting planet and not a dimmer companion star or some other anomaly.

More than 20 groups around the world are searching for extrasolar planets with this method. Some researchers are using telescopes as small as one-inch backyard scopes to search for extrasolar planets, teaming with researchers in different parts of the world so they can take photos of the same part of the sky at nighttime around the clock as the Earth turns. Small telescopes look at nearby, bright stars. Seager's team uses more powerful telescopes in a complementary approach: Looking at fainter, more distant stars. Scheduling time on the few large optical telescopes around the world appropriate for this kind of research is a constant challenge. Seager's team uses the Carnegie one-meter telescope in Chile and has used the National Optical Astronomical Observatory's four-meter telescopes at Kitt Peak, Arizona, and the Cerro Tololo Inter-American Observatory near La Serena, Chile. Seager's team and other groups such as the Optical Gravitational Lensing Experiment (OGLE) at Princeton University have found three planets with the transit search technique. They monitor up to tens of thousands of stars at one time. The team is perfecting its techniques and has been studying stars in large groups called open star clusters to maximize the chances of seeing a star with a transiting planet.

One of Dr. Seager's long-term research goals is to learn how to detect signs of life elsewhere in the universe. To recognize planets with oceans like Earth, more needs to be known about what the Earth and the rest of this solar system look like from space. There is a lot of dust in and around this solar system from asteroids and comets. What does this look like from far away? If scientists saw an extrasolar planetary system likely to hold planets like Earth, how would they recognize it? Perhaps the small planets like Earth, so hard to detect, leave wakes in the dust as they orbit, so observers could look

(continues)

Dr. Sara Seager and the Search for Extrasolar Planets (continued)

for wakes. After finding a small, dark planet, perhaps its atmospheric characteristics will indicate the presence of liquid water.

Seager's main line of research is about extrasolar planetary atmospheres. Her work was used to help detect an extrasolar planet atmosphere for the first time. She studies the theory of atmospheres and planetary systems to determine what scientists on Earth can detect about extrasolar atmospheres, and she is continuing to work on characterizing the atmospheres of planets that transit their parent stars. The formation and persistence of atmospheres are little understood, even in this solar system. Can a planet orbiting at 0.05 AU (seven times closer to its star than Mercury is to the Sun) have an atmosphere? How can an observer tell if an extrasolar planet has clouds? Most importantly, how can an observer tell from these great distances whether an extrasolar planet has life?

Dr. Seager is involved with NASA's Terrestrial Planet Finder mission to locate extrasolar planets. Looking at distant stars is much easier outside the blurring influence of the Earth's atmosphere, and there are plans to launch an instrument into orbit to look for planets. She is on the mission's scientific working group, which decides which stars and how many stars the instrument should look at, and what kinds of measurements it needs to be able to make to detect what the science team wants it to. They think about how to detect small, dark planets like Earth, and collaborate with the mission's engineers to come up with an instrument that can do the necessary work. When *Terrestrial Planet Finder* is launched in the next decade, Dr. Seager hopes to be able to find planets like Earth, small and dark when seen from a great distance, and thus locate the best chances for finding other life in the universe.

star from the human point of view, never passing in front of it. Requiring a transit narrows the candidate extrasolar systems considerably. This kind of detection is far more desirable, though, because as the planet passes in front of the star the star's light is also changed by the planet's atmosphere, if it has one, and much more can be learned about the planet. The mass, size, and atmospheric compositions of transiting planets can be determined. For more, see the sidebar "Dr. Sara Seager and the Search for Extrasolar Planets" on page 110.

An example of a giant planet orbiting close to its star is found at HD209458, a faint star in the constellation Pegasus. The giant planet orbiting this star makes a transit of the star from the viewpoint of Earth. During transit of the planet, the star's light is dimmed by 2 percent (an Earth-size planet would only dim the starlight by about 0.02 percent). This regular dip in light is the clue that allowed scientists to identify the planet, since it is far too small and dim to be seen with telescopes from Earth. The size and mass of the planet were then determined by studying the pattern of light from the star and the wobble of the star as the orbiting planet circles it. This planet appears to be 35 percent larger than Jupiter, but it has 30 percent less mass. This strange, low-density giant planet is nothing like any planet in this solar system. As it cools over the age of the solar system, Jupiter is contracting. Its current rate of contraction is three millimeters per year. How, then, can this distant system maintain a larger, lower-density planet? Perhaps the heat from the star may be keeping the planet hot and inflated. This system raises the question of Jupiter's future: Will it eventually migrate inward in the solar system, disrupting the inner planets, to take up an orbit closer to the Sun?

Of the many extrasolar planets now known, only two Earth-size and one Moon-size planets have been detected. More than 5 percent of nearby stars show evidence of giant orbiting planets, but these are actually the least likely to have Earth-size planets. Giant planets close to their stars are likely to have thrown smaller planets out of their solar systems through gravitational interference. To find smaller, Earth-like planet around other stars, some scientists are more closely watching the inner planets Mercury and Venus. Mercury transits the Sun from the Earth's point of view several times per century, and Venus transits the Sun once or twice per century. By watching these transits, scientists hope to learn how to detect Earth-like planets transiting other stars.

Finding Earth-like planets that may harbor life is an even larger challenge. Sara Seager from the Carnegie Institute would like to identify habitability from spectral analyses of the atmospheres of extrasolar planets. Oxygen is the big signal on Earth: There are no known nonbiological sources that can create large amounts of O_2 in an atmosphere. Nitrogen is another important atmospheric tracer of life: Only microbes on Earth manufacture nitrogen oxide (N_2O). Water clouds might signal oceans, and high *albedo* contrasts on the surface may indicate oceans and continents. To learn to identify these signals from other planets, scientists would like to see the spectra of Earth from a distance. There is a way to do this from Earth: Scientists measure the light that is reflected off the Earth, shines onto the Moon, and is bounced back to Earth. This light, called Earthshine, gives the spectral signature of Earth from space. Earthshine needs to be distinguished from sunshine, though; during a full Moon, the light shining back to Earth comes from the Sun. Earthshine can only be measured from the relatively dark portions of the Moon when the Moon is not full.

Scientists and nations around the world are becoming involved in the search for extrasolar planets. In 2007 NASA is launching a mission called *Kepler* to examine stars from outside the Earth's atmosphere. The European Space Agency will launch a similar mission, *Eddington,* in 2008, and in 2006 the French space agency (CNES) will launch a mission called *Corot.* Together these missions will be able to examine 100,000 stars over three years, searching for signs of life outside the solar system.

Part Two: The Moon

The Moon: Fast Facts about the Earth's Moon in Orbit

6

The Moon's radius is 1,079.6 miles (1,737.4 km), about a quarter the size of the Earth's. The Moon would fit between New York City and Denver, Colorado, or between the east and west coasts of Australia. How did the Earth come to have such a huge moon, relative to its size? With a couple of exceptions, the other planets all have satellites much smaller than themselves, compared to the Earth and Moon (*satellite* means anything orbiting a planet; in this case the topic is natural satellites, also called moons). The table on page 118 lists the nine planets, the name of their largest natural satellite, and the ratio of the radius of the largest satellite to the radius of the planet. Only Charon is larger in relation to Pluto than the Moon is to Earth, but Pluto and Charon are better described as a two-body system rather than a planet-moon system, since they are each like the many Kuiper belt bodies that orbit near them.

Barring Pluto and Charon, the Moon is by far the largest natural satellite in comparison to its planet. The Moon's radius and other important physical parameters are listed in the table on page 121. The Moon's large size raises questions about how it was formed: Could the Moon have formed from the same material as the Earth, at the same time the Earth formed? Computer models show that the Moon could never have become so large, or to have its particular characteristics of spin, if the Earth and Moon had formed from the same material at the same time. The Moon is now thought to have formed from the debris left when a giant impactor, perhaps the size of Mars, struck the Earth

Many solar system objects have simple symbols; this is the symbol for the Moon.

Symbol for the Moon

PLANETS AND THEIR MOONS

Planet	Planetary radius (miles [km])	Largest satellite	Satellite radius (miles [km])	Ratio of radii (moon/planet)
Mercury		(no satellites)		
Venus		(no satellites)		
Earth	3,986 (6,377)	Moon	1,079 (1,736)	0.27
Mars	2,110 (3,395)	Phobos	8.8 (14)	0.0004
Jupiter	44,423 (71,492)	Ganymede	1,649 (2,638)	0.04
Saturn	37,449 (60,268)	Titan	1,609 (2,575)	0.04
Uranus	15,882 (25,959)	Titania	494 (790)	0.03
Neptune	15,379 (24,750)	Triton	846 (1,353)	0.06
Pluto	747 (1,195)	Charon	371 (593)	0.50

when it was largely formed. The giant impactor theory is discussed in chapter 8.

Formation of the Moon

From the Earth the Moon has looked the same throughout human history. Looking up on clear nights, the Moon's familiar face is reassuring in its constancy. Comparing the Moon to the Earth strengthens that image: The Earth has hurricanes that change shorelines, volcanoes that make new islands, clouds that move and change, and plants whose colors change with the seasons. Above us, the Moon has no atmosphere to make weather, and therefore no oxygen to support life, and it has no volcanoes. Aside from its waxing and waning each month, regularly and smoothly, the Moon never seems to change.

This was not always the case. The origins of the Moon are hugely violent and hot, and for billions of years it had active volcanoes dotting its surface. The large dark areas filling the Moon's craters are seeing the largest volcanic flows in the Earth-Moon system, more volcanic rock than can be seen at a glance anywhere else in the solar system. The huge dark basalt flows exist almost exclusively on the near side of the Moon (see the photo below), while the far side has fewer giant craters and almost no dark basalt flows (see the photo on page 120). The

The near side of the Moon shows the familiar dark mare basalt flows filling ancient impact craters. (NASA)

The Moon's far side, never visible from Earth, has fewer distinctive features than does the familiar near side. (NASA)

reasons for the differences between the two sides are not agreed upon in the scientific community. Basic physical parameters for the Moon are given in the table on page 121.

Each planet and some other bodies in the solar system (the Sun and certain asteroids) have been given its own symbol as a shorthand in scientific writing. The symbol for the Moon is shown on page 118.

The orbital relationships of the Earth, Sun, and Moon create the gorgeous phenomenon of the eclipse, as shown in the figure on page 122. There are lunar eclipses, in which the shadow of the Earth is cast over the Moon, making it dark when seen from the Earth. More spectacularly, there are solar eclipses, in which the Moon moves between the Sun and the Earth, covering the Sun from the vantage point of people on parts of the Earth. Because the shadow of the Moon (the umbra) is relatively small on the surface of the Earth, solar eclipses are seen only in narrow paths that curve across the Earth's surface. The path over the Earth's surface where the Sun completely disappears behind the Moon is called the path of totality, and the regions adjacent to it where a partial eclipse is seen are known as the penumbra.

As implied by the terms *near side* and *far side,* the same side of the Moon faces toward the Earth at all times. This relationship is called synchronous rotation, and is created by the period of the moon's rotation on its axis being the same as the period of the moon's orbit around its planet. Information about the Moon's orbit is given in the table on page 123.

Tidal locking causes synchronous rotation. Gravitational attraction between the Moon and the Earth produces a tidal force on each of them, stretching each very slightly along the axis oriented toward its partner. The tidal force causes each to become slightly egg-shaped; the extra stretch is called a tidal bulge. If either of the two bodies is rotating relative to the other, this tidal bulge is not stable. The rotation of the body will cause the long axis of the bulge to move out of alignment with the other object, and gravitational force will work to reshape the rotating body. Because of the relative rotation

FUNDAMENTAL FACTS ABOUT THE MOON

equatorial radius	1,079.6 miles (1,737.4 km), or 0.25 Earth's
polar radius	1,077.4 miles (1,733.93 km)
ellipticity ([equatorial radius − polar radius]/polar radius)	0.002
volume	5.267 × 10^9 cubic miles (2.197 × 10^{10} km^3), or 0.02 times Earth's
mass	1.6186 × 10^{23} pounds (7.3483 × 10^{22} kg); just over 1 percent Earth's mass
average density	210 pounds per cubic foot (3,341 kg/m^3)
acceleration of gravity on the surface at the equator	5.32 feet per square seconds (1.62 m/sec^2)
magnetic field strength at the surface	varies from 6 to 313 × 10^{-9} T (about 1,000 times weaker than Earth's)

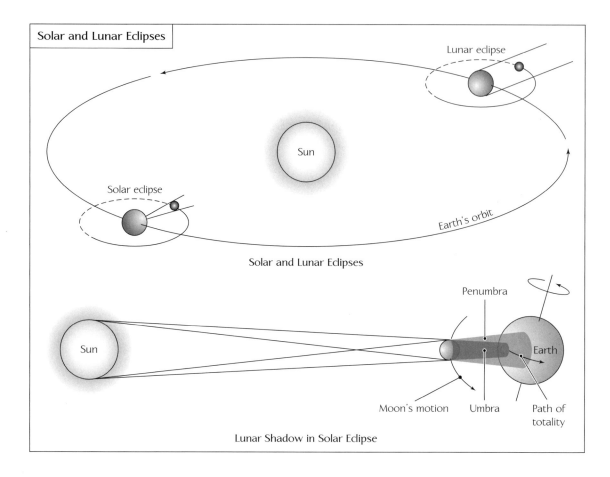

Solar and Lunar Eclipses

Lunar eclipse

Sun

Solar eclipse

Earth's orbit

Solar and Lunar Eclipses

Penumbra

Sun

Earth

Moon's motion   Umbra   Path of totality

Lunar Shadow in Solar Eclipse

Solar and lunar eclipses are caused by the interactions of the shadows of the Earth and Moon. When the Moon is between the Earth and Sun, it can eclipse the Sun from a small portion of the Earth's surface; when the Earth's shadow crosses the Moon, it can cause a lunar eclipse.

between the bodies, the tidal bulges move around the rotating body to stay in alignment with the gravitational force between the bodies. This is why ocean tides on Earth rise and fall with the rising and setting of its Moon; the same effect occurs to some extent on all rotating orbiting bodies.

Since the bulge requires a small amount of time to shift position, the tidal bulge of the Moon is always located at a slight angle to the line between the closest points of the Moon and Earth. The misalignment of the tidal bulge with the body that caused it results in a small but significant gravitational force on the bulge, acting in the opposite direction of its rotation. The rotation of the satellite slowly decreases (and its orbital momentum simultaneously increases). This is the case where the Moon's rotational period is faster than its orbital period around its planet. If the opposite is true, tidal forces increase its rate of rotation and decrease its orbital momentum.

Almost all moons in the solar system are tidally locked with their primaries, since they orbit closely and tidal force strengthens rapidly with decreasing distance. In addition, Mercury is tidally locked with the Sun in a 3:2 *resonance*. Mercury is the only solar system body in a 3:2 resonance with the Sun. For every two times Mercury revolves around the Sun, it rotates on its own axis three times. In a more subtle way the planet Venus is tidally locked with the planet Earth, so that whenever the two are at their closest approach to each other in their orbits Venus always has the same face toward Earth (the tidal forces involved in this lock are extremely small). In general any object that orbits another massive object closely for long periods is likely to be tidally locked to it.

The Moon's tidal lock to the Earth made its far side even more mysterious: What could be there, on the unseen face of the Moon?

THE MOON'S ORBIT

rotation on its axis	27.32166 Earth days
rotation speed at equator	10.34 miles per hour (16.65 km/hr)
rotation direction	prograde (counterclockwise when viewed from above the North Pole)
orbital period around the Earth	27.32166 Earth days (rotates in the same amount of time it takes to orbit the Earth; this is called synchronous rotation)
orbital velocity (average)	0.636 miles per second (1.023 km/sec)
average distance from the Earth	238,862 miles (384,401 km)
perigee	225,700 miles (363,300 km)
aphelion	252,000 miles (405,500 km)
orbital eccentricity	0.05490049
orbital inclination to the ecliptic	5.145 degrees (oscillates 0.15 degrees in a 173-day cycle)
obliquity (inclination of equator to orbit)	6.68 degrees

Humankind did not see the far side of the Moon until the launch of the Soviet space mission *Luna 3* in October 1959. This mission flew around the back of the Moon and photographed its mysterious far side, finding an equally old and cratered surface, but one largely lacking the giant dark pools of mare basalts. This problem is still an active one in the lunar scientific community: Why does only the front of the Moon carry large volcanic surface flows? Theories include larger amounts of heat-producing radiogenic elements in the Moon's near-side mantle, a thicker crust that inhibits eruptions on the far side, and a preferential eruption pattern inside the Moon that happens to face toward the Earth. All these possibilities are tied to processes described in the section on the formation of the Moon, in chapter 7.

Formation and Evolution of the Moon

For a long time people thought the Moon was a large asteroid that happened into the Earth's orbit and was captured by the Earth's gravity. After careful calculations it was shown that no asteroid captured by the Earth could have exactly the orbit around the Earth that the Moon has. Now scientists have decided that the only way the Moon could have formed with its current rotation and orbital characteristics is if a giant meteorite smashed into the Earth and created a cloud of heated material around the Earth that slowly fell together again to form the outer portions of the Earth and its giant satellite, the Moon. How is this known? Angular momentum is the key.

Angular momentum is a measure of both how fast a rotating object is rotating, and how hard it would be to change its rotation (how much force would be required to slow it down, for example). Figure skating provides the classic example of angular momentum. Imagine a skater spinning in place with his arms out. This skater is rotating, has a mass, is spinning at a particular speed, and his arms measure a length from his center to the tip of his fingers, and so he has some amount of angular momentum. As changes occur to the spinning skater, the amount of angular momentum must stay the same (this is called conservation of angular momentum and is a physical law). Imagine the skater pulls his arms in tightly to his body. The length from the center to the edge of the spinning person has gotten shorter, and so to keep the angular momentum the same the skater's spin speeds up. The skater does nothing but pull his arms in; physics does the rest.

The spinning, orbiting system of the Earth and the Moon has angular momentum, as well. (The angular momentum of the Earth-Moon system

The Earth's tidal bulge is at a small angle to the Moon, forming torques that cause the Earth's rotation to slow and the Moon to recede from the Earth.

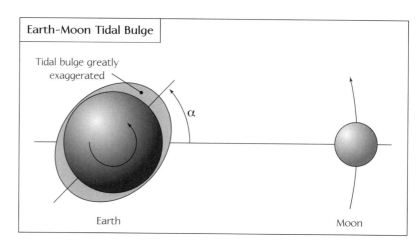

Earth-Moon Tidal Bulge

Tidal bulge greatly exaggerated

α

Earth

Moon

is 3.5×10^{42} kg/m^{2}sec.) The law of conservation of angular momentum works almost perfectly for the Earth-Moon system, though a small amount of energy is lost in tidal friction, and the total angular momentum in the system has stayed almost the same for the last 4.5 billion years. Though the total angular momentum has stayed the same, as in the case of the skater the spin rate and the distance between the bodies may have changed, and in fact they have.

The tidal bulge of water pulled up from the Earth's surface by the gravitational attraction of the Moon leads the Earth-Moon axis by a small angle α, and the Moon exerts a gravitational torque on the bulge, slowing the Earth's rotation, as shown in the figure here. In its turn, the tidal bulge exerts a torque on the Moon, accelerating the Moon's orbital speed, and causing the Moon to move away from the Earth in order to preserve angular momentum.

There are very thin layers of sandstone or siltstone called tidal rhythmites, one layer of which is created each time the tide goes in and out. If these thin layers (called laminae) are buried and baked into rock over time then it is possible for scientists to count the layers and determine how many lunar months per year there were when that rock was made. If the rock can also be dated absolutely using a radiometric method (see the sidebar "Determining Age from Radioactive Isotopes" on page 76), then the rhythmites can determine how many months there were in a year at a given time in the past.

Based on these and similar analyses, scientists have determined that 2.45 billion years ago, or about half the age of the Earth, a day on Earth was only about 19 hours long. This means that every nineteen hours the Earth rotated and passed through a daylight time and a nighttime. Slowly, in the 4.56 billion years since the Earth first formed, the rotation of the Earth has slowed and days have gotten longer. Days are still getting longer, because of conservation of angular momentum: As the Moon pulls the tides around the Earth, the Earth's rotation is slowed by tidal friction. As the rotation slows, to conserve angular momentum, the Moon moves slightly farther from the Earth. This is the same effect as a skater slowing his spinning by extending his arms. By analyzing the tidal rhythmites and other rocks that also record tides or days scientists have created a record of day length over the past 2.5 billion years. Previously only a few data points were available, and scientists extrapolated the data back to try to determine the day length at the beginning of Earth formation. It was then thought that day length in the early solar system was only about five hours! Now, with more data, it seems that the Earth was never spinning that rapidly (which by the law of conservation of angular momentum, would have required that the Moon be very close to the Earth, the subject of a fantastical short story by Italian writer Italo Calvino). It appears, instead, that the Moon and Earth are moving away from each other increasingly rapidly, and so the lengthening of Earth's days is accelerating. Two and a half billion years ago the rate of recession of the Moon was only one third what it is today, and 620 million years ago it was only two thirds what it is today. By measuring the distance from the Moon to the Earth today by laser ranging (bouncing lasers off mirrors left on the Moon by Apollo astronauts), it is known that the Moon is receding from the Earth at a rate of 1.5 ± 0.03 inches (3.82 ± 0.07 cm) per year!

While this may seem a shocking rate of change in the apparently unchanging Earth-Moon system, it is actually a very old idea. Immanuel Kant, the great philosopher, postulated in 1754 that friction from tides have to slow the Earth's rotation, but as he was a writer and thinker and not a scientist, he did not carry the idea further, and it languished forgotten until the mid-19th century.

Angular momentum is also an important constraint for ideas of how the Moon was made. Whatever model a scientist has for the formation of the Earth-Moon system, that model has to result in an Earth-Moon system with the right amount of angular momentum. The theory of an asteroid being captured into Earth orbit does not produce a system with the correct amount of angular momentum, but the theory of a giant impact does. A giant impactor the size of Mars smashed into the young Earth, it is now believed, and pieces of the pulverized, heated impactor and the outside of the Earth fell back together to form the Moon.

A scientist named Robin Canup, working at Arizona State University, has made a huge computer program to model this process. Her program keeps track of the speed, direction, and temperature of the Earth and the asteroid that hits it, called the Giant Impactor. After the Giant Impactor hits the Earth, the program keeps track of the speed, direction, and temperature of tens of thousands of fragments that fly off the Earth. The energy of the impact is so huge that a large portion of the Earth and all of the Giant Impactor simply melt. The Earth then splashes back into the shape of a ball, and fragments of the Earth and the Giant Impactor fly into orbits around the Earth. Gradually the largest of these orbiting fragments run into each other to form larger planetesimals (meaning "little planets" or planet fragments), the planetesimals collide or are drawn together by gravity to form the Moon. Canup has used her computer model to calculate that the Giant Impactor that hit the Earth would have to have been about the size of Mars. This impact had to be early enough in the formation of the solar system that there were giant impactors orbiting erratically in the inner solar system, not yet in stable orbits of their own. It had to have happened before the oldest known rocks on Earth formed, since the entire outside of the Earth was shocked and liquefied by the giant impact. The oldest known rocks on Earth are about 4 billion years old. The giant impact also had to have happened before the oldest known rocks on the Moon were formed. Thanks to the Apollo missions, which brought back about 1,540 pounds (700 kg) of material from the Moon, scientists have rocks from the Moon that can be dated. The oldest rock dated from the Moon is about 4.4 billion years old. Therefore the formation of the Moon happened after the initial planet formation in the solar system, at 4.56 billion years ago, and before 4.4 billion years ago, when the oldest known Moon rocks formed.

Formation and Crystallization of the Lunar Magma Ocean

According to the giant impactor theory, the Moon and the Earth formed from a mixture of the early Earth and the giant impactor. What would be expected for the compositions of two planets that shared material when they were forming? Part One of this volume discussed how the Earth's iron core formed, leaving lighter, nonmetallic elements above the core in the mantle and crust. The Moon, on the other hand, has either no iron core or a very small one. If the material from the Earth and the giant impactor were completely mixed and then separated into the Earth and the Moon, then they would have the same amounts of iron in them relative to their sizes. With its giant iron core, the Earth has much more iron in it than the Moon has. Because of this, people think that the giant impact that made the Moon happened after the Earth's core had formed, and that the Earth's core was left inside the Earth during the event. The Moon, then, ended up with mostly the lighter, silicon-rich mantle material and material from the giant impactor, and therefore has less iron than the Earth.

The Earth's core is thought to have formed within 5 to 20 million years after the Earth accreted (accumulated out of planetesimals), and the Moon-forming giant impact is thought to have occurred right afterward, at between 10 to 30 million years after formation of the planets. Ten million years is an eye-blink of geologic time: Ten million years is just 0.02 percent of the age of the solar system, equivalent to three minutes out of a 24-hour day. As the planetesimals formed by the giant Earth impact collided and stuck together to form the proto-Moon (meaning early, or pre-Moon), the proto-Moon heated up from the energy of the impacts and from heat given off by radioactive decay of some elements. The Moon is thought to have been molten to some depth when it was first formed. Its surface would literally have been a sea of liquid rock. This stage of lunar formation is called the magma ocean (the Earth may have had one as well; so may the other terrestrial planets).

After the majority of the planetesimals had been accreted to form the Moon, the Moon began to cool. The magma ocean, which was at first literally a red-hot ocean of liquid rock covering the entire Moon, began to crystallize into minerals. Because pressure encourages liquid to freeze into crystals by pressing the atoms together, crystallization begins at the bottom of the magma ocean. The liquid of the magma ocean first crystallized a mineral called olivine (this is the same mineral as the gemstone peridot; it is made of magnesium, silicon, iron, and oxygen). Olivine probably made a dense layer at the bottom of the magma ocean. As the magma ocean cooled further, a mineral called orthopyroxene also crystallized, and then finally two more minerals, called clinopyroxene and plagioclase, accompanied at the end by high-density titanium-rich oxides such as ilmenite. The minerals that formed from the magma ocean are called cumulates, because they are the solid residue of cooling liquid.

All of the cumulate minerals listed here are denser than magma and so would sink to the bottom of the magma ocean except the plagioclase ($NaAlSi_3O_8$ to $CaAl_2Si_2O_8$), which is more buoyant than the liquid it crystallized from, and so it may have floated up to the surface of the Moon. In fact, the white areas of the Moon surrounding the dark round craters are called the lunar highlands (shown in the lower color insert on page C-8) and they are made mainly of this mineral. Since plagioclase is lighter than magma and since the lunar highlands are made mainly of plagioclase, these highlands are thought to be a prime piece of evidence that the magma ocean did once exist on the Moon. Without flotation in a magma ocean, accounting for plagioclase-rich highlands is difficult.

There are different estimates of how deep the magma ocean probably was on the moon: These estimates vary from 190 miles (300 km) deep to the whole depth of the Moon (imagine a completely molten blob of liquid rock in the sky where the Moon is now!). At the final stage of magma ocean cooling, a strangely composed final liquid is thought to have crystallized fairly close to the bottom of the lunar plagioclase crust. This final liquid was rich with potassium, a family of elements called the rare earth elements, and phosphorus. Lunar researchers in the 1970s named this material KREEP, after the scientific symbol of potassium (K), REE for the rare earth elements, and P for phosphorus. After KREEP crystallized, the Moon was mostly solid, with only a deep, partly melted area forming later as the interior of the moon began to heat from radioactivity.

The idea of a magma ocean resulting from the heat of accretion and core formation for many of the terrestrial planets is controversial, as it is for the Earth, but there is very good evidence for a magma ocean having occurred on the Moon. The existence of KREEP indicates that some large amount of magma was crystallized until only the dregs were left; there seems to be no other reasonable way to make KREEP.

An element called europium provides further evidence. In the very low oxygen environment of the Moon, europium loses an electron and thus becomes electrically compatible with the crystal structure of the mineral plagioclase. Europium does not fit into olivine, orthopyroxene, or clinopyroxene crystals, even when it has lost an electron. When olivine and the pyroxene minerals crystallized out of the magma ocean, they left the europium behind, making the magma ocean more concentrated in this element. The samples returned from the Apollo missions show that the plagioclase in the highlands is very much enriched in europium compared to elements on either side of it in the periodic table; this is called the positive europium anomaly. The dark lavas that fill the craters on the face of the Moon (these are called mare—pronounced "mah-rey"—basalts, after the Latin word *mare,* meaning sea) have a conspicuous lack of europium: The corresponding negative europium anomaly. The mare basalts melted from material deep in the Moon, europium-poor olivine and pyroxene that crystallized from the magma ocean before plagioclase did. Apparently these two materials, the highlands plagioclase and the deep mantle that melted to make the basalts, are two halves of the same original reservoir of material. A magma ocean, crystallizing and differentiating, is the most effective way to create these separate reservoirs.

Thus, many scientists think that the Moon began as a homogeneous mass: Any part of it contained the same mixture of elements as any other part of it. Through the gradual crystallization of the magma ocean and the settling or rising of cumulate minerals, the Moon began the process of differentiation. In this case, crystallization, settling, and floating are the processes that differentiated the early Moon. Later, when the interior of the Moon remelted to form the basalts that erupted into the giant craters on the near side of the Moon, another step in the differentiation of the Moon occurred.

Highlands

The lunar highlands are the pale, elevated regions around the giant basins that are filled with dark basalt. Since the giant impacts basins are formed within the highlands, the highlands are necessarily older than the basins. Their composition was unknown until the Apollo missions, particularly *Apollo 16,* which returned a large quantity of samples from a part of the highlands. Their composition is truly intriguing to planetary scientists. All the rocks retrieved are igneous, that is, they crystallized from a liquid silicate magma. Unlike the dark basalts, a common lava composition on many planets (the Earth, Venus, Mars, and the Moon), the highlands are composed of a number of more exotic rock types.

The palest rocks on the Moon are anorthosites. These igneous rocks are composed of 90 percent or more of plagioclase, as described above in the section on the lunar magma ocean. The rocks are called anorthosites because their plagioclase is of a particular composition called *anorthite,* the calcium-rich type of plagioclase ($CaAl_2Si_2O_8$). Anorthite requires a strange composition of magma to crystallize, and anorthosites on Earth are rare. The magma needs to be highly enriched in aluminum and in calcium to make anorthite, but more problematically, the magma has to be very poor in iron and magnesium to produce a rock with 90 percent or more anorthite. With more iron and magnesium, minerals such as olivine and pyroxene will also crystallize from the magma, reducing the percentage of anorthite. Unfortunately, the production of such a magma is a major problem to petrologists, the branch of earth scientists who specialize in minerals and rock compositions.

Assuming the Moon began with a magma ocean requires that the initial magma ocean have a high iron and magnesium composition: It was likely close to the composition of primordial Earth material, minus a large portion of its iron, which sank to depths to form the core. When this initial magma begins to cool it will produce olivine crystals, which are rich in iron and magnesium themselves. Each batch of minerals that crystallize from the magma ocean and settle to the bottom change the composition of the remaining magma a little bit: If the olivine incorporates a lot of magnesium, then the magma left behind will be somewhat depleted in magnesium.

Generations of petrologists have done experiments with rocks and have developed the thermodynamic rules that govern the order of minerals that crystallize from a magma ocean, along with their compositions. The order of minerals and the evolution of the remaining liquid is now known in some level of detail. After olivine and pyroxene have crystallized from the magma ocean to the point that about 70 percent of the magma ocean is solid, the remaining liquid has become enriched enough in aluminum and calcium that plagioclase begins to crystallize.

This is the moment that scientists wait for to make the anorthosite highlands: Once plagioclase begins to crystallize, it can float and make the highlands. Pyroxene and olivine are also still crystallizing from the magma ocean, preventing the plagioclase from ever attaining 90 percent of the crystallizing minerals. There is no magma composition, in fact, at any point in the evolution of a magma ocean that would simply produce a rock with 90 percent anorthite. This problem makes the idea of a magma ocean all the more compelling: If there is no magma that can crystallize 90 percent plagioclase, then the plagioclase has to simply float to the top of the crystallizing magma ocean, separating itself from the more iron- and magnesium-rich minerals. Marc Norman at the Australian National University, Lars Borg at the Institute for Meteorites at the University of New Mexico, and colleagues at the Johnson Space Center have been determining the formation ages of anorthosites from the *Apollo 16* landing site. This site is the only one that resembles the large anorthositic (feldspar-rich) regions of the lunar highlands, so detailed study of the anorthositic rocks from the site can shed light on the formation of the oldest lunar crust. The four anorthosites dated so far have ages determined by the samarium-neodymium radiometric system of 4.29 to 4.54 billion years.

Norman noted that the plagioclase in the rocks has been compositionally modified by exchange after crystallization, most likely by a large impact event around 3.9 billion years ago, but that pyroxene is more likely to have remained unchanged. The pyroxene isotopic data alone from all four rocks define a precise age of 4.456 billion years, well within the possible time of magma ocean crystallization. He suggested that this is a robust estimate for the crystallization age of lunar anorthosites.

Borg, however, is convinced by the care taken with the anorthosite dates and states that the young age of 4.29 billion years is a good date describing a crystallization age. Therefore there may be two problems with the plagioclase flotation model. First, the anorthosites with radiometric dates of 4.29 billion years are far younger than any likely magma ocean would have survived. If those dates are correct, then those anorthosites must have been made in an event that came later than the magma ocean. The total time needed for crystallizing the magma ocean is difficult to calculate, but is highly unlikely to be more than 50 million years. Some scientists estimate complete crystallization in as little as a few million years. These anorthosites are younger than the last possible magma ocean liquids by over 100 million years. Second, by the time plagioclase began to crystallize from the magma ocean, the entire remaining ocean was filled with crystals and had formed a sort of stiff crystal mush. Plagioclase is physically unlikely to have been able to float out of such a dense stiff mush. On Earth in

A time line of early events on the Moon shows the progression from early anorthosite crust formation to more iron-rich crustal materials to the eventual eruption of the mare basalts and fire-fountaining volcanic glasses.

such cases plagioclase forms clumps with dense pyroxene and olivine crystals and sinks under the influence of their density. Because of the late ages, shown in the figure here called "Time Line of Early Lunar Events," and because of the physical constraint of a highly crystalline magma ocean, some scientists are suggesting that the anorthosite highlands formed in a second event.

As minerals crystallize from the magma ocean they preferentially take magnesium out of the remaining magma, causing it to be relatively enriched in iron. Eventually the magma is sufficiently depleted in magnesium that the minerals are forced to incorporate more iron, becoming increasingly iron-rich. As the minerals become more iron-rich, they become more dense, since iron is denser than magnesium.

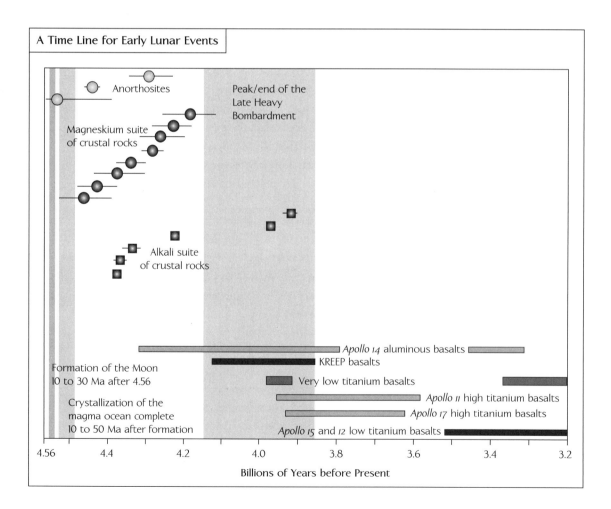

A Time Line for Early Lunar Events

Anorthosites

Peak/end of the Late Heavy Bombardment

Magneskium suite of crustal rocks

Alkali suite of crustal rocks

Formation of the Moon 10 to 30 Ma after 4.56

Crystallization of the magma ocean complete 10 to 50 Ma after formation

Apollo 14 aluminous basalts

KREEP basalts

Very low titanium basalts

Apollo 11 high titanium basalts

Apollo 17 high titanium basalts

Apollo 15 and *12* low titanium basalts

4.56 4.4 4.2 4.0 3.8 3.6 3.4 3.2

Billions of Years before Present

Their increasing density means that the last minerals to crystallize from the magma ocean, near the top, are far denser than those below them. These dense minerals are driven by gravity to sink as blobs through the more buoyant minerals underneath. These cumulate minerals sink and rise as solids, flowing slowly by human standards, but completing their overturn in about 1 million years (for more, see the sidebar "Rheology, or How Solids Can Flow" on page 38).

As deeper cumulates rise toward the surface through buoyancy, they can also melt through decompression as they come closer to the surface (see the sidebar "What Is Pressure?" on page 52). This may be the process that forms these younger anorthosites: Melting during magma ocean overturn. Overturn may also produce some other enigmatic rocks found in the lunar highland crust, known as the mafic- and alkali-rich suites (the word *suite* is used for a group of related rocks). These are also intrusive igneous rocks; that is, they cooled within the crust rather than erupting onto the surface as volcanics. The mafic-rich suite has more magnesium- (*ma*) and iron-rich (*fic,* from *ferrous,* meaning iron-rich) minerals than do the anorthosites, and the alkali-rich suite is enriched in sodium and potassium relative to other highlands rocks. Many of these are younger than the anorthositic highlands, as shown in the figure on page 134. Many of the mafic and alkali suit rocks have ages far younger than the likely completion of magma ocean crystallization, and may therefore be another indicator for melting during magma ocean overturn.

No matter what their age, the lunar anorthosites are compelling evidence for the existence of a magma ocean early in lunar evolution. They may have formed through flotation from the crystallizing magma ocean, or they may have formed by melting during magma ocean overturn. By 150 million years after formation of the Earth and Moon, at the latest, the Moon had a fully formed plagioclase-rich crust, much of which can be seen today.

The Late Heavy Meteorite Bombardment

There was a period of time early in solar system development when all the bodies in the inner solar system were repeatedly impacted by large bolides. This high-activity period might be anticipated by thinking about how the planets formed, accreting from smaller bodies into larger and larger bodies—it may seem intuitive that there would be a time even after most of the planets formed when there was still

Fossa, Sulci, and Other Terms for Planetary Landforms

On Earth the names for geological features often connote how they were formed and what they mean in terms of surface and planetary evolution. A caldera, for example, is a round depression formed by volcanic activity and generally encompassing volcanic vents. Though a round depression on another planet may remind a planetary geologist of a terrestrial caldera, it would be misleading to call that feature a caldera until its volcanic nature was proven. Images of other planets are not always clear and seldom include topography, so at times the details of the shape in question cannot be determined, making their definition even harder.

To avoid assigning causes to the shapes of landforms on other planets, scientists have resorted to creating a new series of names largely based on Latin, many of which are listed in the following table, that are used to describe planetary features. Some are used mainly on a single planet with unusual features, and others can be found throughout the solar system. Chaos terrain, for example, can be found on Mars, Mercury, and Jupiter's moon Europa. The Moon has a number of names for its exclusive use, including lacus, palus, rille, oceanus, and mare. New names for planetary objects must be submitted to and approved by the International Astronomical Union's (IAU) Working Group for Planetary System Nomenclature.

NOMENCLATURE FOR PLANETARY FEATURES

Feature	Description
astrum, astra	radial-patterned features on Venus
catena, catenae	chains of craters
chaos	distinctive area of broken terrain
chasma, chasmata	a deep, elongated, steep-sided valley or gorge
colles	small hills or knobs
corona, coronae	oval-shaped feature
crater, craters	a circular depression not necessarily created by impact
dorsum, dorsa	ridge
facula, faculae	bright spot
fluctus	flow terrain

Feature	Description
fossa, fossae	narrow, shallow, linear depression
labes	landslide
labyrinthus, labyrinthi	complex of intersecting valleys
lacus	small plain on the Moon; name means "lake"
lenticula, lenticulae	small dark spots on Europa (Latin for freckles); may be domes or pits
linea, lineae	a dark or bright elongate marking, may be curved or straight
macula, maculae	dark spot, may be irregular
mare, maria	large circular plain on the Moon; name means "sea"
mensa, mensae	a flat-topped hill with cliff-like edges
mons, montes	mountain
oceanus	a very large dark plain on the Moon; name means "ocean"
palus, paludes	small plain on the Moon; name means "swamp"
patera, paterae	an irregular crater
planitia, planitiae	low plain
planum, plana	plateau or high plain
reticulum, reticula	reticular (netlike) pattern on Venus
rille	narrow valley
rima, rimae	fissure on the Moon
rupes	scarp
sinus	small rounded plain; name means "bay"
sulcus, sulci	subparallel furrows and ridges
terra, terrae	extensive land mass
tessera, tesserae	tile-like, polygonal terrain
tholus, tholi	small dome-shaped mountain or hill
undae	dunes
vallis, valles	valley
vastitas, vastitates	extensive plain

(continues)

Fossa, Sulci, and Other Terms for Planetary Landforms (continued)

The IAU has designated categories of names from which to choose for each planetary body, and in some cases, for each type of feature on a given planetary body. On Mercury, craters are named for famous deceased artists of various stripes, while rupes are named for scientific expeditions. On Venus, craters larger than 12.4 miles (20 km) are named for famous women, and those smaller than 12.4 miles (20 km) are given common female first names. Colles are named for sea goddesses, dorsa are named for sky goddesses, fossae are named for goddesses of war, and fluctus are named for miscellaneous goddesses.

The gas giant planets do not have features permanent enough to merit a nomenclature of features, but some of their solid moons do. Io's features are named after characters from Dante's *Inferno*. Europa's features are named after characters from Celtic myth. Guidelines can become even more explicit: Features on the moon Mimas are named after people and places from Malory's *Le Morte d'Arthur* legends, Baines translation. A number of asteroids also have naming guidelines. Features on 253 Mathilde, for example, are named after the coalfields and basins of Earth.

enough material left over in the early solar system to continue bombarding and cratering the early planets.

Beyond this theory, though, there is visible evidence on Mercury, the Moon, and Mars in the form of ancient surfaces that are far more heavily cratered than any fresher surface on the planet (Venus, on the other hand, has been resurfaced by volcanic activity, and plate tectonics and surface weathering have wiped out all record of early impacts on Earth). The giant basins on the Moon, filled with dark basalt and so visible to the eye from Earth, are left over from that early period of heavy impacts, called the Late Heavy Bombardment.

Crater density on the sheet of impact *ejecta* from the Mare Imbrium Basin (actually an immense impact crater, as are all the basins on the Moon; see the sidebar "Fossa, Sulci, and Other Terms for Planetary Landforms" on page 136) is six times greater than that on lava flows formed 600 million years later. This decrease can be modeled as a 50 percent decrease every 100 million years (the 50 percent per 100 million years model assumes that cratering rates dropped off evenly, rather than abruptly).

Dating rocks from the Moon using radioactive isotopes and carefully determining the age relationships of different crater's ejecta blankets indicates that the lunar Late Heavy Bombardment lasted until about 3.8 billion years ago. Some scientists believe that the Late Heavy Bombardment was a specific period of very heavy impact activity that lasted from about 4.2 to 3.8 billion years ago, after a pause in bombardment following initial planetary formation at about 4.56 billion years ago, while other scientists believe that the Late Heavy Bombardment was just the tail end of a continuously decreasing rate of bombardment that began at the beginning of the solar system. Cratering rate before about 4 billion years before the present cannot be known by today's methods because older rocks on the Moon have been so severely pulverized by impact.

In the continual bombardment model, the last giant impacts from 4.2 to 3.8 billion years ago simply erased the evidence of all the earlier bombardment. If, alternatively, the Late Heavy Bombardment was a discrete event, then some reason for the sudden invasion of the inner solar system by giant bolides must be discovered. Were they bodies perturbed from the outer solar system by the giant planets there? The bodies may have been planetesimals left over from Earth accretion, or they could have been asteroids perturbed out of the asteroid belt, or they could have been broken-up planetesimals from Uranus or Neptune's formation.

On Earth the age of a rock can often be determined exactly by measuring its radioactive isotopes and their daughter products, and thereby knowing how long the radioactive elements have been in the rock, decaying to form their daughters. Before the discovery of radioactivity and its application to determining the age of rocks, all of which happened in the 20th century, geologists spent a few centuries working out the relative ages of rocks, that is, which ones were formed first and in what order the others came. Between 1785 and 1800, James Hutton and William Smith introduced and labored over the idea of geologic time: That the rock record describes events that happened over a long time period.

Fossils were the best and easiest way to correlate between rocks that did not touch each other directly. Some species of fossil life can be found in many locations around the world, and so form important markers in the geologic record. Relative time was broken into sections divided by changes in the rock record, for example, times when many species apparently went extinct, since their fossils were no longer found in younger rocks. This is why, for example, the extinction of the dinosaurs lies directly on the Cretaceous-Tertiary boundary: The boundary was set to mark their loss. The largest sections of geologic history were further divided into small sections, and so on, from epochs, to eras, to periods. For centuries a debate raged in the scientific community over how much time was represented by these geologic divisions. With the development of radioactive dating methods, those relative time markers could be converted to absolute time; for example, that the oldest known rock on Earth is 3.96 billion years old, and the Cretaceous-Tertiary boundary lies at about 66.5 million years ago.

As discussed in the chapter "The Visible Planet" in Part One of this book, by using detailed images of the Moon scientists have worked out the relative ages of many of the crustal features. By carefully examining images researchers can determine "superposition," that is, which rock unit was formed first, and which later formed on top of it. Impact craters and canyons are very helpful in determining superposition. Through this sort of meticulous photogeology, scientists have developed relative timescales for other planets. (A rough set of geological epochs has been built up for the Moon and is shown in the figure on page 74.) From oldest to youngest, epochs on the Moon are called the Pre-Nectarian, Nectarian, Imbrian, and Copernican, named after craters. Events and objects on the Moon tend to be approximately located in time by these epochs. The Late Heavy Bombardment began in the Pre-Nectarian, bridged the Nectarian with its most intense activity, and ended in the Imbrian.

Basins and Volcanism

The largest of the Moon's great basalt-filled basins were all formed during the Late Heavy Bombardment. These and some lesser basins are listed in the table on page 142. These large ancient impact craters are traditionally called mare, meaning sea, since they have the appearance of dark oceans when viewed from Earth. The dark material is basalt, formed by melting in the Moon's interior that erupted into the low areas excavated by the large impacts of the Late Heavy Bombardment. The low elevations of the craters along with their

The lunar basins Imbrium (left), Serenitatis (center), and Crisium (right) are all filled with dark mare basalts. (NASA/Galileo)

large size and basalt fill has also led them to be called basins. Small basins were named palus, meaning swamps, though of course they are perfectly dry areas with pools of frozen basalt. Some examples are the Palus Epidemiarum (the marsh of epidemics), the Palus Putredinis (the marsh of decay) and the Palus Somni (the marsh of sleep). The Apollo 15 mission landed near the Palus Putredinis.

This image from the Galileo mission in 1992 clearly shows a number of the larger basins. The North Polar region is near the top part of the photomosaic. Mare Imbrium is the dark area on the left, Mare Serenitatis is at center, and Mare Crisium is the circular dark area to the right. Bright crater rim and ray deposits are from Copernicus, an impact crater about 60 miles (95 km) in diameter.

In the table on page 142 the mare are listed in approximate order of size, though measuring the size of an ancient crater is an inexact science. Similarly, estimating the ages of the basins is a difficult exercise. In the best case, melt caused by the heat and shock of impact is

IMPACT BASINS ON THE MOON

Latin name	English name	Latitude (degrees)	Longitude (degrees)	Diameter (miles [km])	Approx. age (billion years)
Oceanus Procellarum	Ocean of Storms	18.4N	57.4W	1,605 (2,568)	
Mare Frigoris	Sea of Cold	56.0N	1.4E	998 (1,596)	
Mare Imbrium	Sea of Showers	32.8N	15.6W	702 (1,123)	3.85
Mare Fecunditatis	Sea of Fecundity	7.8S	51.3E	568 (909)	4.0
Mare Tranquillitatis	Sea of Tranquility	8.5N	31.4E	546 (873)	3.99
Mare Nubium	Sea of Clouds	21.3S	16.6W	447 (715)	3.98
Mare Serenitatis	Sea of Serenity	28.0N	17.5E	442 (707)	3.87
Mare Australe	Southern Sea	38.9S	93.0E	377 (603)	4.05
Mare Insularum	Sea of Islands	7.5N	30.9W	321 (513)	
Mare Marginis	Sea of the Edge	13.3N	86.1E	263 (420)	
Mare Crisium	Sea of Crises	17.0N	59.1E	261 (418)	3.84
Mare Humorum	Sea of Moisture	24.4S	38.6W	243 (389)	3.87
Mare Cognitum	Known Sea	10.0S	23.1W	235 (376)	
Mare Smythii	Sea of William Henry Smyth	1.3N	87.5E	233 (373)	3.97
Mare Nectaris	Sea of Nectar	15.2S	35.5E	208 (333)	3.91
Mare Orientale	Eastern sea	19.4S	92.8W	204 (327)	3.80
Mare Ingenii	Sea of Cleverness	33.7S	163.5E	199 (318)	
Mare Moscoviense	Sea of Muscovy	27.3N	147.9E	173 (277)	3.91
Mare Humboldtianum	Sea of Alexander von Humboldt	56.8N	81.5E	171 (273)	3.89
Mare Vaporum	Sea of Vapors	13.3N	3.6E	153 (245)	
Mare Anguis	Serpent Sea	22.6N	67.7E	94 (150)	
Mare Spumans	Foaming Sea	1.1N	65.1E	87 (139)	

found in some rock near the crater and dated using radioisotopes. This kind of high-precision field geology is almost completely unavailable for the Moon, and so crater ages are estimated by the relationships among craters (often judged by their overlapping ejecta), combined with whatever radiodates that can be obtained. This table also lists some age estimates for the craters. The ages listed all have possible errors of at least plus or minus 25 million years (0.02 billion years). Some of the ages come from radiometric dating of crater ejecta returned by Apollo missions, and other ages come from relationships among craters judged from overlapping crater ejecta. The ages have been compiled and analyzed by Greg Neumann and Maria Zuber at the Massachusetts Institute of Technology with David Smith and Frank Lemoine at the Laboratory for Terrestrial Physics at the NASA/ Goddard Space Flight Center, using the extensive mapping and analysis of the Moon done by Don Wilhelms, an astrogeologist with the United States Geological Survey.

Mare Orientale is the youngest of the large impact basins, and makes a striking image. In the left image of this pair from the Galileo mission Orientale is centered on the Moon. Its complex rings can be seen but its center contains only a small pool of mare basalt. By

These two views of Mare Orientale, taken by the Galileo spacecraft, also show large regions of dark mare basalt. (NASA/JPL/Galileo)

contrast, the older Oceanus Procellarum covers the upper right of the Moon in this image, with the Mare Imbrium above it and the small Mare Humorum beneath. In the right image Imbrium lies on the extreme left limb of the Moon.

The Apollo samples returned from the Moon include pieces of the dark mare basalts sufficient to analyze and learn a significant amount about their origins and age. The majority of the basalts appear to date from the time of the Late Heavy Bombardment, corresponding to the times of formation of the great basins that they fill. Other basalts are younger, with ages that stretch through the period from 4.3 to around 3 billion years ago (a collection of age data for basalts is shown in the figure titled "Time Line of Lunar Events" on page 134). Lunar volcanic eruptions peaked in the Imbrian Epoch (3.85 to 3.2 billion years ago), the majority of the basalts lie on the near side, and the total volume of mare basalt is about 2.4 million cubic miles (10 million km^3). Though most scientists believe that the mare basalts finished erupting by about 3 billion years ago, some others say they have found evidence for eruptions as recent as 2 billion years ago, through comparisons of crater ejecta relationships and cratering intensities (the fewer craters on a surface, the younger it is).

Some of these basalts closely resemble Earth basalts, but others have exceptionally high titanium contents. This high titanium is again thought to tie the basalts back to the fundamental processes of magma ocean crystallization: As the magma ocean liquids evolved further and further toward the end of crystallization, they were progressively enriched in titanium because it does not fit well into the common mantle forming minerals. After the magma ocean was about 94 percent crystalline the remaining liquids were sufficiently enriched in titanium to start crystallizing ilmenite, a titanium oxide mineral. This process produced a region enriched in titanium.

Planetary scientists immediately saw the possibility that the high-titanium mare basalts could have formed by melting this titanium-rich region. This gave a simple explanation for the existence of such strangely titanium-rich magmas, while tying them to magma ocean processes. Experimental petrologists started conducting high-pressure experiments using synthetic rock compositions identical to the high-titanium basalts to see if they could form from an ilmenite-rich source (see the sidebar "High-Pressure Experiments" on page 36). Much to their surprise, they found that the high-titanium basalts

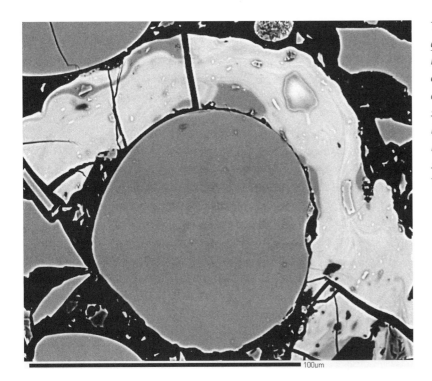

100µm

The dark beads are volcanic glasses from an Apollo 15 lunar soil sample, and the central bead is mantled by an agglutinate, a mix of melted soil components caused by heat from the bead as it landed, or possibly by a separate small impact. (Linda T. Elkins-Tanton/NASA/JSC)

cannot be made by simply melting an ilmenite-rich source: All the resulting magmas were much to high in calcium. While most lunar scientists remain convinced that the titanium-rich basalts must be related to the titanium-rich layer produced in magma ocean crystallization, the exact process that made the basalts remains unknown.

Along with the pieces of basalt returned by the Apollo missions came samples of lunar soil. The lunar soil is properly called regolith since it consists of many tiny rock fragments without any organic material. By examining the regolith with microscopes and analyzing the pieces with an instrument called an electron microprobe, which can measure the compositions of rocks as small as 10 microns across, a whole new world of lunar data was discovered. One of the most exciting discoveries was a large assortment of beads of glass, each just a few tens of microns across. Some are bright green, and others yellow, red, or black.

These beads, it appeared after they were analyzed with an electron microprobe, are volcanic in origin. They are thought to have been erupted in fire fountains like those that sometimes spew from the volcanic vents in Hawaii. When the magma in the fire fountains hit the frozen near-vacuum at the lunar surface they chilled so quickly ("quenched") that there was no time for crystals to form, and the beads froze as glass. The image of glass beads from an *Apollo 15* soil sample

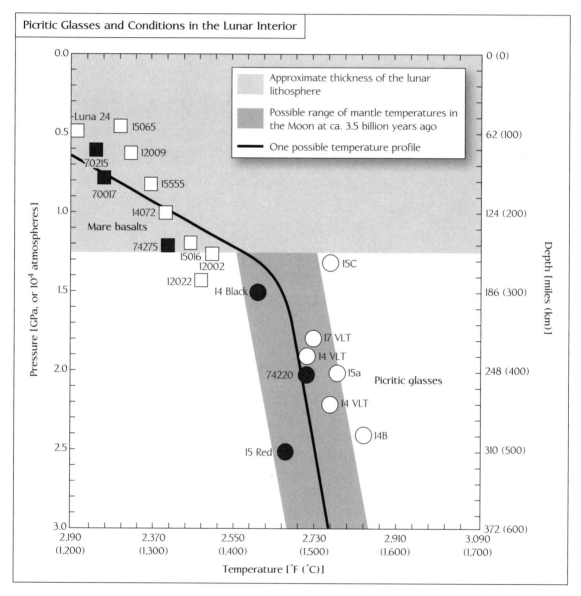

Experimental work on the lunar picritic glasses has created an image of pressure, temperature, and compositional conditions in the lunar interior around 3.5 billion years ago.

(see page 145) was taken by the author using an electron microprobe in the laboratory of Tim Grove at the Massachusetts Institute of Technology. The large, round, gray objects are glass beads that would appear bright green in visible light, though in this image their color indicates their density (the image is created by bouncing beams of electrons off the small samples, and recording how many of the electrons bounce back; the denser the material, the more electrons bounce back). The central glass bead in the image is cloaked with a mantle of brighter material containing spots and swirls. This is termed an *agglutinate,* material created by the melting and mixing soil components.

These beads have become perhaps the most important window into the lunar interior. Many of them are near-pristine melts of mantle material and have experienced almost no later processing (magmas can cool on their way to the surface and precipitate crystals, or they can heat, melt, and assimilate rocks that they pass through; these processes cloud the clear record of mantle melting that the original magma carried). Pure mantle melts are rich in magnesium, as are picritic glasses, picritic being the geologic term for high magnesium.

Doing high-pressure experiments on synthetic versions of these picritic beads provides information about the pressure and temperature of melting that produced the magmas, as well as the material that melted. The experiments are time-consuming: The time needed to obtain this information for just one picritic bead takes months of work and between 20 and 40 separate experiments. Over the years since the Apollo missions a number of scientists in different laboratories have conducted studies on these beads and have thus produced a kind of picture of the interior of the Moon at about 3.5 billion years ago, shown in the figure on page 146.

This figure also shows the same information for the mare basalts. The mare basalts originated at shallower depths, and the picritic glasses came from deep in the Moon. All of the lunar interior was hot at that time, almost hot enough to melt. Just a little addition of heat, for example from radiogenic elements, or a little depressurization in a convective upwelling, would be enough to allow the mantle to melt.

An important result of these studies is also the knowledge that basalts and picritic glasses with different compositions can erupt from about the same depth in the Moon. Jeffrey Gillis, a professor at the Washington University in St. Louis, used Clementine and Prospector mission orbital data to investigate the nature of the lunar maria. He reported that there are basaltic rocks in Mare Australe that are distinctly different from other maria. They are lower in iron and contain significant amounts of low-calcium pyroxene. This implies that they formed by melting of compositionally and mineralogically distinctive regions in the lunar mantle. Harry Hiesinger, a researcher at Brown University, and his colleagues have also been making detailed studies of the lunar maria, including determining their ages by counting craters. They find no correlation between age and composition. In fact, high-titanium and low-titanium lava flows can occur almost simultaneously. Age is, however, correlated with location: The flows in the western maria are youngest. According to Paul Spudis, then at the Lunar and Planetary Institute and now at the Applied Physics Laboratory at Johns Hopkins University, the eastern maria, such as Mare Smythii, are also relatively young.

Models of magma ocean crystallization produced by the author and her colleagues Marc Parmentier and Sarah Zaranek at Brown University indicate that during magma ocean cumulate overturn mantle parcels with different compositions but the same buoyancy end up at the same depths in the shallow Moon, making a mantle with distinct compositional regions. This theoretical model is consistent with the differing compositions of the mare basalts and picritic glasses.

Both the mare basalts and the picritic glasses may have had a difficult time erupting to the surface. Remember that the lunar crust is largely made of plagioclase, which is an unusually buoyant mineral. On Earth, mantle melts are generally more buoyant than the crust they are attempting to erupt through, so magma moves onto the surface relatively easily. On the Moon in many cases the thick plagioclase crust is actually more buoyant the almost all the mantle melts, meaning that additional force is needed to move the melts onto the surface. The picritic glasses were clearly blasted onto the surface by some sort of propellant that sprayed them into fountains above the lunar surface. Tiny films on the surface of the beads provide evidence for the sort of propellant that caused the eruptions. Mac Rutherford, a professor at Brown University, and his colleague Michael Nicholis studied the orange glass beads, and believe their strong eruption was driven by carbon. The carbon started as graphite in the magma at depth, and then as pressure decreased, the graphite converted to a CO and CO_2 gas mix, driving the eruption much the way bubbles make soda bottles squirt.

The author and her colleagues at the Massachusetts Institute of Technology studied green glass beads from the *Apollo 15* landing site and suggested that fluorine was partly the driving force, possibly in addition to carbon. These traces of volatile gases expand catastrophically as they leave the pressure of the lunar interior and reach the near-vacuum of the surface. Their violent expansion raises the pressure in the liquid magma catastrophically, driving it out onto the surface and breaking it into tiny drops. Newer work by Michael Nicholis and Mac Rutherford at Brown University shows that a small proportion of carbon in the magma is a highly effective way to drive firefountaining eruptions, because at an appropriate depth the carbon breaks down to carbon dioxide and other volatile compounds, the pressure of which drives eruption.

Without additional driving force, the mare basalts had to find a way to move onto the surface through buoyancy, with little volatile driving force. The giant impact basins made the eruption of the mare basalts possible. When these huge impactors struck the Moon, they removed a large fraction of the anorthositic crust from the site of impact and threw it elsewhere on the Moon as ejecta. The mare basalts had just enough buoyancy to seep into these holes, when they could not erupt onto the higher anorthosite highlands. This process for eruption and explanation for the basalt fill in the basins was proposed early on by Sean Solomon, now director of the Carnegie Institute in Washington, D.C. Marc Wieczorek, at the time a researcher at the Massachusetts Institute of Technology, made a series of calculations of magma buoyancy and proved that the magmas could just seep into the basins, while they could not rise onto the highlands.

The early history of the Moon contains almost all its dynamic action. The Moon was probably formed in a catastrophic giant impact that partly destroyed the early Earth and heated the early Moon until it was a molten magma ocean. This magma ocean crystallized over 10 or 20 million years, producing a mantle made of cumulate minerals layered by density and composition. Magma ocean crystallization also formed the anorthositic highlands, probably by flotation of plagioclase in the magma ocean, though possibly through secondary melting when the gravitationally unstable mantle overturned to a stable stratification. Between about 4 and 3.8 billion years ago, in the Pre-Nectarian and Nectarian, at least 400 million years after the magma ocean crystallized, came the peak of the Late Heavy Bombardment. The basins formed by these catastrophic impacts filled with mare basalts between then and about 3 billion years ago, after which magmatism on the Moon tailed off. Today the Moon is largely inactive. There is no more volcanic activity and cratering has tailed off as debris becomes less and less common in the inner solar system.

The Moon's Interior and Surface Today

8

Today, in the Copernican, the Moon is largely unchanging. The time of volcanism is over and there are few bodies left to make giant impacts on the surface. The story of the Moon's surface today is one of tiny gradual changes wrought by the solar wind striking its surface, unprotected as it is by magnetic field or atmosphere.

The Interior

Though the Moon has no plate tectonics, the most common cause of quakes on Earth, the Moon still experiences many small quakes. A seismometer placed on the Moon by one of the Apollo missions measured 3,000 quakes per year, though each was orders of magnitude less powerful than normal quakes on Earth. The quakes seem to occur at depths of 375 to 500 miles (600 to 800 km). Many of these quakes occur on a monthly cycle, and are therefore caused by tidal stresses. The seismometer also recorded between 70 and 150 meteorite impacts per year. By measuring the length of time it takes a laser to bounce off reflectors left on the Moon by the Apollo missions, and come back to Earth, scientists recently discovered that the Moon expands and contracts by 3.9 inches (10 cm) every 27 days. This distortion is caused by tides from the gravity of the Earth and Sun. This information, along with evidence that moonquake waves lose energy at depth, indicates that the inside of the Moon is still partly molten, or at least close to the temperature required for melting. Only cold, brittle material can create quakes, which are the result of energy being released when rocks break in a brittle fashion, as they do on the Earth's surface. Warm rocks will flow in response to stress. The expansion and contraction of the Moon is allowed by flowing warm interior rocks, while the quakes occur in cold, brittle regions. The crust of the Moon has been investigated using gravity signatures. Where gravity is strong, the crust must be thinner and the mantle material closer to the surface, because the mantle material is denser and creates a larger gravitational pull. The Clementine orbiter mission recorded the Moon's gravity field in detail. Based on modeling from this gravitational data, the Moon's crust appears to be between about 13 and 75 miles (20 and 120 km) thick. The crust is thickest on the far side by an average of about eight miles (12 km) (which is perhaps part of the reason there are so few mare basalt flows on the far side), thinner on the near side, and thinnest under the basins. There is no clear explanation now for the difference in crustal thickness between the near and far sides.

Gravity data also reveals that there is a strong gravity increase over each of the mare basins, as well as a few craters without mare fill. The gravity highs, as they are called, correspond to areas of high density that are known as lunar mascons. Mascons and their attendant high gravity signature are thought to be the result of the giant impacts: The giant impact thinned the crust by ejecting mass from the site of impact. After thinning, the crust at the site of impact rose in elevation to its level of buoyancy, as a ship rises in the water when its freight is removed. When the crust rose the mantle flowed upward to fill in the new dome in the bottom of the crust. The mantle material is denser than the crust it replaced, and causes the high gravity. The Moon today has a crust consisting of anorthosite and the mafic and alkali suites of highlands rocks, along with mare basalts. Beneath the crust is a deep mantle of silicate minerals, mainly olivine and pyroxene, but apparently divided into regions with different compositions both by depth and laterally at the same depth. Judging from the laser ranging and seismic evidence, the upper mantle is cold and brittle, but at some depth the mantle becomes warm enough to flow, and perhaps to be partly molten.

Surface Features

Though the Moon appears bright in the night sky, its surface is actually dark. The albedo of the lunar surface is 0.07, meaning that it absorbs 93 percent of the sunlight that strikes it. (Albedo is a measure of the light reflected by an object as a fraction of the light shining on an object; mirrors have high albedo, while charcoal has low albedo.) The

Astronaut Harrison (Jack) Schmitt stands by a lunar boulder while on the Apollo 17 mission. (NASA/Apollo 17/ NSSDC)

Moon simply appears bright from Earth because it is so relatively large and close, and stands in comparison to the deep dark of space.

The surface of the Moon consists of rock in various stages of pulverization by impacts. The outer shell of the Moon's crust is regolith, a region some one to six miles (2 to 10 km) deep made of giant blocks of bedrock broken by the Late Heavy Bombardment covered by a three- and 60-foot-deep (1- and 20-m-deep) regolith made of small rock fragments from impacts and volcanic glass beads, all altered by gardening from the solar wind. It is called regolith rather than soil, though, since it has none of the water or organic components so crucial to Earth's soil. The Moon's soil was created by millennia of meteorite bombardments.

The wide size range of rock fragments that make up the lunar regolith can be seen in this photograph of lunar module pilot Harrison Schmitt standing in front of a large boulder on the Moon, taken by Eugene Cernan, commander of *Apollo 17*. The lunar rover is in the foreground at left. *Apollo 17,* launched on December 7, 1972, was the last of the Apollo Moon landing missions.

This soil sample from the Apollo 15 mission shows rounded and broken beads of volcanic glass, some with skeletal olivine crystals, and soil agglutines caused by melting. (Linda T. Elkins-Tanton/NASA/JSC)

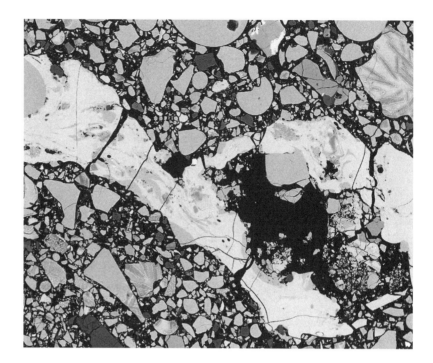

While the image of Jack Schmitt shows a large boulder making up part of the lunar regolith, the photomicrograph here shows the other size extreme in the lunar regolith. The image shows round volcanic glass beads, sharp-cornered broken fragments of glass and rock, and swirly mixtures of materials created by heat of impact into the surface. A bead of volcanic glass in the upper right corner of the image also shows dark bar-shaped crystals of olivine, indicating that the glass cooled slowly enough to allow crystals to form.

All the rocks on the lunar surface are igneous, the cooled result of rock heated enough to be completely liquid. No rocks on the Moon are sedimentary; without atmosphere and water, the Moon lacks the processes that create sedimentary rocks. No rocks on the Moon are metamorphic, either, since the Moon lacks the tectonic processes to bury rocks under heat and pressure and then bring them back to the surface in their changed form. Knowledge of lunar surface compositions comes from orbital data, material returned by the Apollo and Soviet Luna missions, and from a small collection of lunar meteorites that have landed on Earth, the result of large impacts on the Moon spalling off smaller pieces.

The more that is learned the more complicated the lunar surface appears. Tom Prettyman, David Vaniman, and their colleagues at Los Alamos National Laboratory have used special data processing techniques to determine the concentrations of major elements from Lunar Prospector gamma-ray data. They show that the most abundant compositions on the surface are matched by some of the rarer rocks in collections. Lunar meteorites, for example, seem to be more characteristic of the lunar highlands than samples of the surface soil collected by Apollo astronauts.

Even more curiously, rocks with high ratios of magnesium to iron and low concentrations of thorium may be quite abundant in some regions of the Moon, especially in the North Polar regions. The anorthosite-rich highlands rocks are by comparison unusually low in magnesium and so are completely different from the high magnesium rocks spotted in orbital data. Not everyone is convinced that the magnesium determination is calibrated sufficiently, but these preliminary results are interesting and, if they survive careful scrutiny, may have important implications for the origin of the lunar crust. Characterization of the rocks in these areas will have to wait for future missions to test the magnesium concentration by independent techniques (for example, orbital X-ray spectrometry and sample return missions; for more, see the sidebar "Remote Sensing" on page 156), but it shows that the Moon's crust is compositionally diverse.

Though the lunar surface is continually bombarded by the solar wind, this is the only continuous process acting to change the surface. With no wind, rain, ice, or volcanic activity, the Moon's craters are the cleanest in the solar system, and they make a convenient natural laboratory for Earth scientists to study cratering.

Two of the youngest craters on the Moon are Copernicus and Tycho, each of which can be seen on the near side. Tycho, with a diameter of 53 miles (85 km), is particularly prominent because of its bright white ejecta rays that reach almost around the Moon. Tycho is visible on the near side of the Moon near its South Pole. Tycho's exceptional brightness is due to its young age. One such ray crosses the *Apollo 17* landing site, about 1,300 miles (2,000 km) from Tycho. The impacts of this ejected material from Tycho are thought to have triggered a landslide near the *Apollo 17* landing site. Laboratory analysis of returned samples from this landslide suggests that Tycho's age is

Remote Sensing

Remote sensing is the name given to a wide variety of techniques that allow observers to make measurements of a place they are physically far from. The most familiar type of remote sensing is the photograph taken by spacecraft or by giant telescopes on Earth. These photos can tell scientists a lot about a planet; by looking at surface topography and coloration photo geologists can locate faults, craters, lava flows, chasms, and other features that indicate the weather, volcanism, and tectonics of the body being studied. There are, however, critical questions about planets and moons that cannot be answered with visible-light photographs, such as the composition and temperature of the surface or atmosphere. Some planets, such as Venus, have clouds covering their faces, and so even photography of the surface is impossible.

For remote sensing of solar system objects, each wavelength of radiation can yield different information. Scientists frequently find it necessary to send detectors into space rather than making measurements from Earth, first because not all types of electromagnetic radiation can pass through the Earth's atmosphere (see figure, opposite page), and second, because some electromagnetic emissions must be measured close to their sources, because they are weak, or in order to make detailed maps of the surface being measured.

Spectrometers are instruments that spread light out into spectra, in which the energy being emitted at each wavelength is measured separately. The spectrum often ends up looking like a bar graph, in which the height of each bar shows how strongly that wavelength is present in the light. These bars are called spectral lines. Each type of atom can only absorb or emit light at certain wavelengths, so the location and spacing of the spectral lines indicate which atoms are present in the object absorbing and emitting the light. In this way, scientists can determine the composition of something simply from the light shining from it.

Below are examples of the uses of a number of types of electromagnetic radiation in remote sensing.

Gamma rays

Gamma rays are a form of electromagnetic radiation; they have the shortest wavelength and highest energy. High-energy radiation such as X-rays and gamma rays are absorbed to a great degree by the Earth's atmosphere, so it is not possible to measure their production by solar system bodies without sending measuring devices into space. These high-energy radiations are created only by high-energy events, such as matter heated to millions of degrees, high-speed collisions, or cosmic explosions. These wavelengths, then, are used to investigate the hottest regions of the Sun. The effects of gamma rays on other

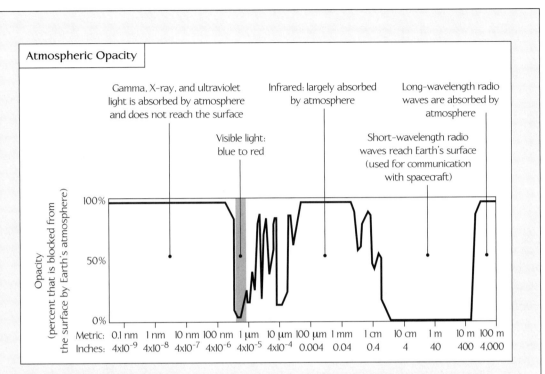

Atmospheric Opacity

Gamma, X-ray, and ultraviolet light is absorbed by atmosphere and does not reach the surface

Infrared: largely absorbed by atmosphere

Long-wavelength radio waves are absorbed by atmosphere

Visible light: blue to red

Short-wavelength radio waves reach Earth's surface (used for communication with spacecraft)

Opacity (percent that is blocked from the surface by Earth's atmosphere)

Metric:	0.1 nm	1 nm	10 nm	100 nm	1 μm	10 μm	100 μm	1 mm	1 cm	10 cm	1 m	10 m 100 m
Inches:	4×10^{-9}	4×10^{-8}	4×10^{-7}	4×10^{-6}	4×10^{-5}	4×10^{-4}	0.004	0.04	0.4	4	40	400 4,000

The Earth's atmosphere is opaque to many wavelengths of radiation but allows the visible and short radio wavelengths through to the surface.

solar systems bodies, those without protective atmospheres, can be measured and used to infer compositions. This technique searches for radioactivity induced by the gamma rays.

Though in the solar system gamma rays are produced mainly by the hottest regions of the Sun, they can also be produced by colder bodies through a chain reaction of events, starting with high-energy cosmic rays. Space objects are continuously bombarded with cosmic rays, mostly high-energy protons. These high-energy protons strike the surface materials, such as dust and rocks, causing nuclear reactions in the atoms of the surface material. The reactions produce neutrons, which collide with surrounding nuclei. The nuclei become excited by the added energy of neutron impacts, and reemit gamma rays as they return to their original, lower-energy state. The energy of the resultant gamma rays is characteristic of specific nuclear interactions in

(continues)

Remote Sensing (continued)

the surface, so measuring their intensity and wavelength allow a measurement of the abundance of several elements. One of these is hydrogen, which has a prominent gamma-ray emission at 2.223 million electron volts (a measure of the energy of the gamma ray). This can be measured from orbit, as it has been in the Mars Odyssey mission using a Gamma-Ray Spectrometer. The neutrons produced by the cosmic ray interactions discussed earlier start out with high energies, so they are called fast neutrons. As they interact with the nuclei of other atoms, the neutrons begin to slow down, reaching an intermediate range called epithermal neutrons. The slowing-down process is not too efficient because the neutrons bounce off large nuclei without losing much energy (hence speed). However, when neutrons interact with hydrogen nuclei, which are about the same mass as neutrons, they lose considerable energy, becoming thermal, or slow, neutrons. (The thermal neutrons can be captured by other atomic nuclei, which then can emit additional gamma rays.) The more hydrogen there is in the surface, the more thermal neutrons relative to epithermal neutrons. Many neutrons escape from the surface, flying up into space where they can be detected by the neutron detector on Mars Odyssey. The same technique was used to identify hydrogen enrichments, interpreted as water ice, in the polar regions of the Moon.

X-rays

When an X-ray strikes an atom, its energy can be transferred to the electrons or biting the atom. This addition of energy to the electrons makes one or more electrons leap from their normal orbital shells around the nucleus of the atom to higher orbital shells, leaving vacant shells at lower energy values. Having vacant, lower-energy orbital shells is an unstable state for an atom, and so in a short period of time the electrons fall back into their original orbital shells, and in the process emit another X-ray. This X-ray has energy equivalent to the difference in energies between the higher and lower orbital shells that the electron moved between. Because each element has a unique set of energy levels between electron orbitals, each element produces X-rays with energies that are characteristic of itself and no other element. This method can be used remotely from a satellite, and it can also be used directly on tiny samples of material placed in a laboratory instrument called an electron microprobe, which measures the composition of the material based on the X-rays the atoms emit when struck with electrons.

Visible and near-infrared

The most commonly seen type of remote sensing is, of course, visible light photography. Even visible light, when measured and analyzed according to wavelength and intensity, can be used to learn more about the body reflecting it.

Visible and near-infrared reflectance spectroscopy can help identify minerals that are crystals made of many elements, while other types of spectrometry identify individual types of atoms. When light shines on a mineral, some wavelengths are absorbed by the mineral, while other wavelengths are reflected back or transmitted through the mineral. This is why things have color to the eye: Eyes see and brains decode the wavelengths, or colors, that are not absorbed. The wavelengths of light that are absorbed are effectively a fingerprint of each mineral, so an analysis of absorbed versus reflected light can be used to identify minerals. This is not commonly used in laboratories to identify minerals, but it is used in remote sensing observations of planets.

The primary association of infrared radiation is heat, also called thermal radiation. Any material made of atoms and molecules at a temperature above absolute zero produces infrared radiation, which is produced by the motion of its atoms and molecules. At absolute zero, –459.67°F (–273.15°C), all atomic and molecular motion ceases. The higher the temperature, the more they move, and the more infrared radiation they produce. Therefore, even extremely cold objects, like the surface of Pluto, emit infrared radiation. Hot objects, like metal heated by a welder's torch, emit radiation in the visible spectrum as well as in the infrared.

In 1879 Josef Stefan, an Austrian scientist, deduced the relation between temperature and infrared emissions from empirical measurements. In 1884 his student, Ludwig Boltzmann derived the same law from thermodynamic theory. The relation gives the total energy emitted by an object (E) in terms of its absolute temperature in Kelvin (T), and a constant called the Stefan-Boltzman constant (equal to 5.670400×10^{-8} W m^{-2} K^{-4}, and denoted with the Greek letter sigma, σ):

$$E = \sigma T^4 .$$

This total energy E is spread out at various wavelengths of radiation, but the energy peaks at a wavelength characteristic of the temperature of the body emitting the energy. The relation between wavelength and total energy, Planck's Law, allows scientists to determine the temperature of a body by measuring the energy it emits.

(continues)

Remote Sensing (continued)

The hotter the body, the more energy it emits at shorter wavelengths. The surface temperature of the Sun is 9,900°F (5,500°C), and its Planck curve peaks in the visible wavelength range. For bodies cooler than the Sun, the peak of the Planck curve shifts to longer wavelengths, until a temperature is reached such that very little radiant energy is emitted in the visible range.

Humans radiate most strongly at an infrared wavelength of 10 microns (*micron* is another word for micrometer, one millionth of a meter). This infrared radiation is what makes night vision goggles possible: Humans are usually at a different temperature than their surroundings, and so their shapes can be seen in the infrared.

Only a few narrow bands of infrared light make it through the Earth's atmosphere without being absorbed, and can be measured by devices on Earth. To measure infrared emissions, the detectors themselves must be cooled to very low temperatures, or their own infrared emissions will swamp those they are trying to measure from elsewhere.

In thermal emission spectroscopy, a technique for remote sensing, the detector takes photos using infrared wavelengths and records how much of the light at each wavelength the material reflects from its surface. This technique can identify minerals and also estimate some physical properties, such as grain size. Minerals at temperatures above absolute zero emit radiation in the infrared, with characteristic peaks and valleys on plots of emission intensity versus wavelength. Though overall emission intensity is determined by temperature, the relationships between wavelength and emission intensity are determined by composition. The imager for *Mars Pathfinder*, a camera of this type, went to Mars in July 1997 to take measurements of light reflecting off the surfaces of Martian rocks (called reflectance spectra), and this data was used to infer what minerals the rocks contain.

When imaging in the optical or near-infrared wavelengths, the image gains information about only the upper microns of the surface. The thermal infrared gives information about the upper few centimeters, but to get information about deeper materials, even longer wavelengths must be used.

Radio waves

Radio waves from outside the Earth do reach through the atmosphere and can be detected both day and night, cloudy or clear, from Earth-based observatories using huge metal dishes. In this way, astronomers observe the universe as it appears in radio waves. Images like photographs can be made from any wavelength of radiation coming from a body: Bright regions on the image can correspond to more intense radiation, and dark parts, to

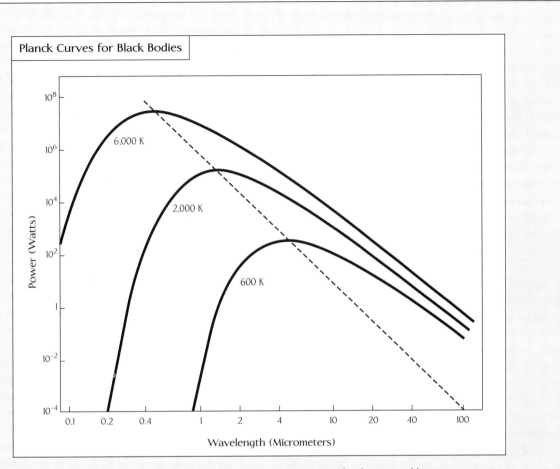

Planck Curves for Black Bodies

The infrared radiation emitted by a body allows its temperature to be determined by remote sensing. The curves showing the relationship between infrared and temperature are known as Planck curves.

less intense regions. It is as if observers are looking at the object through eyes that "see" in the radio, or ultraviolet, or any other wavelength, rather than just visible. Because of a lingering feeling that humankind still observes the universe exclusively through our own eyes and ears, scientists still often refer to "seeing" a body in visible wavelengths and to "listening" to it in radio wavelengths.

Radio waves can also be used to examine planets' surfaces, using the technique called radar (radio detection and ranging). Radar measures the strength and round-trip time of

(continues)

Remote Sensing (continued)

microwave or radio waves that are emitted by a radar antenna and bounced off a distant surface or object, thereby gaining information about the material of the target. The radar antenna alternately transmits and receives pulses at particular wavelengths (in the range 1 cm to 1 m) and polarizations (waves polarized in a single vertical or horizontal plane). For an imaging radar system, about 1,500 high-power pulses per second are transmitted toward the target or imaging area. At the Earth's surface, the energy in the radar pulse is scattered in all directions, with some reflected back toward the antenna. This backscatter returns to the radar as a weaker radar echo and is received by the antenna in a specific polarization (horizontal or vertical, not necessarily the same as the transmitted pulse). Given that the radar pulse travels at the speed of light, the measured time for the round trip of a particular pulse can be used to calculate the distance to the target.

Radar can be used to examine the composition, size, shape, and surface roughness of the target. The antenna measures the ratio of horizontally polarized radio waves sent to the surface to the horizontally polarized waves reflected back, and the same for vertically polarized waves. The difference between these ratios helps to measure the roughness of the surface. The composition of the target helps determine the amount of energy that is returned to the antenna: Ice is "low loss" to radar, in other words, the radio waves pass straight through it the way light passes through window glass. Water, on the other hand, is reflective. Therefore, by measuring the intensity of the returned signal and its polarization, information about the composition and roughness of the surface can be obtained. Radar can even penetrate surfaces and give information about material deeper in the target: By using wavelengths of 3, 12.6, and 70 centimeters, scientists can examine the Moon's surface to a depth of 32 feet (10 m), at a resolution of 330 to 985 feet (100 to 300 m), from the Earth-based U.S. National Astronomy and Ionosphere Center's Arecibo Observatory!

about 100 million years. Over time gardening from the solar wind dulls the brightness of ejecta rays.

Copernicus, about 60 miles (95 km) in diameter, is a large young crater visible just northwest of the center of the Moon's Earth-facing side. Though at about 1 billion years old it is not as bright and fresh as Tycho, Copernicus also has many bright ejecta rays surrounding it. The image of Copernicus shown on page 164 was taken by the *Lunar*

Venus is imaged almost exclusively in radar because of its dense, complete, permanent cloud cover. Radar images of Venus have been taken by several spacecraft and can also be taken from Arecibo Observatory on Earth. The image below makes a comparison between the resolution possible from Earth using Arecibo (left), and the resolution from the *Magellan* spacecraft (right). Arecibo's image is 560 miles (900 km) across and has a resolution of 1.9 miles (3 km). The *Magellan* image corresponds to the small white rectangle in the Arecibo image, 12 × 94 miles (20 × 120 km) in area. Magellan's resolution is a mere 400 feet (120 m) per pixel.

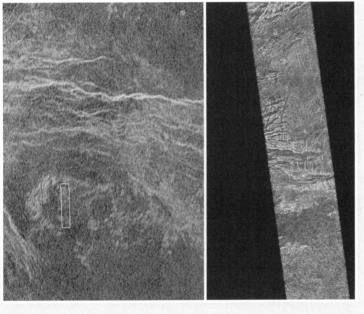

The far greater resolution obtained by the Magellan *craft (right) shows the relative disadvantage of taking images of Venus from the Earth (left) using the Arecibo Observatory.* (NASA/Magellan/JPL)

Orbiter 2. Copernicus has no basalt filling and its prominent central peak is easily seen in the image.

If an impact is made by a small object, less than a few kilometers in diameter (but greater than a few meters, the minimum needed to make a crater), the resulting crater is shaped like a bowl, and referred to as a simple crater. Larger craters undergo more complicated rebounding during impact, and end with circular rims, terraced inner

Copernicus crater is relatively young. as shown by its bright ejecta rays not yet dimmed by the action of the solar wind and disturbance from other impacts. (NASA/JPL/ Lunar Orbiter 2)

wall slopes, well-developed ejecta deposits, and flat floors with a central peak or peak ring. These craters are called complex craters. On the Moon, where erosion does not wear down craters as it does on Earth and the acceleration of gravity is only about 5.2 feet per square seconds (1.6 m/sec²) compared to Earth's 32 feet per square seconds (9.8 m/sec²), the central peaks of craters can be several kilometers high. By comparison, Mount Everest is 5.5 miles (8.8 km) high. A large central peak can be seen in the photo on page 165 of the Taruntius crater on the Moon. In this image the large Taruntius crater (35 miles [56 km] in diameter) is in the upper left, and smaller simple craters can be seen in the lava plains below.

While Taruntius and its neighbors demonstrate the differences between simple and complex craters, the lunar craters Herschel and Ptolomaeus show that some lunar craters are flooded with basalt while others nearby are not. In the image on page 165 from the *Apollo 12,* Herschel crater, 25 miles (40 km) in diameter, is at the center of this frame. Herschel lies at 5.7 degrees south and 2.1 degrees west in the lunar highlands. To the right is the 102 miles (164 km) diameter crater Ptolemaeus.

Herschel's floor is well defined and covered with rubble, showing a clear central peak and terraced walls. Ptolomaeus's floor, on the other hand, is relatively smooth and flat, despite the fact that it is a larger crater. The flatness of Ptolomaeus's floor is due to a basalt filling, much as the large mare basins are filled. Ptolomaeus's basalt filling is pocked with small impacts that are thought to have been caused by

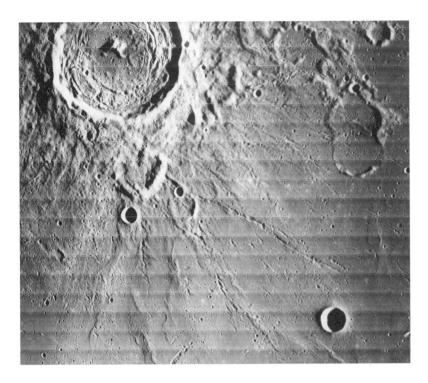

The Moon's Taruntius crater
has a high central peak.
(NASA/Lunar Orbiter 1/NSSDC)

The lunar crater Herschel
is bare of lava, while its
neighbor Ptolomaeus has
a smooth lava filling.
(NASA/Apollo 12/NSSDC)

material excavated by Herschel (these are called Herschel's "secondaries").

In the above section on basins the hypothesis is discussed that crater excavation allowed the basalt magmas to erupt onto the surface. In this case Ptolomaeus, being the larger crater, would have excavated more of the crust and therefore is more likely to have allowed basalt magma to flow onto the surface. This may seem to be a simple explanation for the basalt in Ptolomaeus and the lack of it in Herschel, but two other considerations must also be made: First, the Moon has been cooling over time, and at some point the interior became too cool for basalt lava to be available to flow into the craters. Perhaps Herschel is simply much younger, and by the time it was formed there was no more basalt to flow. The second question might then follow: At the time of the great basins, was the upper mantle of the Moon partly melted at all times? Why was there basalt available to flow into the craters?

It is possible that there was liquid basalt lying under the crust waiting for giant impacts to allow it to flow to the surface—but all

These ancient sinuous rilles east of Aristarchus Plateau are thought to have been created by flowing magma during the time of the mare basalt eruptions, over 3 billion years ago. (NASA/Apollo 15/NSSDC)

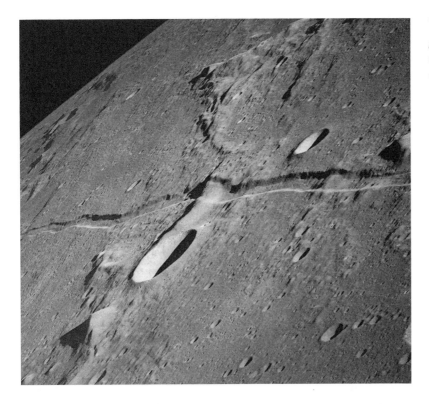

This large lunar rille was probably formed by the collapse of a lava tube. (NASA/Apollo 10/GRIN)

the time that the basalt is waiting it is cooling and crystallizing. Another possibility is that the impact craters themselves caused the lunar mantle to melt. When the giant impacts that created the basins excavated crustal material, the bottom of the crust arched upward and made a dome in its bottom, as described in the section on basins above. The impact and the dome in the crust can influence the mantle beneath to start convecting, moving up into the dome and down off the rim. It is possible that the basalt formed by melting in these convection currents, and that is why basalt was available to erupt into the basins: The basin formation itself caused the mantle to melt.

The lunar surface is also marked with rilles, linear or curving features with the appearance of channels or perhaps collapsed lava tubes. They are thought to represent features created by moving magma at the time of the mare basalts, particularly because many originate at craters. The image on page 166 was taken on the *Apollo 15* east of the Aristarchus Plateau. The largest rille in this southward-looking view is Rima Prinz, which starts at the center of the image at the crater Prinz (about 28 miles, or 46 km, in diameter).

This image on page 167, from *Apollo 10,* shows a more perplexing rille, which appears to run up and over a small ridge. This rille may well be a collapsed lava tube. If the ceiling of a lava tube collapsed along its length, it would create the appearance of a channel running over all the topography above it.

The Insignificant Magnetic Fields and Atmosphere

The Moon has a magnetic field less than 0.001 that of the Earth. This field is not an active one being produced inside the planet, but simply the record of a magnetic field from the past. Some lunar samples preserve old magnetic fields as remanent magnetization. A rock obtains a magnetic field by crystallizing in a larger field, for example, the field of the planet it is on. When the rock cools fully, its iron-based minerals (such as magnetite) hold the record of the magnetic field frozen for as long as the rock remains cool. If the rock is heated above a certain temperature called the Curie temperature, the minerals lose their record of the magnetic field. These frozen remanent fields can thus remain in rocks after the planet's own magnetic field has ceased. This is probably what happened on the Moon: It may have had a planetary magnetic field early in its history, and this field remains recorded in certain crustal rocks even though the Moon has only the tiniest magnetic field now (for more on planetary magnetic fields, see the section "Magnetic Field" on page 46).

The fact that the Moon had any magnetic field in the past was a surprise to some scientists, since until recently many scientists thought the Moon entirely lacked an iron core, and an iron core was thought necessary for the production of a magnetic field. Now it appears that the Moon likely has a small iron core, no larger than 10 or 20 percent of the Moon's radius. Any magnetic field created on the Moon occurred early in its evolution and lasted only a brief time. Today there is no magnetic field being created by the body.

The atmospheres of Venus, the Earth, and Mars, as well as those of all the gas giant planets, are protected by their magnetic fields. The planet's magnetic field creates a *magnetosphere,* a region around the planet in space from which the solar wind is blocked. When energetic particles from the Sun strike the magnetic field, they are carried along the field lines rather than passing through to the planet. If the energetic solar wind were able to strike the planet's atmosphere, the gases in the atmosphere would be knocked off into space and depleted over a short period of time. Without a magnetic field and atmosphere the planet's surface would also be bombarded by high-energy radiation from the Sun.

The Moon has almost no atmosphere now. There is a small region around the Moon that has a few tenuous gases, made from radon and a few other elements degassing from the Moon's interior, and from the solar wind itself. The solar wind contributes mainly hydrogen and helium to the planet's surface. The *Apollo 17* specifically measured the lunar atmosphere, and found that the three primary gases in the lunar atmosphere are neon, helium, and hydrogen, in approximately equal amounts. Methane, carbon dioxide, ammonia, and water are also present in smaller amounts. Argon was also detected, and its abundance appears to coincide with quakes on the Moon. Moonquakes may cause new fractures in the lunar crust, allowing ^{40}Ar to escape from the lunar interior, which it had previously been produced by decay of potassium-40 (^{40}K). Each atom in the lunar atmosphere has a lifetime of only a few months on average before it escapes into space. Some atoms or molecules, however, get caught in "cold traps," that is, cold areas in permanent or semipermanent shadow in which molecules freeze and where they are unlikely to be struck by energetic particles or heated by radiation. These molecules can remain stuck in the cold traps indefinitely.

Unlike Mars, which apparently started with a significant atmosphere, the Moon probably never had one. The tiny gravity field of the Moon was almost certainly incapable of retaining any atmosphere after the giant impact that created the Moon, especially because at the time of the impact all the matter was highly energized and liable to be lost to space or to the Earth's greater gravity field. While the side of the Moon facing the Sun obtains a few atoms from the solar wind, on the far side of the Moon from the Sun is a region called the plasma umbra that may be the most complete vacuum in the solar system. The Moon itself shields this region of space from corpuscular radiation, and in the absence of solar heating and radiation the Moon itself contributes almost no particles to this region.

The exceptional heat of formation of the Moon is thought to have driven off some fraction of the planet's oxygen. With no oxygen atmosphere and with an oxygen-depleted interior, the Moon is highly reduced, meaning that fewer atoms are bonded to oxygens than they are on Earth. Where on Earth iron would commonly be bonded with oxygen as Fe_2O_3 or as FeO, on the Moon iron is often so reduced that it is simply metallic iron. On Earth metallic iron on the surface is rapidly oxidized into rust.

Without an atmosphere and a magnetosphere, the temperature on the lunar surface is controlled by the cycles of heating by the Sun and cooling into space at night. In the day, the temperature of the Moon averages 225°F (107°C), although it rises as high as 253°F (123°C). At night the surface cools to an average of −243°F (−153°C), and an extreme of −387°F (−233°C) in the permanently shaded South Polar basin. A typical minimum temperature at the nonpolar *Apollo 15* landing site was −294°F (−181°C). These extreme temperature swings of 200 to 300 degrees between night and day make the lunar surface an inhospitable place and highly stressful on materials.

Water on the Moon?

A number of decades ago some scientists predicted the existence of frozen water on the Moon, based on calculations they made of temperatures in the shadowed interiors of craters. The Clementine and Lunar Prospector missions and radar measurements with the Arecibo radio telescope appear to have confirmed the predictions, though not all scientists agree that the measurements made absolutely confirm the presence of water. Measurements by the Prospector neutron spectrometer show that concentrations of hydrogen are highest in permanently shadowed craters, strong evidence for water in those permanently cool places. The H may be in water ice or in some other form, and the total amount is not known. It may have come from the solar wind or from cometary impacts. Richard Vondrak of the Goddard Space Flight Center reported on a model he has been developing with Dana Crider of the Catholic University of America. They conclude that all the observed hydrogen at the poles could be derived from implanted hydrogen that has been mobilized by micrometeorite impacts and sputtering by cosmic rays, and therefore there is no need to call upon water delivery by comets. This is surprising because comets are loaded with water ice and organic compounds (hence hydrogen) and, in the natural course of solar system collisions, have been colliding with the Moon for billions of years. Where, then, is all the additional water the comets delivered to the Moon? Crider and

Vondrak suggest a comet impact might produce such a hot, gaseous plume that almost all the water escapes.

If there is water on the Moon, it will be frozen in areas of permanent shadow. A permanent shadow in a crater on the Moon is defined as an area on the surface of the Moon that never receives sunlight. This happens at the poles because the Moon's axis of rotation is nearly perpendicular to the plane of its orbit around the Sun, so the Sun is always low, close to the horizon, casting long shadows off the crater rims or any other high point. Because temperatures in these polar shadows do not exceed about −380°F (−230°C), water in them is cold enough at all times that it cannot evaporate or even sublimate (move from solid ice to gas, as happens to the ice in frost-free freezers).

In their simulations of lunar topography, Ben Bussey of the Johns Hopkins University Applied Physics Lab and colleagues superimposed the shapes of simple craters onto a sphere the size of the Moon. Simulations were run for craters ranging in diameter from 1.5 to 13 miles (2.5 km to 20 km) to see how the amount of permanent shadow varies with crater size. For each size, simulations were run on craters placed at latitudes from 70 degrees to 90 degrees at one degree increments. Seasonal variations were studied by moving the position of the Sun's direct ray 1.5 degrees above or below the equator, to represent summer and winter for the Northern Hemisphere. The researchers assumed in their simulations that the craters were fresh and that they did not lie on a regional slope (slopes would expose a crater rim to more or less sunlight, thus affecting the size and shape of the internal shadow). They found that for a given latitude, larger craters have slightly more relative permanent shadow in them than smaller craters, simply because larger craters have higher rims. More than crater size, they found that latitude is the dominant parameter affecting the amount of permanent shadow in a simple crater. Craters as far as 20 degrees away from a pole still have significant amounts (22 to 27 percent) of permanent shadow. Craters near the poles can remain up to 80 percent in shadow even in the lunar summer. Their next step was to examine images of the Moon and identify all the fresh-looking simple craters larger than one kilometer within 12 degrees of each pole. By measuring the diameters of these craters and using their calculations for permanent darkness, they calculated the total amount of permanent shadow on the Moon.

The 832 craters at the North Pole have a total surface area of approximately 4,900 square miles (12,500 km²), and contain about 2,900 square miles (7,500 km²) of permanent shadow. This value is a lower limit because it is based solely on simple craters, excluding complex craters and craters on slopes. More shadow is contributed by poleward-facing walls of complex (multi-ringed) craters. The 547 craters identified at the South Pole have about 2,500 square miles (6,500 km²) of permanent shadow. If all the permanently shadowed regions contain water ice at a concentration suggested by *Lunar Prospector* data, about 1.5 weight percent, then the volume of ice on the Moon might be nearly one-quarter cubic mile (one cubic kilometer). While reports of ice on the Moon have created excitement in the community of people who want to place permanent human habitation on the Moon, the quantity of ice and its distribution in minute amounts over large land areas makes this idea less than practical.

The ancient lunar surface changes little in the present day but it perfectly preserves the record of the processes that occurred on the Moon 4 billion and more years ago. On the Moon are written the events that undoubtedly also happened to the Earth, where their evidence was wiped away by erosion and plate tectonics: Magma ocean crystallization, the Late Heavy Bombardment, active and voluminous volcanism. The Earth has progressed to become a world of oxygen and water, but the Moon lost its magnetic field and whatever thin atmosphere it ever possessed, and now lies exposed to extremes of temperature and the battering of the solar wind.

Missions to the Moon

9

More than 60 lunar spacecraft missions have been attempted, 12 astronauts have walked on the surface, and more than 840 pounds (382 kg) of lunar rock and soil have been brought to Earth. The contributions of these missions to scientific understanding of the solar system is incalculable; understanding something about the history and evolution of the Moon has added a second planetary body to the short list of bodies that people have touched. This second data point, so to speak, adds immeasurably to scientists' abilities to hypothesize about other planets. As shown in the figure on page 174, the Moon is by far the most visited of solar system bodies.

The tremendous effort and risk of space travel has cost lives. Valentin Bondarenko was selected in 1960 as a military pilot cosmonaut, and on March 23, 1961, he was killed when fire broke out in his spacecraft simulator, driven by its pure oxygen atmosphere. On April 23, 1967, Colonel Engineer Vladimir Mikhailovich Komarov of the Soviet Air Force was launched as pilot of *Soyuz 1,* a solo mission. On April 24 he became the first person to die during a space mission. On January 27, 1967, a fire occurred on *Apollo 1* and killed American astronauts Gus Grissom, Ed White, and Roger Chaffee. On June 6, 1971, Lieutenant Colonel Georgi Timofeyevich Dobrovolsky was launched as commander of *Soyuz 11* along with crewmates Vladislav Volkov (the flight engineer) and Viktor Patsayev (the research engineer). They became the first crew of the world's first space station, *Salyut 1.* After a 23-day mission, the crew was killed during preparations for reentry to Earth's atmosphere.

The Soviets worked flat out to win the space race with the United States. They sent more than 30 missions to the Moon over the years 1959 through 1973, severely straining the Soviet economy. As one Soviet

The approximate number of successful space missions from all nations to each of the planets and the Moon shows that the Moon is by far the most visited body: only Pluto has had no missions, and Mercury is as neglected as Uranus and Neptune. The definition of a successful mission is arguable, so the total for Mars and the Moon in particular may be disputed by a small number.

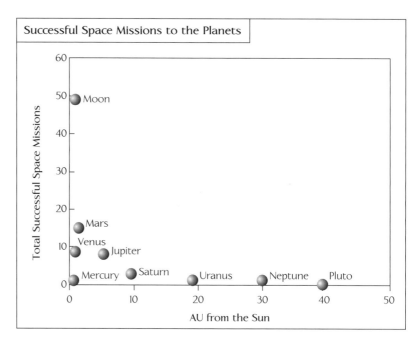

Successful Space Missions to the Planets

scientist from the era explains, it was a simple equation: more rockets, fewer cars; more rockets, fewer clothes. Their extensive Luna series (*Lunik* in Russian) made a large number of significant scientific discoveries, including returning the first lunar sample to Earth (an unmanned lander did the work), taking the first photographs of the lunar far side, and determining that the Moon has no current magnetic field. The Luna series included three landers (numbers *16, 20,* and *24*); one of the Soviet remotely controlled landers operated for about a year, an amazing longevity record. Soviet missions returned about seven tenths of a pound (310 g) of surface material and a drill core into the regolith five feet (160 cm) long.

The Soyuz orbiters and Zond missions were meant to converge with sending men to the Moon, but Soyuz had several tragic explosions, and Sergei Korolev, the chief designer, died, and the push by the Soviets to land men on the Moon ended. All the studies that followed were robotic. Soyuz rockets are still in production, marketed by a joint French and Russian consortium called STARSEM.

In reaction to the Soviet launch of *Sputnik,* the Americans became determined to land the first man on the Moon, and by that single symbolic act, prove themselves as the leaders of the space age. The Apollo series of launches included five successful manned landings with large sample returns (*11, 12, 14, 15, 16,* and *17*). These missions returned 2,000 samples, totaling 840 pounds (382 kg) of material. Instruments left on the Moon operated for up to eight years, and laser reflectors placed there are still in use.

The Japanese have been active in launches since 1970. Initially, their space agency (the Institute of Space and Astronautical Science, recently integrated into the Japan Aerospace Exploration Agency) focused on Earth satellites. In 1980 the Japanese entered the arena of missions to the Moon with a mission named HITEN (MUSES-A), launched on January 24 from the Kagoshima Space Center. The aim of the mission was to practice orbital techniques, including a swing-by using the Moon's gravitation. When *HITEN* approached the Moon, the spacecraft released a tiny lunar orbiter, *HAGOROMO*, into orbit around the Moon. *HAGOMORO* orbited the Moon until April 11, 1993, when it crashed into the lunar surface. Several missions to the Moon are planned by the Japan Aerospace Exploration Agency for the next decade. Missions to the Moon are summarized in the table below, and discussed in more detail below. The list of lunar missions here omits a number of missions by both the United States and the Soviet Union that failed at or soon after launch.

MISSIONS TO THE MOON

Year	Launch date	Mission	Country	Comments
1959	January 2, 1959	*Luna 1*	USSR	flyby
	March 3, 1959	*Pioneer 4*	U.S.	flyby
	September 12, 1959	*Luna 2*	USSR	first human-made object to reach the Moon
	October 4, 1959	*Luna 3*	USSR	probe
1961	August 23, 1961	*Ranger 1*	U.S.	attempted test flight
	November 18, 1961	*Ranger 2*	U.S.	attempted test flight
1962	January 26, 1962	*Ranger 3*	U.S.	attempted impact
	April 23, 1962	*Ranger 4*	U.S.	impact
	October 18, 1962	*Ranger 5*	U.S.	attempted impact

(continues)

MISSIONS TO THE MOON (continued)

Year	Launch date	Mission	Country	Comments
1963	April 2, 1963	Luna 4	USSR	flyby
1964	January 30, 1964	Ranger 6	U.S.	impact
	July 28, 1964	Ranger 7	U.S.	impact
1965	February 17, 1965	Ranger 8	U.S.	impact
	March 21, 1965	Ranger 9	U.S.	impact
	May 9, 1965	Luna 5	USSR	impact
	June 8, 1965	Luna 6	USSR	attempted lander
	July 18, 1965	Zond 3	USSR	flyby
	October 4, 1965	Luna 7	USSR	impact
	December 3, 1965	Luna 8	USSR	impact
1966	January 31, 1966	Luna 9	USSR	first soft landing in space history
	March 31, 1966	Luna 10	USSR	orbiter
	May 30, 1966	Surveyor 1	U.S.	lander
	August 10, 1966	Lunar Orbiter 1	U.S.	orbiter
	August 24, 1966	Luna 11	USSR	orbiter
	September 20, 1966	Surveyor 2	U.S.	attempted lander
	October 22, 1966	Luna 12	USSR	orbiter
	November 6, 1966	Lunar Orbiter 2	U.S.	orbiter
	December 21, 1966	Luna 13	USSR	lander
1967	February 4, 1967	Lunar Orbiter 3	U.S.	orbiter
	April 17, 1967	Surveyor 3	U.S.	lander
	May 8, 1967	Lunar Orbiter 4	U.S.	orbiter
	July 14, 1967	Surveyor 4	U.S.	attempted lander
	August 1, 1967	Lunar Orbiter 5	U.S.	orbiter
	September 8, 1967	Surveyor 5	U.S.	lander
	November 7, 1967	Surveyor 6	U.S.	lander
1968	January 7, 1968	Surveyor 7	U.S.	lander
	April 7, 1968	Luna 14	USSR	orbiter

Year	Launch date	Mission	Country	Comments
	September 15, 1968	Zond 5	USSR	return probe
	November 10, 1968	Zond 6	USSR	return probe
	December 21, 1968	Apollo 8	U.S.	crewed orbiter
1969	May 18, 1969	Apollo 10	U.S.	orbiter
	July 13, 1969	Luna 15	USSR	orbiter
	July 16, 1969	Apollo 11	U.S.	first crewed landing and sample return in space history
	August 7, 1969	Zond 7	USSR	return probe
	November 14, 1969	Apollo 12	U.S.	crewed landing and sample return
1970	April 11, 1970	Apollo 13	U.S.	attempted crewed landing (aborted)
	September 12, 1970	Luna 16	USSR	first Soviet sample return
	October 20, 1970	Zond 8	USSR	return probe
	November 10, 1970	Luna 17	USSR	first robotic rover in space history
1971	January 31, 1971	Apollo 14	U.S.	crewed landing and sample return
	July 26, 1971	Apollo 15	U.S.	crewed landing and sample return
	September 2, 1971	Luna 18	USSR	impact
	September 28, 1971	Luna 19	USSR	orbiter
1972	February 14, 1972	Luna 20	USSR	sample return
	April 16, 1972	Apollo 16	U.S.	crewed landing and sample return
	December 7, 1972	Apollo 17	U.S.	crewed landing and sample return
1973	January 8, 1973	Luna 21	USSR	rover

(continues)

MISSIONS TO THE MOON (continued)

Year	Launch date	Mission	Country	Comments
1974	June 2, 1974	*Luna 22*	USSR	orbiter
	October 28, 1974	*Luna 23*	USSR	lander
1976	August 14, 1976	*Luna 24*	USSR	sample return
1990	January 24, 1990	*HITEN*	Japan	flyby and orbiter
1994	January 25, 1994	*Clementine*	U.S.	orbiter
1997	December 24, 1997	*AsiaSat 3/HGS-1*	Hong Kong/PRC	lunar flyby
1998	January 7, 1998	*Lunar Prospector*	U.S.	orbiter
2003	September, 2003	*SMART 1*	ESA	lunar orbiter

Sputnik 1   *October 1957*
Soviet

Sputnik was the mission that started the great race between the United States and the Soviet Union. When in 1957 the rocket was ready but not the satellite, Sergei Korolev, the chief designer, simply told the engineers to immediately make a sphere and put a radio in it. This simple design allowed the study of radio waves in the atmosphere and the structure of the Earth's upper atmosphere, previously unexplored areas. *Sputnik 1* was launched on October 4, 1957, and history changed. The world's first artificial satellite was about the size of a basketball, weighed only 183 pounds (82 kg), and took about 98 minutes to orbit the Earth on its elliptical path. That launch ushered in new political, military, technological, and scientific developments. Though *Sputnik 1* was not a mission to the Moon, its launch inspired both countries to aim for that goal.

Pioneer missions   *1958–1959*
American

The early American lunar attempts, named Pioneer, began in the summer of 1958. *Pioneer 1A, 1B, 2,* and *3* all either exploded or fell back to Earth. In 1959 *Pioneer 4* finally made a successful lunar flyby.

Ranger 7, 8, 9 1964–1965
American

The *Ranger* were deliberately crash-landed on the Moon in the years 1964 and 1965, obtaining the first close-up pictures of the Moon showing boulders and meter-size craters.

Luna missions 1958–1974
Soviet

The Soviet Luna missions began in September 1958 and continued through 1974. Two early Soviet missions named Luna failed in the fall of 1958 before *Luna 1* launched successfully in 1959. *Luna 1* missed the Moon by 3,750 miles (6,000 km), and thus became the first artificial satellite of the Sun. In the same year *Luna 2* became the first human artifact to reach the Moon. It landed at 1 degree west longitude and 30 degrees north latitude, and determined that the Moon has no magnetic field. *Luna 3* then took the first pictures of the far side of the Moon, and showed that there are no maria (floods of dark mare basalts) on the far side. Soviet aerospace had a watershed year in 1959, with several unique achievements and impressive data returns.

From 1963 through 1965, *Luna 4* through *8* all failed: *Luna 4* missed the Moon by 5,250 miles (8,400 km); the retrorocket on *Luna 5* failed, and it crashed into the Moon; *Luna 6* was given an incorrect midcourse correction, and it missed the Moon by 100,000 miles (160,000 km); and both *Luna 7* and *Luna 8* crashed in the Oceanus Procellarum.

In 1966 the Luna missions achieved another major milestone: the first soft landing on the Moon. *Luna 9* landed softly in the Oceanus Procellarum, at 64.37 degrees west longitude and 7.13 degrees north latitude. This mission also provided the first television programming from a space mission, and showed that the soil had enough strength to support a lander: Arthur C. Clarke had written about seas of dust on the Moon, and some scientists also thought that a lander might simply sink. This lander was a sphere that landed on airbags that then deflated. Four petal-shape panels of metal unfolded to form braces on each side, revealing the camera at the top of the sphere. This is a simple, effective design, similar to that later used in *Mars Pathfinder*. Later the same year *Luna 10* became the first lunar satellite (meaning it orbited the Moon). It carried a gamma-ray composition sensor (see the sidebar "Remote Sensing" on page 156). *Luna 11* followed, another lunar orbiter, carrying X-ray, plasma, and micrometeorite sensors. *Luna 12* was the third lunar orbiter in the series, carrying an onboard television and making crater measurements. *Luna 13,* launched at the end of 1966, made another soft landing in Oceanus Procellarum at 18.87 degrees north latitude and 62.05 degrees west longitude. It transmitted television panoramas, and made measurements of soil mechanics.

Luna 14, launched in 1968, also orbited the Moon, making gravity measurements and measuring plasma and particles in space. Following *Luna 14,* serious attempts at sample returns from the Moon began. *Luna 15* attempted a sample return from Mare Crisium. The intended soft landing failed, and the geologists were blamed because the spacecraft hit a mountain. Later it was determined that the Doppler radar device failed. Quickly, though, success followed: *Luna 16* was the Soviet Union's first successful unmanned sample return, from Mare Fecunditatis in 1970. The great achievement of a robotic sample return was somewhat overshadowed by the United States' *Apollo 11* the previous year, which had successfully landed the first men on the Moon and returned the first samples. The Soviets followed *Luna 16* in 1970 with *Luna 17,* which carried the *Lunokhod 1* rover. This was the first robotic rover in the history of space travel, and it was a tremendous success: It functioned for more than a year, traveling about six miles (10 km) around Mare Imbrium.

In 1972 *Luna 20* completed an unmanned sample return from the highlands. The capsule fell back to Earth in a snowy swamp in Siberia, and the scientists were relieved to be able to detect its beacon. The following year *Luna 21* carried the *Lunokhod 2* rover to the Moon. The rover traveled around the crater Le Monier, near Serenitatis basin. It worked for about four months, traveling about 19 miles (30 km). *Luna 24,* the final Luna mission, was the third robotic sample return (from Mare Crisium to a landing in western Siberia), and a fittingly successful ending to this marathon series of space missions.

Zond missions 1965–1970

Soviet

Zond 3 was designed to fly to Mars in the 1964 launch window, which would certainly have panicked the Americans even more than they were. Instead, *Zond 3* repeated in 1965 the flight of *Luna 3,* taking photos of both sides of the Moon. *Zond 5,* in 1968, was the first lunar flyby with an Earth return; previous missions all remained in space. *Zond 5* carried turtles and returned them to Earth. *Zond 7* and *Zond 8* were flyby missions in 1970 and took photographs that were the best photos of the far side until the American Clementine mission in 1994.

Surveyor missions *1966–1968*
American

Surveyor 1, in 1966, was America's first successful soft landing on the Moon, four months after the Soviets achieved a soft landing. *Surveyor 3* through 7 all landed successfully on the Moon. *Surveyor 3* took soil samples (without returning them), and all four missions prepared the American space program for manned missions to the Moon.

Lunar Orbiters 1 through 5 *1966–1967*
American

The series of Lunar Orbiters in 1966 and 1967 were all used to make photographs of possible landing sites for later missions.

Soyuz 1 *April 22 and 23, 1967*
Soviet

Once in orbit, *Soyuz 1,* piloted by Valeri Komarov, was to have docked with *Soyuz 2* and its crew of three. After the docking was complete, two engineers from *Soyuz 2* were to transfer from *Soyuz 2* to *Soyuz 1* and return home with Komarov. The launch of *Soyuz 2* never happened, it is believed, because of some trouble *Soyuz 1* experienced on reaching orbit. Immediately after reaching orbit, one of the solar panels on *Soyuz 1* failed to deploy. Although *Soyuz 1* received only half of the planned solar power, an attempt was made to maneuver the spacecraft.

The decision was then made to bring Komarov back. Reentry was successful and the drag chute deployed. However, due to a failure of a pressure sensor, the main parachute would not deploy. Komarov released the reserve chute, but it became tangled with the drag chute. The descent module crashed into a field near Orenburg at 7 A.M., killing Komarov. There had been discussions of problems and dangers before the flight, and some sources claim that Komarov himself did not expect to survive the flight. Controversy followed the disaster, of course, including poignant claims that the crash site was not handled correctly and that Young Pioneers later came to give some of

Komarov's abandoned remains a good burial. This terrible space disaster put back Soviet lunar program 18 months. Despite the tragedy of the early flight, the Soyuz spacecraft went on to become the longest-serving spacecraft in history, continuing to be in use well past the turn of the millennium.

Apollo missions 1963–1972
American

NASA Administrator James Webb wrote the following excellent description of the challenges facing the Apollo mission teams:

> *The Apollo requirement was to take off from a point on the surface of the Earth that was traveling 1,000 miles per hour as the Earth rotated, to go into orbit at 18,000 miles an hour, to speed up at the proper time to 25,000 miles an hour, to travel to a body in space 240,000 miles distant which was itself traveling 2,000 miles per hour relative to the Earth, to go into orbit around this body, and to drop a specialized landing vehicle to its surface.*

Apollo 7 and *9* were Earth-orbiting missions to test the Command and Lunar Modules, and did not return lunar data. In 1968 *Apollo 8* made the first manned orbits of the Moon, and it and *Apollo 10* tested various components while orbiting the Moon, and returned photography of the lunar surface.

Apollo 11 was the historic first manned landing of a man on any planetary body beyond the Earth, and the first sample return to Earth from any planetary body. *Apollo 11* landed at Mare Tranquillitatis and accomplished a safe return and sample return. *Apollo 12* completed a manned landing and exploration of the Oceanus Procellarum region, with a successful return with samples. *Apollo 13,* the subject of many documentaries, was meant to continue this run of manned landings, but the explosion of an oxygen tank resulted in serious damage to the craft while still on its way to the Moon. Through a series of heroic efforts on the parts of the crew and ground support, the craft returned all astronauts safely to the Earth.

Apollo 14 followed in 1971 with a manned landing and exploration of the Fra Mauro highlands with a sample return. *Apollo 15* repeated the effort at Hadley Rille, *Apollo 16* at the Cayley-

Descartes region, and *Apollo 17* in the southeastern rim of Mare Serenitatis. Together the Apollo missions returned more than 840 pounds (382 kg) of rock and soil (the Soviet Luna robotic returns contributed an additional few grams, though from locales unvisited by the Apollo missions).

Clementine *1994*
American
Clementine, launched in 1994, was an orbiter with multispectral imaging, allowing determination of surface compositions, and altimetry, measuring elevation.

Lunar Prospector *1997*
American
Lunar Prospector, launched in 1997, was a polar orbiter able to make multispectral imaging, gravity, and magnetic field measurements.

Planned Missions

When Project Apollo ended in 1972, the era of Moon missions appeared to have ended. The hiatus ended with the Clementine mission in 1994, followed by the Lunar Prospector mission in 1997. Several new missions are now planned. These missions will obtain data that are much needed. They will deploy seismometers to determine the size of the lunar core, analyze the surface composition for elements not determined precisely, study volatile substances and the geology of the polar regions, and return samples from the largest lunar basin. The missions are being planned by the Japanese space agency and the European Space Agency. The U.S. National Research Council has recommended that a sample-return mission to the South Pole-Aitken basin be given a high priority in NASA's mission planning.

The NASA Exploration Team (NExT) is developing exciting plans for a human return to the Moon. A centerpiece of the planning is the use of the Earth-Moon Lagrangian point, L1. From this gravitationally balanced place in space astronauts will have easy access to anywhere in the Earth-Moon system, opening up endless possibilities.

10

Conclusions: The Known and the Unknown

Geologists have walked over and inspected the vast majority of the Earth's surface, mapping and describing its rocks, mapping its structures, and collecting samples for analysis and dating. Seismologists measure earthquakes and use the data to understand the structure of the Earth's interior. Petrologists and mineralogists have measured the compositions of terrestrial rocks and meteorites to estimate the composition of the Earth's interior and the timing of its formation. Though far more is known about the Earth than about any other planet, many questions remain about its formation, evolution, and current processes.

1. What will be the future of the Earth's climate, and what will it mean for life on Earth?

Over the history of the Earth, even the recent history of Earth, temperatures have fluctuated violently. Initially this may seem a comforting fact in the face of the dire warnings about mankind's contributions to global warming, but historical temperature fluctuations appear to have wreaked havoc on the Earth's weather and climate. The half- to one-degree increase in average global temperatures that mankind's chemical contributions have thus far added seems already to have added violence and irregularity to weather patterns. Beyond this immediate, controllable concern, long-term and very long-term climate changes caused by orbital variability, solar output changes, and other effects will also change climate in the long term.

Life on Earth has adapted to many unusual circumstances. Single-celled organisms known as extremophiles have adapted to life in otherwise entirely inhospitable places. Some bacteria, called chemolithoautotrophs ("those that live on energy they extract themselves from rock or inorganic chemicals"), live with less than 1 percent oxygen and without sunlight and derive their energy from methane, manganese, iron, or even arsenic. Some eat sulfide minerals and excrete sulfuric acid. Some bacteria live meters or even kilometers deep in bedrock; they may make up half of the Earth's biomass. Bacteria on Earth can live in water with a high-acid pH of 2.3, such as the Rio Tinto River, (the pH of most water is around 7); the organism *Ferroplasma* can even live at pH equal to 0. Extremophiles on Earth have been shown to live at temperatures ranging from –4°F (–20°C) to 250°F (121°C), that is, from well below freezing to well above the boiling point of water. On Earth life has adapted to every environment except high temperatures still, and extreme dryness.

These examples of single-celled life show that the most extreme climate changes will not easily deter Earth life. Mankind, however, has greater needs for life than do these single-celled organisms. To retain the societies and habits of the developed world and to continue to spread technology, health, and food to emerging countries, mankind must act to limit its own damaging effects on climate.

2. What are the interactions among large igneous provinces, giant impacts, and extinctions?

Though other planets and moons are covered with impact craters from meteorite bombardment, the Earth has relatively few recognizable craters. They have been eroded away over time. Because there are so few to be seen on the Earth, it took centuries for scientists to agree that giant meteorites have in fact struck the Earth. The reigning paradigm for the previous three centuries had been gradualism and uniformitarianism: the ideas that Earth processes happened gradually and incrementally over vast amounts of time, leading in the end to the dramatic formations seen today. Now scientists think there are several good examples of the converse, catastrophism. Sudden catastrophic processes that alter landforms include meteorite impacts, volcanic explosions, giant landslides, earthquakes, and storms. Giant impacts, in fact, are the only known natural disaster that has the ability to entirely sterilize the Earth of life.

Throughout Earth history there have been a number of large extinctions of multiple species, most notably, the extinction at the end of the Permian, at 250 million years ago, when 90 percent of the species on Earth went extinct over a geologically brief time, perhaps a few million years. This extinction, the extinction that killed the dinosaurs at 65 million years ago, and several other extinctions all occurred simultaneously with another phenomenon, eruptions of large igneous provinces. Perhaps 10 times through Earth history a large outpouring of basalt occurred onto a continent, an event in which 1 or more million cubic kilometers of lava poured onto the crust in less than a million years. Several of these large igneous provinces appear to coincide in time with extinctions. The processes that create large igneous provinces are not fully understood, and some scientists believe they may be triggered by giant meteorite impacts. The reasons for large igneous province development, the exact processes that cause extinctions, and any possible links between them and to giant meteorite impacts are not well understood, though they are the topics of heated debates at scientific conferences. While the extinction that killed the dinosaurs is clearly linked to a large meteorite impact, other extinctions have not been explained.

3. Why is the Moon asymmetrical?

The Moon's crust is, on average, thicker on its far side than on its near side. The most obvious large impact basins are on the near side. The vast majority of mare basalts are on its near side, as it the largest quantity of radiogenic elements near the lunar surface. What caused this asymmetry in lunar formation? The early development of the asymmetrical crust may have influenced the other asymmetries, in that the crust on the near side may have been just thin enough that giant impacts could allow the basalt to erupt. Even if this is the case, a reason for the asymmetrical formation of the crust needs to be found.

Even this most studied planet and its large, close Moon are not thoroughly understood. The Earth and Moon had a common formation when the early Earth was struck by a giant impactor, about the size of Mars, and the resulting spray of superheated material partly settled back onto the Earth and partly reformed to make the

Moon, or at least this is believed to be the case. As effectively as scientists can look into the most distant past of the solar system and infer the timing of core formation for the Earth, the process of magma ocean crystallization for the Moon (and quite likely for the Earth as well), and as effective as researchers are at learning about the Earth's mantle, slow-moving processes, atmospheric movements, and climate changes over time, they do not know with any assurance conditions in the Earth's deepest interior, or the complexity of interactions among the weather, climate, oceans, and orbit of the planet, or about the deeply complicated and critically important effects that mankind is having on the Earth's ecosystems and climate. Indications are unequivocal that mankind is damaging the environment and endangering the planet through climate change.

On a geologic timescale, none of this really matters: The Earth will continue to orbit the Sun, plates will continue to move, and heat will slowly leave the planet and move into space. The large-scale processes continue unabated; from a cosmic distance nothing will change. From a human perspective, however, the big picture is unimportant and only the details really matter. If humankind's changes cause more violent hurricanes and a lack of protection from dangerous solar radiation, then coastal houses will be repeatedly destroyed, lives will be lost, and cancer rates will soar. If global temperatures rise, then ice caps will melt and continents will flood. Life as it is now will no longer exist. Even if catastrophes of this size have occurred in Earth's past, the only catastrophes that will matter are those happening to humankind now.

Appendix 1:
Units and Measurements

Fundamental Units

The system of measurements most commonly used in science is called both the SI (for Système International d'Unités) and the International System of Units (it is also sometimes called the MKS system). The SI system is based upon the metric units meter (abbreviated m), kilogram (kg), second (sec), kelvin (K), mole (mol), candela (cd), and ampere (A), used to measure length, time, mass, temperature, amount of a substance, light intensity, and electric current, respectively. This system was agreed upon in 1974 at an international general conference. There is another metric system, CGS, which stands for centimeter, gram, second; that system simply uses the hundredth of a meter (the centimeter) and the hundredth of the kilogram (the gram). The CGS system, formally introduced by the British Association for the Advancement of Science in 1874, is particularly useful to scientists making measurements of small quantities in laboratories, but it is less useful for space science. In this set, the SI system is used with the exception that temperatures will be presented in Celsius (C), instead of Kelvin. (The conversions between Celsius, Kelvin, and Fahrenheit temperatures are given below.) Often the standard unit of measure in the SI system, the meter, is too small when talking about the great distances in the solar system; kilometers (thousands of meters) or AU (astronomical units, defined below) will often be used instead of meters.

How is a unit defined? At one time a "meter" was defined as the length of a special metal ruler kept under strict conditions of temperature and humidity. That perfect meter could not be measured, however, without changing its temperature by opening the box, which would change its length, through thermal expansion or contraction. Today a meter is no longer defined according to a physical object; the only

189

FUNDAMENTAL UNITS

Measurement	Unit	Symbol	Definition
length	meter	m	The meter is the distance traveled by light in a vacuum during 1/299,792,458 of a second.
time	second	sec	The second is defined as the period of time in which the oscillations of cesium atoms, under specified conditions, complete exactly 9,192,631,770 cycles. The length of a second was thought to be a constant before Einstein developed theories in physics that show that the closer to the speed of light an object is traveling, the slower time is for that object. For the velocities on Earth, time is quite accurately still considered a constant.
mass	kilogram	kg	The International Bureau of Weights and Measures keeps the world's standard kilogram in Paris, and that object is the definition of the kilogram.
temperature	kelvin	K	A degree in Kelvin (and Celsius) is 1/273.16 of the thermodynamic temperature of the triple point of water (the temperature at which, under one atmosphere pressure, water coexists as water vapor, liquid, and solid ice). In 1967, the General Conference on Weights and Measures defined this temperature as 273.16 kelvin.
amount of a substance	mole	mol	The mole is the amount of a substance that contains as many units as there are atoms in 0.012 kilogram of carbon 12 (that is, Avogadro's number, or 6.02205×10^{23}). The units may be atoms, molecules, ions, or other particles.
electric current	ampere	A	The ampere is that constant current which, if maintained in two straight parallel conductors of infinite length, of negligible circular cross section, and placed one meter apart in a vacuum, would produce between these conductors a force equal to 2×10^{-7} newtons per meter of length.
light intensity	candela	cd	The candela is the luminous intensity of a source that emits monochromatic radiation with a wavelength of 555.17 nm and that has a radiant intensity of 1/683 watt per steradian. Normal human eyes are more sensitive to the yellow-green light of this wavelength than to any other.

fundamental measurement that still is defined by a physical object is the kilogram. All of these units have had long and complex histories of attempts to define them. Some of the modern definitions, along with the use and abbreviation of each, are listed in the table here.

Mass and weight are often confused. Weight is proportional to the force of gravity: Your weight on Earth is about six times your weight on the Moon because Earth's gravity is about six times that of the Moon's. Mass, on the other hand, is a quantity of matter, measured independently of gravity. In fact, weight has different units from mass: Weight is actually measured as a force (newtons, in SI, or pounds, in the English system).

The table "Fundamental Units" lists the fundamental units of the SI system. These are units that need to be defined in order to make other measurements. For example, the meter and the second are fundamental units (they are not based on any other units). To measure velocity, use a derived unit, meters per second (m/sec), a combination of fundamental units. Later in this section there is a list of common derived units.

The systems of temperature are capitalized (Fahrenheit, Celsius, and Kelvin), but the units are not (degree and kelvin). Unit abbreviations are capitalized only when they are named after a person, such as K for Lord Kelvin, or A for André-Marie Ampère. The units themselves are always lowercase, even when named for a person: one newton, or one N. Throughout these tables a small dot indicates multiplication, as in N · m, which means a newton (N) times a meter (m). A space between the symbols can also be used to indicate multiplication, as in N · m. When a small letter is placed in front of a symbol, it is a prefix meaning some multiplication factor. For example, J stands for the unit of energy called a joule, and a mJ indicates a millijoule, or 10^{-3} joules. The table of prefixes is given at the end of this section.

Comparisons among Kelvin, Celsius, and Fahrenheit

One kelvin represents the same temperature difference as 1°C, and the temperature in kelvins is always equal to 273.15 plus the temperature in degrees Celsius. The Celsius scale was designed around the behavior of water. The freezing point of water (at one atmosphere of pressure) was originally defined to be 0°C, while the boiling point is 100°C. The kelvin equals exactly 1.8°F.

To convert temperatures in the Fahrenheit scale to the Celsius scale, use the following equation, where F is degrees Fahrenheit, and C is degrees Celsius:

$$C = (F - 32)/1.8.$$

And to convert Celsius to Fahrenheit, use this equation:

$$F = 1.8C + 32.$$

To convert temperatures in the Celsius scale to the Kelvin scale, add 273.16. By convention, the degree symbol (°) is used for Celsius and Fahrenheit temperatures but not for temperatures given in Kelvin, for example, 0°C equals 273K.

What exactly is temperature? Qualitatively, it is a measurement of how hot something feels, and this definition is so easy to relate to that people seldom take it further. What is really happening in a substance as it gets hot or cold, and how does that change make temperature? When a fixed amount of energy is put into a substance, it heats up by an amount depending on what it is. The temperature of an object, then, has something to do with how the material responds to energy, and that response is called entropy. The entropy of a material (entropy is usually denoted S) is a measure of atomic wiggling and disorder of the atoms in the material. Formally, temperature is defined as

$$\frac{1}{T} = \left(\frac{dS}{dU} \right)_N,$$

meaning one over temperature (the reciprocal of temperature) is defined as the change in entropy (dS, in differential notation) per change in energy (dU), for a given number of atoms (N). What this means in less technical terms is that temperature is a measure of how much heat it takes to increase the entropy (atomic wiggling and disorder) of a substance. Some materials get hotter with less energy, and others require more to reach the same temperature.

The theoretical lower limit of temperature is −459.67°F (−273.15°C, or 0K), known also as absolute zero. This is the temperature at which all atomic movement stops. The Prussian physicist Walther Nernst showed that it is impossible to actually reach absolute zero, though with laboratory methods using nuclear magnetization it is possible to reach 10^{-6}K (0.000001K).

Useful Measures of Distance

A *kilometer* is a thousand meters (see the table "International System Prefixes"), and a *light-year* is the distance light travels in a vacuum during one year (exactly 299,792,458 m/sec, but commonly rounded to 300,000,000 m/sec). A light-year, therefore, is the distance that light can travel in one year, or:

$$299,792,458 \ m/sec \times 60 \ sec/min \times 60 \ min/hr \times 24 \ hr/day \times 365 \ days/yr = 9.4543 \ 3 \ 10^{15} \ m/yr.$$

For shorter distances, some astronomers use light minutes and even light seconds. A light minute is 17,998,775 km, and a light second is 299,812.59 km. The nearest star to Earth, Proxima Centauri, is 4.2 light-years away from the Sun. The next, Rigil Centaurs, is 4.3 light-years away.

An *angstrom* (10^{-10}m) is a unit of length most commonly used in nuclear or particle physics. Its symbol is Å. The diameter of an atom is about one angstrom (though each element and isotope is slightly different).

An astronomical unit (AU) is a unit of distance used by astronomers to measure distances in the solar system. One astronomical unit equals the average distance from the center of the Earth to the center of the Sun. The currently accepted value, made standard in 1996, is 149,597,870,691 meters, plus or minus 30 meters.

One kilometer equals 0.62 miles, and one mile equals 1.61 kilometers.

The following table gives the most commonly used of the units derived from the fundamental units above (there are many more derived units not listed here because they have been developed for specific situations and are little-used elsewhere; for example, in the metric world, the curvature of a railroad track is measured with a unit called "degree of curvature," defined as the angle between two points in a curving track that are separated by a chord of 20 meters).

Though the units are given in alphabetical order for ease of reference, many can fit into one of several broad categories: dimensional units (angle, area, volume), material properties (density, viscosity,

DERIVED UNITS

Measurement	Unit symbol (derivation)	Comments
acceleration	unnamed (m/sec^2)	
angle	radian rad (m/m)	One radian is the angle centered in a circle that includes an arc of length equal to the radius. Since the circumference equals two pi times the radius, one radian equals $1/(2\,pi)$ of the circle, or approximately $57.296°$.
	steradian sr (m^2/m^2)	The steradian is a unit of solid angle. There are four pi steradians in a sphere. Thus one steradian equals about 0.079577 sphere, or about 3282.806 square degrees.
angular velocity	unnamed (rad/sec)	
area	unnamed (m^2)	
density	unnamed (kg/m^3)	Density is mass per volume. Lead is dense, styrofoam is not. Water has a density of one gram per cubic centimeter or 1,000 kilograms per cubic meter.
electric charge or electric flux	coulomb C ($A \cdot sec$)	One coulomb is the amount of charge accumulated in one second by a current of one ampere. One coulomb is also the amount of charge on 6.241506×10^{18} electrons.
electric field strength	unnamed $[(kg \cdot m)/(sec^3 \cdot A) = V/m]$	Electric field strength is a measure of the intensity of an electric field at a particular location. A field strength of one V/m represents a potential difference of one volt between points separated by one meter.
electric potential, or electromotive force (often called voltage)	volt V $[(kg \cdot m^2)/(sec^3 \cdot A) = J/C = W/A]$	Voltage is an expression of the potential difference in charge between two points in an electrical field. Electric potential is defined as the amount of potential energy present per unit of charge. One volt is a potential of one joule per coulomb of charge. The greater the voltage, the greater the flow of electrical current.

Measurement	Unit symbol (derivation)	Comments
energy, work, or heat	joule J [N·m (= kg·m^2/sec^2)]	
	electron volt eV	The electron volt, being so much smaller than the joule (one eV= 1.6 × 10^{-17} J), is useful for describing small systems.
force	newton N (kg·m/sec^2)	This unit is the equivalent to the pound in the English system, since the pound is a measure of force and not mass.
frequency	hertz Hz (cycles/sec)	Frequency is related to wavelength as follows: kilohertz × wavelength in meters = 300,000.
inductance	henry H (Wb/A)	Inductance is the amount of magnetic flux a material produces for a given current of electricity. Metal wire with an electric current passing through it creates a magnetic field; different types of metal make magnetic fields with different strengths and therefore have different inductances.
magnetic field strength	unnamed (A/m)	Magnetic field strength is the force that a magnetic field exerts on a theoretical unit magnetic pole.
magnetic flux	weber Wb [(kg·m^2)/(sec^2·A) = V·sec]	The magnetic flux across a perpendicular surface is the product of the magnetic flux density, in teslas, and the surface area, in square meters.
magnetic flux density	tesla T [kg/(sec^2·A) = Wb/m^2]	A magnetic field of one tesla is strong: The strongest artificial fields made in laboratories are about 20 teslas, and the Earth's magnetic flux density, at its surface, is about 50 microteslas (μT). Planetary magnetic fields are sometimes measured in gammas, which are nanoteslas (10^{-9} teslas).
momentum, or impulse	unnamed [N·sec (= kg· m/sec)]	Momentum is a measure of moving mass: how much mass and how fast it is moving.

(continues)

DERIVED UNITS (*continued*)

Measurement	Unit symbol (derivation)	Comments
power	watt W [J/s (= (kg·m²)/sec³))]	Power is the rate at which energy is spent. Power can be mechanical (as in horsepower) or electrical (a watt is produced by a current of one ampere flowing through an electric potential of one volt).
pressure, or stress	pascal Pa (N/m²)	The high pressures inside planets are often measured in gigapascals (10^9 pascals), abbreviated GPa. ~10,000 atm = one GPa.
	atmosphere atm	The atmosphere is a handy unit because one atmosphere is approximately the pressure felt from the air at sea level on Earth; one standard atm = 101,325 Pa; one metric atm = 98,066 Pa; one atm ~ one bar.
radiation per unit mass receiving it	gray (J/kg)	The amount of radiation energy absorbed per kilogram of mass. One gray = 100 rads, an older unit.
radiation (effect of)	sievert Sv	This unit is meant to make comparable the biological effects of different doses and types of radiation. It is the energy of radiation received per kilogram, in grays, multiplied by a factor that takes into consideration the damage done by the particular type of radiation.
radioactivity (amount)	becquerel Bq	One atomic decay per second
	curie Ci	The curie is the older unit of measure but is still frequently seen. One Ci = 3.7×10^{10} Bq.
resistance	ohm Ω (V/A)	Resistance is a material's unwillingness to pass electric current. Materials with high resistance become hot rather than allowing the current to pass and can make excellent heaters.
thermal expansivity	unnamed (/°)	This unit is per degree, measuring the change in volume of a substance with the rise in temperature.
vacuum	torr	Vacuum is atmospheric pressure below one atm (one torr = 1/760 atm). Given a pool of mercury with a glass tube standing in it, one torr of pressure on the pool will press the mercury one millimeter up into the tube, where one standard atmosphere will push up 760 millimeters of mercury.

Measurement	Unit symbol (derivation)	Comments
velocity	unnamed (m/sec)	
viscosity	unnamed [Pa·sec (= kg/ (m·sec))]	Viscosity is a measure of resistance to flow. If a force of one newton is needed to move one square meter of the liquid or gas relative to a second layer one meter away at a speed of one meter per second, then its viscosity is one Pa·s, often simply written Pa·s or Pas. The cgs unit for viscosity is the poise, equal to 0.1Pa s.
volume	cubic meter (m^3)	

thermal expansivity), properties of motion (velocity, acceleration, angular velocity), electrical properties (frequency, electric charge, electric potential, resistance, inductance, electric field strength), magnetic properties (magnetic field strength, magnetic flux, magnetic flux density), and properties of radioactivity (amount of radioactivity and effect of radioactivity).

Definitions for Electricity and Magnetism

When two objects in each other's vicinity have different electrical charges, an *electric field* exists between them. An electric field also forms around any single object that is electrically charged with respect to its environment. An object is negatively charged (−) if it has an excess of electrons relative to its surroundings. An object is positively charged (+) if it is deficient in electrons with respect to its surroundings.

An electric field has an effect on other charged objects in the vicinity. The field strength at a particular distance from an object is directly proportional to the electric charge of that object, in coulombs. The field strength is inversely proportional to the distance from a charged object.

Flux is the rate (per unit of time) in which something flowing crosses a surface perpendicular to the direction of flow.

An alternative expression for the intensity of an electric field is *electric flux density*. This refers to the number of lines of electric flux passing at right angles through a given surface area, usually one meter squared (1 m²). Electric flux density, like electric field strength, is directly proportional to the charge on the object. But flux density diminishes with distance according to the inverse-square law because it is specified in terms of a surface area (per meter squared) rather than a linear displacement (per meter).

INTERNATIONAL SYSTEM PREFIXES

SI prefix	Symbol	Multiplying factor
exa-	E	10^{18} = 1,000,000,000,000,000,000
peta-	P	10^{15} = 1,000,000,000,000,000
tera-	T	10^{12} = 1,000,000,000,000
giga-	G	10^{9} = 1,000,000,000
mega-	M	10^{6} = 1,000,000
kilo-	K	10^{3} = 1,000
hecto-	h	10^{2} = 100
deca-	da	10 = 10
deci-	d	10^{-1} = 0.1
centi-	c	10^{-2} = 0.01
milli-	m	10^{-3} = 0.001
micro-	μ or u	10^{-6} = 0.000,001
nano-	n	10^{-9} = 0.000,000,001
pico-	p	10^{-12} = 0.000,000,000,001
femto-	f	10^{-15} = 0.000,000,000,000,001
atto-	a	10^{-18} = 0.000,000,000,000,000,001

A note on nonmetric prefixes: In the United States, the word billion means the number 1,000,000,000, or 10^9. In most countries of Europe and Latin America, this number is called "one milliard" or "one thousand million," and "billion" means the number 1,000,000,000,000, or 10^{12}, which is what Americans call a "trillion." In this set, a billion is 10^9.

NAMES FOR LARGE NUMBERS

Number	American	European	SI prefix
10^9	billion	milliard	giga-
10^{12}	trillion	billion	tera-
10^{15}	quadrillion	billiard	peta-
10^{18}	quintillion	trillion	exa-
10^{21}	sextillion	trilliard	zetta-
10^{24}	septillion	quadrillion	yotta-
10^{27}	octillion	quadrilliard	
10^{30}	nonillion	quintillion	
10^{33}	decillion	quintilliard	
10^{36}	undecillion	sextillion	
10^{39}	duodecillion	sextilliard	
10^{42}	tredecillion	septillion	
10^{45}	quattuordecillion	septilliard	

This naming system is designed to expand indefinitely by factors of powers of three. Then, there is also the googol, the number 10^{100} (one followed by 100 zeroes). The googol was invented for fun by the eight-year-old nephew of the American mathematician Edward Kasner. The googolplex is 10^{googol}, or one followed by a googol of zeroes. Both it and the googol are numbers larger than the total number of atoms in the universe, thought to be about 10^{80}.

A *magnetic field* is generated when electric charge carriers such as electrons move through space or within an electrical conductor. The geometric shapes of the magnetic flux lines produced by moving charge carriers (electric current) are similar to the shapes of the flux lines in an electrostatic field. But there are differences in the ways electrostatic and magnetic fields interact with the environment.

Electrostatic flux is impeded or blocked by metallic objects. *Magnetic flux* passes through most metals with little or no effect, with certain exceptions, notably iron and nickel. These two metals, and alloys and mixtures containing them, are known as ferromagnetic materials because they concentrate magnetic lines of flux.

Magnetic flux density and *magnetic force* are related to *magnetic field strength*. In general, the magnetic field strength diminishes with increasing distance from the axis of a magnetic dipole in which the flux field is stable. The function defining the rate at which this field-strength decrease occurs depends on the geometry of the magnetic lines of flux (the shape of the flux field).

Prefixes

Adding a prefix to the name of that unit forms a multiple of a unit in the International System (see the table "International System Prefixes"). The prefixes change the magnitude of the unit by orders of 10 from 10^{18} to 10^{-18}.

Very small concentrations of chemicals are also measured in parts per million (ppm) or parts per billion (ppb), which mean just what they sound like: If there are four parts per million of lead in a rock (4 ppm), then out of every million atoms in that rock, on average four of them will be lead.

Appendix 2:
Light, Wavelength, and Radiation

Electromagnetic radiation is energy given off by matter, traveling in the form of waves or particles. Electromagnetic energy exists in a wide range of energy values, of which visible light is one small part of the total spectrum. The source of radiation may be the hot and therefore highly energized atoms of the Sun, pouring out radiation across a wide range of energy values, including of course visible light, and they may also be unstable (radioactive) elements giving off radiation as they decay.

Radiation is called "electromagnetic" because it moves as interlocked waves of electrical and magnetic fields. A wave is a disturbance traveling through space, transferring energy from one point to the next. In a vacuum, all electromagnetic radiation travels at the speed of light, 983,319,262 feet per second (299,792,458 m/sec, often approximated as 300,000,000 m/sec). Depending on the type of radiation, the waves have different wavelengths, energies, and frequencies (see the following figure). The wavelength is the distance between individual waves, from one peak to another. The frequency is the number of waves that pass a stationary point each second. Notice in the graphic how the wave undulates up and down from peaks to valleys to peaks. The time from one peak to the next peak is called one cycle. A single unit of frequency is equal to one cycle per second. Scientists refer to a single cycle as one hertz, which commemorates 19th-century German physicist Heinrich Hertz, whose discovery of electromagnetic waves led to the development of radio. The frequency of a wave is related to its energy: The higher the frequency of a wave, the higher its energy, though its speed in a vacuum does not change.

The smallest wavelength, highest energy and frequency electromagnetic waves are cosmic rays, then as wavelength increases and energy

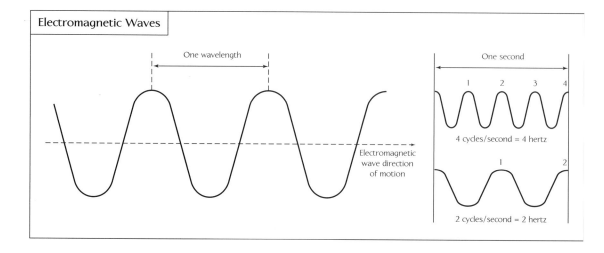

Electromagnetic Waves

One wavelength

Electromagnetic wave direction of motion

One second

4 cycles/second = 4 hertz

2 cycles/second = 2 hertz

Each electromagnetic wave has a measurable wavelength and frequency.

and frequency decrease, come gamma rays, then X-rays, then ultraviolet light, then visible light (moving from violet through indigo, blue, green, yellow, orange, and red), then infrared (divided into near, meaning near to visible, mid-, and far infrared), then microwaves, and then radio waves, which have the longest wavelengths and the lowest energy and frequency. The electromagnetic spectrum is shown in the accompanying figure and table.

As a wave travels and vibrates up and down with its characteristic wavelength, it can be imagined as vibrating up and down in a single plane, such as the plane of this sheet of paper in the case of the simple example in the figure here showing polarization. In nature, some waves change their polarization constantly so that their polarization sweeps through all angles, and they are said to be circularly polarized. In ordinary visible light, the waves are vibrating up and down in numerous random planes. Light can be shone through a special filter called a polarizing filter that blocks out all the light except that polarized in a certain direction, and the light that shines out the other side of the filter is then called polarized light.

Polarization is important in wireless communications systems such as radios, cell phones, and non-cable television. The orientation of the transmitting antenna creates the polarization of the radio waves transmitted by that antenna: A vertical antenna emits vertically polarized waves, and a horizontal antenna emits horizontally polarized waves. Similarly, a horizontal antenna is best at receiving horizontally polarized waves and a vertical antenna at vertically polarized waves. The best communications are obtained when the source and receiver antennas have the same polarization. This is why, when trying to adjust television antennas to get a better signal, having the two antennae at right angles to each other can maximize the chances of receiving a signal.

The human eye stops being able to detect radiation at wavelengths between 3,000 and 4,000 angstroms, which is deep violet—also the

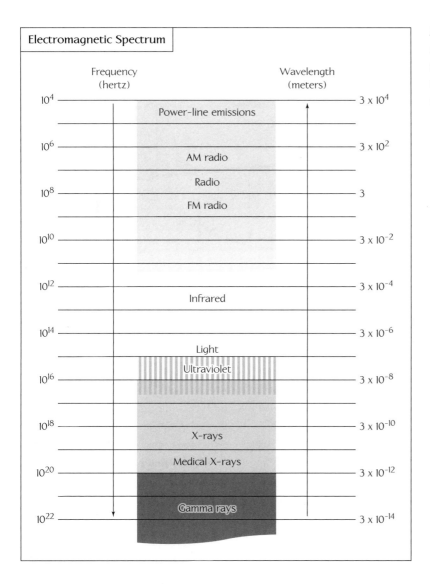

Electromagnetic Spectrum

Frequency (hertz)		Wavelength (meters)
10^4	Power-line emissions	3×10^4
10^6	AM radio	3×10^2
	Radio	
10^8	FM radio	3
10^{10}		3×10^{-2}
10^{12}	Infrared	3×10^{-4}
10^{14}	Light	3×10^{-6}
10^{16}	Ultraviolet	3×10^{-8}
10^{18}	X-rays	3×10^{-10}
10^{20}	Medical X-rays	3×10^{-12}
10^{22}	Gamma rays	3×10^{-14}

Electromagnetic spectrum ranges from cosmic rays at the shortest wavelengths to radiowaves at the longest wavelengths.

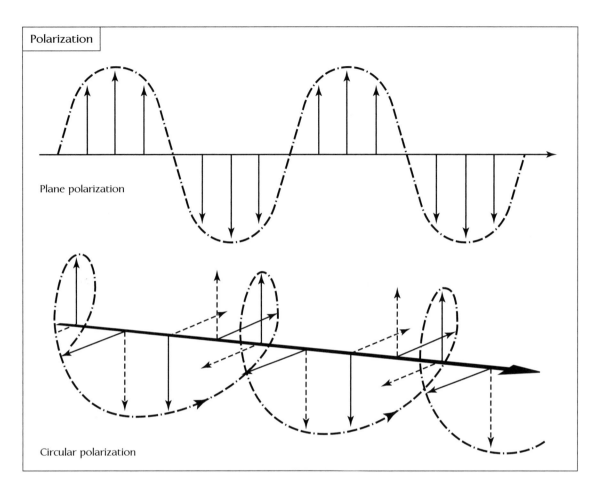

Polarization

Plane polarization

Circular polarization

Waves can be thought of as plane or circularly polarized.

rough limit on transmissions through the atmosphere (see the table "Wavelengths and Frequencies of Visible Light"). (Three thousand to 4,000 angstroms is the same as 300–400 nm because an angstrom is 10^{-9} m, while the prefix nano- or n means 10^{-10}; for more, see appendix 1, "Units and Measurements.") Of visible light, the colors red, orange, yellow, green, blue, indigo, and violet are listed in order from longest wavelength and lowest energy to shortest wavelength and highest energy. Sir Isaac Newton, the spectacular English physicist and mathematician, first found that a glass prism split sunlight into a rainbow of colors. He named this a "spectrum," after the Latin word for ghost.

If visible light strikes molecules of gas as it passes through the atmosphere, it may get absorbed as energy by the molecule. After a short amount of time, the molecule releases the light, most probably in a different direction. The color that is radiated is the same color that was absorbed. All the colors of visible light can be absorbed by atmospheric molecules, but the higher energy blue light is absorbed more often than the lower energy red light. This process is called

WAVELENGTHS AND FREQUENCIES OF VISIBLE LIGHT

Visible light color	Wavelength (in Å, angstroms)	Frequency (times 10^{14} Hz)
violet	4,000–4,600	7.5–6.5
indigo	4,600–4,750	6.5–6.3
blue	4,750–4,900	6.3–6.1
green	4,900–5,650	6.1–5.3
yellow	5,650–5,750	5.3–5.2
orange	5,750–6,000	5.2–5.0
red	6,000–8,000	5.0–3.7

WAVELENGTHS AND FREQUENCIES OF THE ELECTROMAGNETIC SPECTRUM

Energy	Frequency in hertz (Hz)	Wavelength in meters
cosmic rays	everything higher in energy than gamma rays	everything lower in wavelength than gamma rays
gamma rays	10^{20} to 10^{24}	less than 10^{-12} m
X-rays	10^{17} to 10^{20}	1 nm to 1 pm
ultraviolet	10^{15} to 10^{17}	400 nm to 1 nm
visible	4×10^{14} to 7.5×10^{14}	750 nm to 400 nm
near-infrared	1×10^{14} to 4×10^{14}	2.5 μm to 750 nm
infrared	10^{13} to 10^{14}	25 μm to 2.5 μm
microwaves	3×10^{11} to 10^{13}	1 mm to 25 μm
radio waves	less than 3×10^{11}	more than 1 mm

COMMON USES FOR RADIO WAVES

User	Approximate frequency
AM radio	0.535×10^6 to 1.7×10^6 Hz
baby monitors	49×10^6 Hz
cordless phones	49×10^6 Hz
	900×10^6 Hz
	$2,400 \times 10^6$ Hz
television channels 2 through 6	54×10^6 to 88×10^6 Hz
radio-controlled planes	72×10^6 Hz
radio-controlled cars	75×10^6 Hz
FM radio	88×10^6 to 108×10^6 Hz
television channels 7 through 13	174×10^6 to 220×10^6 Hz
wildlife tracking collars	215×10^6 Hz
cell phones	800×10^6 Hz
	$2,400 \times 10^6$ Hz
air traffic control radar	960×10^6 Hz
	$1,215 \times 10^6$ Hz
global positioning systems	$1,227 \times 10^6$ Hz
	$1,575 \times 10^6$ Hz
deep space radio	$2,300 \times 10^6$ Hz

Rayleigh scattering (named after Lord John Rayleigh, an English physicist who first described it in the 1870s).

The blue color of the sky is due to Rayleigh scattering. As light moves through the atmosphere, most of the longer wavelengths pass straight through: The air affects little of the red, orange, and yellow light. The gas molecules absorb much of the shorter wavelength blue light. The absorbed blue light is then radiated in different directions and is scattered all around the sky. Whichever direction you look, some of this scattered blue light reaches you. Since you see the blue light from everywhere overhead, the sky looks blue. Note also that there is a very different kind of scattering, in which the light is simply bounced off larger objects like pieces of dust and water droplets, rather than being absorbed by a molecule of gas in the atmosphere and then reemitted. This bouncing kind of scattering is responsible for red sunrises and sunsets.

Until the end of the 18th century, people thought that visible light was the only kind of light. The amazing amateur astronomer Frederick William Herschel (the discoverer of Uranus) discovered the first non-visible light, the infrared. He thought that each color of visible light had a different temperature and devised an experiment to measure the temperature of each color of light. The temperatures went up as the colors progressed from violet through red, and then Herschel decided to measure past red, where he found the highest temperature yet. This was the first demonstration that there was a kind of radiation that could not be seen by the human eye. Herschel originally named this range of radiation "calorific rays," but the name was later changed to infrared, meaning "below red." Infrared radiation has become an important way of sensing solar system objects and is also used in night-vision goggles and various other practical purposes.

At lower energies and longer wavelengths than the visible and infrared, microwaves are commonly used to transmit energy to food in microwave ovens, as well as for some communications, though radio waves are more common in this use. There is a wide range of frequencies in the radio spectrum, and they are used in many ways, as shown in the table "Common Uses for Radio Waves," including television, radio, and cell phone transmissions. Note that the frequency units are given in terms of 10^6 Hz, without correcting for each coefficient's additional factors of 10. This is because 10^6 Hz corresponds to the unit of megahertz (MHz), which is a commonly used unit of frequency.

Cosmic rays, gamma rays, and X-rays, the three highest-energy radiations, are known as ionizing radiation because they contain enough energy that, when they hit an atom, they may knock an electron off of it or otherwise change the atom's weight or structure. These ionizing radiations, then, are particularly dangerous to living things; for example, they can damage DNA molecules (though good use is made of them as well, to see into bodies with X-rays and to kill cancer cells with gamma rays). Luckily the atmosphere stops most ionizing radiation, but not all of it. Cosmic rays created by the Sun in solar flares, or sent off as a part of the solar wind, are relatively low energy. There are far more energetic cosmic rays, though, that come from distant stars through interstellar space. These are energetic enough to penetrate into an asteroid as deeply as a meter and can often make it through the atmosphere.

When an atom of a radioisotope decays, it gives off some of its excess energy as radiation in the form of X-rays, gamma rays, or fast-moving subatomic particles: alpha particles (two protons and two neutrons, bound together as an atomic *nucleus*), or beta particles (fast-moving electrons), or a combination of two or more of these products. If it decays with emission of an alpha or beta particle, it becomes a new element. These decay products can be described as gamma, beta, and alpha radiation. By decaying, the atom is progressing in one or more steps toward a stable state where it is no longer radioactive.

RADIOACTIVITY OF SELECTED OBJECTS AND MATERIALS

Object or material	Radioactivity
1 adult human (100 Bq/kg)	7,000 Bq
1 kg coffee	1,000 Bq
1 kg high-phosphate fertilizer	5,000 Bq
1 household smoke detector (with the element americium)	30,000 Bq
radioisotope source for cancer therapy	100 million million Bq
1 kg 50-year-old vitrified high-level nuclear waste	10 million million Bq
1 kg uranium ore (Canadian ore, 15% uranium)	25 million Bq
1 kg uranium ore (Australian ore, 0.3% uranium)	500,000 Bq
1 kg granite	1,000 Bq

The X-rays and gamma rays from decaying atoms are identical to those from other natural sources. Like other ionizing radiation, they can damage living tissue but can be blocked by lead sheets or by thick concrete. Alpha particles are much larger and can be blocked more quickly by other material; a sheet of paper or the outer layer of skin on your hand will stop them. If the atom that produces them is taken inside the body, however, such as when a person breathes in radon gas, the alpha particle can do damage to the lungs. Beta particles are more energetic and smaller and can penetrate a couple of centimeters into a person's body.

But why can both radioactive decay that is formed of subatomic particles and heat that travels as a wave of energy be considered radiation? One of Albert Einstein's great discoveries is called the photoelectric effect: Subatomic particles can all behave as either a wave or a particle. The smaller the particle, the more wavelike it is. The best example of this is light itself, which behaves almost entirely as a wave, but there is the particle equivalent for light, the massless photon. Even alpha particles, the largest decay product discussed here, can act like a wave, though their wavelike properties are much harder to detect.

The amount of radioactive material is given in becquerel (Bq), a measure that enables us to compare the typical radioactivity of some natural and other materials. A becquerel is one atomic decay per second. Radioactivity is still sometimes measured using a unit called a Curie; a Becquerel is 27×10^{-12} Curies. There are materials made mainly of radioactive elements, like uranium, but most materials are made mainly of stable atoms. Even materials made mainly of stable atoms, however, almost always have trace amounts of radioactive elements in them, and so even common objects give off some level of radiation, as shown in the following table.

Background radiation is all around us all the time. Naturally occurring radioactive elements are more common in some kinds of rocks than others; for example, *granite* carries more radioactive elements than does sandstone; therefore a person working in a bank built of granite will receive more radiation than someone who works in a wooden building. Similarly, the atmosphere absorbs cosmic rays, but the higher the elevation, the more cosmic-ray exposure there is. A person living in Denver or in the mountains of Tibet is exposed to more cosmic rays than someone living in Boston or in the Netherlands.

Appendix 3:
A List of All Known Moons

Though Mercury and Venus have no moons, the other planets in the solar system have at least one. Some moons, such as Earth's Moon and Jupiter's Galileans satellites, are thought to have formed at the same time as their accompanying planet. Many other moons appear simply to be captured asteroids; for at least half of Jupiter's moons, this seems to be the case. These small, irregular moons are difficult to detect from Earth, and so the lists given in the table below must be considered works in progress for the gas giant planets. More moons will certainly be discovered with longer observation and better instrumentation.

MOONS KNOWN AS OF 2005

Earth	Mars	Jupiter	Saturn	Uranus	Neptune	Pluto
1. Moon	1. Phobos	1. Metis	1. Pan	1. Cordelia	1. Naiad	1. Charon
	2. Diemos	2. Adrastea	2. Atlas	2. Ophelia	2. Thalassa	
		3. Amalthea	3. Prometheus	3. Bianca	3. Despina	
		4. Thebe	4. Pandora	4. Cressida	4. Galatea	
		5. Io	5. Epimetheus	5. Desdemona	5. Larissa	
		6. Europa	6. Janus	6. Juliet	6. Proteus	
		7. Ganymede	7. S/2004 S1	7. Portia	7. Triton	
		8. Callisto	8. S/2004 S2	8. Rosalind	8. Nereid	

Earth	Mars	Jupiter	Saturn	Uranus	Neptune	Pluto
		9. Themisto	9. Mimas	9. 2003 U2	9. S/2002 N1	
		10. Leda	10. Enceladus	10. Belinda	10. S/2002 N2	
		11. Himalia	11. Tethys	11. 1986 U10	11. S/2002 N3	
		12. Lysithea	12. Telesto	12. Puck	12. S/2003 N1	
		13. Elara	13. Calypso	13. 2003 U1	13. S/2002 N4	
		14. S/2000 J11	14. Dione	14. Miranda		
		15. Euporie	15. Helene	15. Ariel		
		16. Orthosie	16. Rhea	16. Umbriel		
		17. Euanthe	17. Titan	17. Titania		
		18. Thyone	18. Hyperion	18. Oberon		
		19. Harpalyke	19. Iapetus	19. 2001 U3		
		20. Hermippe	20. Kiviuq	20. Caliban		
		21. Praxidike	21. Ijiraq	21. Stephano		
		22. Iocaste	22. Phoebe	22. Trinculo		
		23. Ananke	23. Paaliaq	23. Sycorax		
		24. S/2002 J1	24. Skathi	24. 2003 U3		
		25. Pasithee	25. Albiorix	25. Prospero		
		26. Chaldene	26. Erriapo	26. Setebos		
		27. Kale	27. Siarnaq	27. 2001 U2		
		28. Isonoe	28. Tarvos			
		29. Aitne	29. Mundilfari			
		30. Erinome	30. S/2003 S1			
		31. Taygete	31. Suttungr			
		32. Carme	32. Thrymr			
		33. Kalyke	33. Ymir			

Jupiter (continued)

34. Eurydome	35. Autonoe	36. Sponde	37. Pasiphae	38. Magaclite	39. Sinope
40. Calirrhoe	41. S/2003 J1	42. S/2003 J2	43. S/2003 J3	44. S/2003 J4	45. S/2003 J5
46. S/2003 J6	47. S/2003 J7	48. S/2003 J8	49. S/2003 J9	50. S/2003 J10	51. S/2003 J11
52. S/2003 J12	53. S/2003 J13	54. S/2003 J14	55. S/2003 J15	56. S/2003 J16	57. S/2003 J17
58. S/2003 J18	59. S/2003 J19	60. S/2003 J20	61. S/2003 J21	62. S/2003 J22	63. S/2003 J23

Glossary

accretion   The accumulation of celestial gas, dust, or smaller bodies by gravitational attraction into a larger body, such as a planet or an asteroid

albedo   The light reflected by an object as a fraction of the light shining on an object; mirrors have high albedo, while charcoal has low albedo

anorthite   A calcium-rich plagioclase mineral with compositional formula $CaAl_2Si_2O_8$, significant for making up the majority of the rock anorthosite in the crust of the Moon

anticyclone   An area of increased atmospheric pressure relative to the surrounding pressure field in the atmosphere, resulting in circular flow in a clockwise direction north of the equator and in a counterclockwise direction to the south

aphelion   A distance; the farthest from the Sun an object travels in its orbit

apogee   As for aphelion but for any orbital system (not confined to the Sun)

apparent magnitude   The brightness of a celestial object as it would appear from a given distance—the lower the number, the brighter the object

atom   The smallest quantity of an element that can take part in a chemical reaction; consists of a nucleus of protons and neutrons, surrounded by a cloud of electrons; each atom is about 10^{-10} meters in diameter, or one angstrom

atomic number   The number of protons in an atom's nucleus

AU   An AU is an astronomical unit, defined as the distance from the Sun to the Earth; approximately 93 million miles, or 150 million kilometers. For more information, refer to the UNITS AND MEASUREMENTS appendix

basalt   A generally dark-colored extrusive igneous rock most commonly created by melting a planet's mantle; its low silica content indicates that it has not been significantly altered on its passage to the planet's surface

bolide An object falling into a planet's atmosphere, when a specific identification as a comet or asteroid cannot be made

bow shock The area of compression in a flowing fluid when it strikes an object or another fluid flowing at another rate; for example, the bow of a boat and the water, or the magnetic field of a planet and the flowing solar wind

breccia Material that has been shattered from grinding, as in a fault, or from impact, as by meteorites or other solar system bodies

chondrite A class of meteorite thought to contain the most primitive material left from the solar nebula; named after their glassy, super-primitive inclusions called chondrules

chondrule Rounded, glassy, and crystalline bodies incorporated into the more primitive of meteorites; thought to be the condensed droplets of the earliest solar system materials

clinopyroxene A common mineral in the mantle and igneous rocks, with compositional formula $((Ca,Mg,Fe,Al)_2(Si,Al)_2O_6)$

conjunction When the Sun is between the Earth and the planet or another body in question

convection Material circulation upward and downward in a gravity field caused by horizontal gradients in density; an example is the hot, less dense bubbles that form at the bottom of a pot, rise, and are replaced by cooler, denser sinking material

core The innermost material within a differentiated body such as a planet or the Sun

Coriolis force The effect of movement on a rotating sphere; movement in the Northern Hemisphere curves to the right, while movement in the Southern Hemisphere curves to the left

craton The ancient, stable interior cores of the Earth's continents

crust The outermost layer of most differentiated bodies, often consisting of the least dense products of volcanic events or other buoyant material

cryovolcanism Non-silicate materials erupted from icy and gassy bodies in the cold outer solar system; for example, as suspected or seen on the moons Enceladus, Europa, Titan, and Triton

cubewano Any large Kuiper belt object orbiting between about 41 AU and 48 AU but not controlled by orbital resonances with Neptune; the odd name is derived from 1992 QB_1, the first Kuiper belt object found

cyclone   An area in the atmosphere in which the pressures are lower than those of the surrounding region at the same level, resulting in circular motion in a counterclockwise direction north of the equator and in a clockwise direction to the south

differential rotation   Rotation at different rates at different latitudes, requiring a liquid or gassy body, such as the Sun or Jupiter

differentiated body   A spherical body that has a structure of concentric spherical layers, differing in terms of composition, heat, density, and/or motion; caused by gravitational separations and heating events such as planetary accretion

dipole   Two associated magnetic poles, one positive and one negative, creating a magnetic field

direct (prograde)   Rotation or orbit in the same direction as the Earth's, that is, counterclockwise when viewed from above its North Pole

distributary   River channels that branch from the main river channel, carrying flow away from the central channel; usually form fans of channels at a river's delta

eccentricity   The amount by which an ellipse differs from a circle

ecliptic   The imaginary plane that contains the Earth's orbit and from which the planes of other planets' orbits deviate slightly (Pluto the most, by 17 degrees); the ecliptic makes an angle of 7 degrees with the plane of the Sun's equator

ejecta   Material thrown out of the site of a crater by the force of the impactor

element   A family of atoms that all have the same number of positively charged particles in their nuclei (the center of the atom)

ellipticity   The amount by which a planet's shape deviates from a sphere

equinox   One of two points in a planet's orbit when day and night have the same length; vernal equinox occurs in Earth's spring and autumnal equinox in the fall

exosphere   The uppermost layer of a planet's atmosphere

extrasolar   Outside this solar system

garnet   The red, green, or purple mineral that contains the majority of the aluminum in the Earth's upper mantle; its compositional formula is $((Ca,Mg,Fe\ Mn)_3(Al,Fe,Cr,Ti)_2(SiO_4)_3)$

graben   A low area longer than it is wide and bounded from adjoining higher areas by faults; caused by extension in the crust

granite   An intrusive igneous rock with high silica content and some minerals containing water; in this solar system thought to be found only on Earth

half-life   The time it takes for half a population of an unstable isotope to decay

hydrogen burning   The most basic process of nuclear fusion in the cores of stars that produces helium and radiation from hydrogen

igneous rock   Rock that was once hot enough to be completely molten

impactor   A generic term for the object striking and creating a crater in another body

inclination   As commonly used in planetary science, the angle between the plane of a planet's orbit and the plane of the ecliptic

isotope   Atoms with the same number of protons (and are therefore the same type of element) but different numbers of neutrons; may be stable or radioactive and occur in different relative abundances

lander   A spacecraft designed to land on another solar system object rather than flying by, orbiting, or entering the atmosphere and then burning up or crashing

lithosphere   The uppermost layer of a terrestrial planet consisting of stiff material that moves as one unit if there are plate tectonic forces and does not convect internally but transfers heat from the planet's interior through conduction

magnetic moment   The torque (turning force) exerted on a magnet when it is placed in a magnetic field

magnetopause   The surface between the magnetosheath and the magnetosphere of a planet

magnetosheath   The compressed, heated portion of the solar wind where it piles up against a planetary magnetic field

magnetosphere   The volume of a planet's magnetic field, shaped by the internal planetary source of the magnetism and by interactions with the solar wind

magnitude   See APPARENT MAGNITUDE

mantle   The spherical shell of a terrestrial planet between crust and core; thought to consist mainly of silicate minerals

mass number   The number of protons plus neutrons in an atom's nucleus

mesosphere   The atmospheric layer between the stratosphere and the thermosphere

metamorphic rock   Rock that has been changed from its original state by heat or pressure but was never liquid

mid-ocean ridge   The line of active volcanism in oceanic basins from which two oceanic plates are produced, one moving away from each side of the ridge; only exist on Earth

mineral   A naturally occurring inorganic substance having an orderly internal structure (usually crystalline) and characteristic chemical composition

nucleus   The center of the atom, consisting of protons (positively charged) and neutrons (no electric charge); tiny in volume but makes up almost all the mass of the atom

nutation   The slow wobble of a planet's rotation axis along a line of longitude, causing changes in the planet's obliquity

obliquity   The angle between a planet's equatorial plane to its orbit plane

occultation   The movement of one celestial body in front of another from a particular point of view; most commonly the movement of a planet in front of a star from the point of view of an Earth viewer

olivine   Also known as the gem peridot, the green mineral that makes up the majority of the upper mantle; its compositional formula is $((Mg, Fe)_2SiO_4)$

one-plate planet   A planet with lithosphere that forms a continuous spherical shell around the whole planet, not breaking into plates or moving with tectonics; Mercury, Venus, and Mars are examples

opposition   When the Earth is between the Sun and the planet of interest

orbital period   The time required for an object to make a complete circuit along its orbit

parent body   The larger body that has been broken to produce smaller pieces; large bodies in the asteroid belt are thought to be the parent bodies of meteorites that fall to Earth today

perigee   As for perihelion but for any orbital system (not confined to the Sun)

perihelion   A distance; the closest approach to the Sun made in an object's orbit

planetesimal   The small, condensed bodies that formed early in the solar system and presumably accreted to make the planets; probably resembled comets or asteroids

plate tectonics   The movement of lithospheric plates relative to each other, only known on Earth

precession   The movement of a planet's axis of rotation that causes the axis to change its direction of tilt, much as the direction of the axis of a toy top rotates as it slows

prograde (direct)   Rotates or orbits in the same direction the Earth does, that is, counterclockwise when viewed from above its North Pole

protoplanetary disk   The flattened nebular cloud before the planets accrete

radioactive   An atom prone to radiodecay

radio-decay   The conversion of an atom into a different atom or isotope through emission of energy or subatomic particles

red, reddened   A solar system body with a redder color in visible light, but more important, one that has increased albedo at low wavelengths (the "red" end of the spectrum)

refractory   An element that requires unusually high temperatures in order to melt or evaporate; compare to volatile

relief (topographic relief)   The shapes of the surface of land; most especially the high parts such as hills or mountains

resonance   When the ratio of the orbital periods of two bodies is an integer; for example, if one moon orbits its planet once for every two times another moon orbits, the two are said to be in resonance

retrograde   Rotates or orbits in the opposite direction to Earth, that is, clockwise when viewed from above its North Pole

Roche limit   The radius around a given planet that a given satellite must be outside of in order to remain intact; within the Roche limit, the satellite's self-gravity will be overcome by gravitational tidal forces from the planet, and the satellite will be torn apart

rock   Material consisting of the aggregate of minerals

sedimentary rock   Rock made of mineral grains that were transported by water or air

seismic waves   Waves of energy propagating through a planet, caused by earthquakes or other impulsive forces, such as meteorite impacts and human-made explosions

semimajor axis   Half the widest diameter of an orbit

semiminor axis   Half the narrowest diameter of an orbit

silicate   A molecule, crystal, or compound made from the basic building block silica (SiO_2); the Earth's mantle is made of silicates, while its core is made of metals

spectrometer   An instrument that separates electromagnetic radiation, such as light, into wavelengths, creating a spectrum

stratosphere   The layer of the atmosphere located between the troposphere and the mesosphere, characterized by a slight temperature increase and absence of clouds

subduction   Movement of one lithospheric plate beneath another

subduction zone   A compressive boundary between two lithospheric plates, where one plate (usually an oceanic plate) is sliding beneath the other and plunging at an angle into the mantle

synchronous orbit radius   The orbital radius at which the satellite's orbital period is equal to the rotational period of the planet; contrast with synchronous rotation

synchronous rotation   When the same face of a moon is always toward its planet, caused by the period of the moon's rotation about its axis being the same as the period of the moon's orbit around its planet; most moons rotate synchronously due to tidal locking

tacholine   The region in the Sun where differential rotation gives way to solid-body rotation, creating a shear zone and perhaps the body's magnetic field as well; is at the depth of about one-third of the Sun's radius

terrestrial planet   A planet similar to the Earth—rocky and metallic and in the inner solar system; includes Mercury, Venus, Earth, and Mars

thermosphere   The atmospheric layer between the mesosphere and the exosphere

tidal locking   The tidal (gravitational) pull between two closely orbiting bodies that causes the bodies to settle into stable orbits with the same faces toward each other at all times; this final stable state is called synchronous rotation

tomography   The technique of creating images of the interior of the Earth using the slightly different speeds of earthquake waves that have traveled along different paths through the Earth

tropopause   The point in the atmosphere of any planet where the temperature reaches a minimum; both above and below this height, temperatures rise

troposphere   The lower regions of a planetary atmosphere, where convection keeps the gas mixed, and there is a steady decrease in temperature with height above the surface

viscosity   A liquid's resistance to flowing; honey has higher viscosity than water

visual magnitude   The brightness of a celestial body as seen from Earth categorized on a numerical scale; the brightest star has magnitude −1.4 and the faintest visible star has magnitude 6; a decrease of one unit represents an increase in brightness by a factor of 2.512; system begun by Ptolemy in the second century B.C.E.; see also apparent magnitude

volatile   An element that moves into a liquid or gas state at relatively low temperatures; compare with refractory

Bibliography and Further Reading

Beatty, J. K., C. C. Petersen, and A. Chaikin. *The New Solar System.* Cambridge: Sky Publishing and Cambridge University Press, 1999.

Booth, N. *Exploring the Solar System.* Cambridge: Cambridge University Press, 1995.

Boyet, M., J. Blichert-Toft, M. Rosing, M. Storey, P. Télouk, and F. Albarède. "^{142}Nd evidence for early Earth differentiation." *Earth and Planetary Science Letters* 214 (2003): 427–442.

Bussey, D. B. J., P. G. Lucey, D. Steutel, M. S. Robinson, P. D. Spudis, and K. D. Edwards. "Permanent shadow in simple craters near the lunar poles." *Geophysical Research Letters* 30, no. 6 (2003): 1,278.

Canup, R., and E. Asphaug. "Origin of the Moon in a giant impact near the end of the Earth's formation." *Nature* 412 (2001): 708–712.

Dickin, A. P. *Radiogenic Isotope Geology.* Cambridge: Cambridge University Press, 1995.

Dziewonski, A. M., and D. L. Anderson. "Preliminary Earth reference model." *Physics of the Earth and Planetary Interiors* 25 (1982): 297–356.

Elkins-Tanton, L. T., N. Chatterjee, and T. L. Grove. "Experimental and petrological constraints on lunar differentiation from the *Apollo 15* green picritic glasses." *Meteoritics and Planetary Science* 38 (2003): 515–527.

———, B. H. Hager, and T. L. Grove. "Magmatic effects of the Lunar Late Heavy Bombardment." *Earth and Planetary Science Letters* 222 (2004): 17–27.

Harper, C. L., and S. B. Jacobsen. "Evidence from couples ^{147}Sm-^{143}Nd and ^{146}Sm-^{142}Nd systematics for very early (4.5-Gyr) differentiation of the Earth's mantle." *Nature* 360 (1992): 728–732.

Kasting, J. F. "The origins of water on Earth." *Scientific American,* special volume (2003): 28–33.

Kellogg, L. H., B. H. Hager, and R. D. van der Hilst. "Compositional stratification in the deep mantle." *Science* 283 (1999): 1,881–1,884.

Seager, Sara. "The search for extrasolar Earth-like planets." *Earth and Planetary Science Letters* 208 (2003): 113–124.

Spence, P. *The Universe Revealed.* Cambridge: Cambridge University Press, 1998.

Stacey, Frank D. *Physics of the Earth.* Brisbane, Australia: Brookfield Press, 1992.

Van der Hilst, R. D., S. Widiyantoro, and E. R. Engdahl. "Evidence for deep mantle circulation from global tomography" *Nature* 386 (1997): 578.

Wilde, S. A., J. W. Valley, W. H. Peck, and C. M. Graham. "Evidence from detrital zircons for the existence of continental crust and oceans on the Earth 5.5 Gyr ago." *Nature* 409 (2001): 175–178.

Williams, G. E. "Geological constraints on the pre-Cambrian history of the Earth's rotation and the Moon's orbit." *Reviews in Geophysics* 38 (2000): 37–59.

Wolszczan, A., and D. Frail. "A planetary system around the millisecond pulsar PSR1257+12." *Nature* 255 (1992): 145–147.

Yin, Qingzhu, S. B. Jacobsen, J. Blichert-Toft, P. Telouk, and F. Albarède. "A short timescale for terrestrial planet formation from Hf-W chronometry of meteorites." *Nature* 418 (2002): 949–952.

Internet Resources

Blue, Jennifer, and the Working Group for Planetary System Nomenclature. "Gazetteer of Planetary Nomenclature," United States Geological Survey. Available online. URL: http://planetarynames.wr.usgs.gov. Accessed May 17, 2004. Complete and official rules for naming planetary features, along with list of all named planetary features and downloadable images.

LaVoie, Sue, Myche McAuley, and Elizabeth Duxbury Rye. "Planetary Photojournal." Available online. URL: http://photojournal.jpl.nasa.gov. Accessed January 2002. Large database of public-domain images from space missions.

O'Connor, John J., and Edmund F. Robertson. "The MacTutor History of Mathematics Archive." Available online. URL: http://www-gap.dcs.st-and.ac.uk/~history. Accessed January 2002. A scholarly, precise, and eminently accessible compilation of biographies and accomplishments of mathematicians and scientists through the ages.

Rowlett, Russ. "How Many? A Dictionary of Units of Measurement," University of North Carolina at Chapel Hill. Available online. URL: http://www.unc.edu/~rowlett/units. Accessed May 2002. A comprehensive dictionary of units of measurement, from the metric and English systems to the most obscure usages.

United States Navy. "U.S. Naval Observatory Astronomical Applications Department." Available online. URL: http://aa.usno.navy.mil/data/docs/EarthSeasons.html. Accessed January 6, 2004. Astronomical data for practical applications; includes lists of equinoxes, almanacs, and software.

Uranium Information Centre Ltd. Australia. "Radiation and Life." Available online. URL: http://www.uic.com.au/ral.htm. Accessed July 5, 2003. Description of what radiation is and how it interacts with and influences living things.

White, Maura, and Allan Stilwell. "JSC Digital Image Collection." Available online. URL: http://images.jsc.nasa.gov. Accessed January, 2004. A catalog of over 9,000 NASA press release photos from the entirety of the manned space flight program.

Williams, David. "Planetary Sciences at the National Space Science Data Center." NASA. Available online. URL: http://nssdc.gsfc.nasa.gov/planetary. Accessed July 2004. NASA's deep archive and general distribution center for lunar and planetary data and images.

Index

Italic page numbers indicate illustrations. *C* indicates color insert pages.